T0323760

PRAISE FOR *MANAGING THE NEW CUSTOMER RELATIONSHIP*

"Gordon delivers an impressive synthesis of the newest methods for engaging customers in relationships that last. No organization today can succeed without the mastery of customer relationship management strategy fundamentals. But to win in the decades ahead, you must also understand and capitalize on the rapidly evolving social computing, mobility and customer analytics technologies described in this book. Checklists, self-assessments and graphical frameworks deliver pragmatic value for the practicing manager."

—William Band, Vice-President, Principal Analyst,
Forrester Research Inc., Cambridge, MA

"A very comprehensive and practical book on managing relationships with existing customers in the age of social media! I particularly enjoyed reading chapters on teaching customers new behaviors, which were illustrated by excellent case studies."

—Jagdish N. Sheth, Ph.D., Charles H. Kellstadt Professor
of Marketing, Emory University, Atlanta, GA

"The strategic breadth and depth of this book is impressive as Gordon explores the new customer and how to plan and manage the new customer relationship. I found his review of strategies, techniques and technologies for social, mobile, mass customization and customer analytics to be particularly insightful. Gordon urges marketers to live and breathe one-through-one marketing and to master social engagement techniques. The checklists, cases and examples make the content grounded and actionable. This is an important, current and detailed book to which every organization should pay close attention to improve customer relationships and create shareholder value."

—Marcus Ruebsam, Vice-President, Line-of-Business
Marketing Solutions, SAP AG, Walldorf, Germany

"There are many books on CRM, but I recommend this one because Gordon's book does what others do not. He considers CRM strategy and evolves it to recognize a new customer, one who is always connected, socially available and influential. The book doesn't just discuss many point solutions for specific marketing challenges; it integrates technology with strategy, people, process, and customer analytics to develop relationships continuously. This book is a broad and deep exploration of CRM, providing practical, fact-based perspectives that every company can use to validate and rethink their customer and stakeholder relationships."

—Helmuth Cepeda, Small, Medium and Distribution
Director, Microsoft Mexico, Mexico City, Mexico

"Technology has completely changed the nature of social interaction. The new rules of customer relationship management require that companies use new thinking and apply new technologies to engage with customers, keep in contact and build relationships that matter. Gordon shows how companies can create innovative strategies and integrate technology, people and process to interact and collaborate with customers and achieve improved business results. This book is at the cutting edge of CRM and is a must-read for any organization that wants to assess and improve its customer relationships."

—Peter Bergmann, Sales Strategy,
BMW AG, Munich, Germany

"Gordon speaks to the heart of a most important strategic issue for our company as we develop ongoing relationships with customers in a subscription-based pricing model rather than selling software transactions repeatedly. Gordon observes the changing nature of the customer and customer relationship, and describes with great insight how to interact with every customer to create mutually beneficial value. It has never been easier to start a business yet never has it been harder to build a successful company. Gordon understands that customers are bombarded with choice and provides very current and powerful methods for any firm to build relevance and preference, and develop relationships that can lead to lasting success."

—Selwyn Rabins, Co-Founder and CTO,
Alpha Software Inc., Burlington, MA

"Ian Gordon has brilliantly and comprehensively articulated the fundamental strategies that any organization should be applying to turn their customer relationships into strategic and competitive differentiators for long-term growth. This book is a must-read for any company that wishes to build iron-clad customer relationships."

—Vikas Gupta, CEO and President,
TransGaming Inc., Toronto, Canada

"This book provides thoughtful perspectives on what any organization can do to improve customer attraction, engagement and management. The author never loses sight of the customer relationship as he discusses and develops existing theory and goes beyond to explore current issues that affect every marketer, including the technologies firms use and could use, and those their customers and potential customers are using. This is a strategic yet practical and insightful book that gave me a number of useful new ideas."

—Jeremy Fox, Managing Director, Claro Learning Ltd.,
Tavistock, United Kingdom

Managing the New Customer Relationship

ALSO BY IAN GORDON

- *Competitor Targeting: Winning the Battle for Market and Customer Share* (0-471-64410-2; John Wiley & Sons Canada, 2001)
- *Relationship Marketing: New Strategies, Techniques and Technologies to Win the Customers You Want and Keep Them Forever* (0-471-64173-1; John Wiley & Sons Canada, 1998)
- *Beat the Competition: How to Use Competitive Intelligence to Develop Winning Business Strategies* (0-631-15991-6; Oxford: Basil Blackwell, 1989)

Managing the New Customer Relationship

Strategies to Engage the Social Customer and Build Lasting Value

Ian H. Gordon

WILEY

For general information about our other products and services, please contact our Customer Care Department within the United States at (800) 762–2974, outside the United States at (317) 572–3993 or fax (317) 572–4002.

Wiley publishes in a variety of print and electronic formats and by print-on-demand. Some material included with standard print versions of this book may not be included in e-books or in print-on-demand. If this book refers to media such as a CD or DVD that is not included in the version you purchased, you may download this material at http://booksupport.wiley.com. For more information about Wiley products, visit www.wiley.com.

Library and Archives Canada Cataloguing in Publication Data

Gordon, Ian, 1952 June 19-
    Managing the new customer relationship : strategies to engage the social customer and build lasting value / Ian H. Gordon.

Includes index.
Issued also in electronic formats.
ISBN 978-1-118-09221-7

    1. Relationship marketing.   2. Customer relations--Management.
3. Social media--Marketing.   I. Title.

HF5415.55.G66 2013   658.8′12   C2013-900941-8

ISBN: 978-1-118-25589-6 (ebk); 978-1-118-25585-8 (ebk); 978-1-118-25590-2 (ebk)

Production Credits
Acquiring Editor: Karen Milner
Managing Editor: Alison Maclean
Production Editor: Lindsay Humphreys
Cover design: Adrian So
Composition: Thomson Digital
Printer: Friesens Printing

John Wiley & Sons Canada, Ltd.
6045 Freemont Blvd.
Mississauga, Ontario
L5R 4J3

Printed in Canada

1 2 3 4 5 FP 17 16 15 14 13

For Joanne, Lauren and Evan

Contents

Acknowledgments

First and most importantly, thank you for your interest in this subject so close to the hearts of us both, and for investing your time in this book. I hope you will find the time well spent.

This acknowledges and thanks those who have made this book possible: my wonderful family, clients, friends and colleagues at Convergence Management Consultants and more generally. Thanks, too, to the following for their friendly guidance and assistance on aspects of this book: William Band, Vikas Gupta, Paul Hencoski, John Herhalt, Archie Johnston, Robert Love, Robert Paddon, Tim Rideout, Izzy Sobkowski and Dan Trott.

To the professionals at John Wiley & Sons Canada and specifically to Executive Editor Karen Milner, thank you. Karen has patiently, kindly and with great intelligence guided this project to completion while serving as your advocate.

Introduction

"No man is an island, entire of itself; every man is a piece of the continent, a part of the main."

John Donne (1572–1631)

The nature of marketing has changed much in the past few years and, even as we rush to understand the nature of the changes and how to modify what we do, what we expect, how we think and how we plan, the change is accelerating. A few short years ago we observed that the declining costs and increasing performance of technology and associated developments in strategic thinking had enabled an entirely new discipline for marketing: relationship marketing. This discipline offered the company an opportunity to manage each customer as a market of one, over the customer's purchasing lifetime. It held out much promise as the theory and practice addressed several of the problems companies were experiencing, including the low yield some companies were obtaining from their advertising investments, challenges accessing fragmenting markets and developing brand equity in more intensely competitive marketplaces. Relationship marketing principles expected a customer dialog to be initiated and sustained as a learning conversation that would create progressively more value for customer and company over an extended time horizon.

The nature of marketing has shifted in just a few years from a one-way monolog as companies advertised to consumers, to a two-way dialog in which the company sought to understand and communicate with each customer, to engaging with customers in a two-way dialog that recognized the customer's social context. Along the way, the underlying principles of marketing were no longer limited to cognitive psychology. Managing individual customer relationships brought behavioral psychology into the realm of marketing. Now that markets are social, marketing should also consider the implications of social psychology and sociology. The integration of these disciplines changes much about the organization's strategies, technologies and processes and it also invites consideration of what it means to be an employee and what it means to manage. It challenges the organization to revisit its very essence because these categories of knowledge have the potential to renew how an organization conceives itself and how it engages society. This, in turn, invites organizations to consider what philosophy might mean to the enterprise, which has the potential to bring more meaning to everyone with whom the company engages. Meaning, in its own turn, has the potential to make relationships—and the enterprise—more durable.

This book is about creating and sustaining relationships with individual existing customers. It recognizes that social media has profound marketing importance, that social media has revolutionary—not just evolutionary—implications for the marketer. This book seeks to focus on strategies for business-building that other books have not done fully: it broadens and integrates existing relationship management theories, concepts and methods that focus on existing customers with new approaches for managing the social customer; it also includes additional conceptual considerations that are associated with new technologies (such as mobile devices), new methods to develop customer-specific understanding, new roles for the enterprise (such as teaching customers new behaviors) and new perspectives to help the organization to endure by finding meaning beyond a series of transactions—important though these are.

Many companies have already embraced customer relationship management (CRM) strategies, technologies and initiatives to manage individual customers and their relationships with the enterprise. This book recognizes that CRM is no longer novel and adopts the perspective that core CRM principles nevertheless merit revisiting both to solidify the conceptual foundation and to provide a platform from which additional concepts and approaches can be engaged.

Strong relationships are good for customers, the company, shareholders and other stakeholders, and this is now widely acknowledged. But research and one's own experience shows that few companies actually enjoy strong customer relationships. Talk to companies with weak customer relationships and they have a number of things in common. Key relationship management principles, processes or technologies are as yet not fully considered or deployed. Few companies can point to a plan to develop great relationships—they may have a CRM plan but usually this plan focuses more on technology than on customer-specific relationships. So before we deal with the *new* customer and associated management principles—the primary focus of this book—we will consider the core relationship marketing principles that should be a starting point for relationship management in any enterprise. Once we have done so, we will turn to the management of the new customer relationship, the social customer, and then explore related arenas, ending with considerations for an organization to advance stakeholder relationships amid rapid and ongoing marketplace, technological and societal change.

Traditional marketing focused on mass everything—mass production and distribution, and mass communication and positioning. And all the while, no one within the company was listening. Many marketers would be dismissive of the individual, often considering him or her of marginal importance because the business didn't depend on a single customer. Each person mattered less than the market segment that could be economically accessed and influenced in aggregate. If the company thought a customer was in an untargeted segment or in the tail of a segment's bell curve, that customer's voice would never be heard. The company was determined it would give the target market—all of it—what research said customers in this segment wanted.

Mass everything worked well at a time when products were relatively differentiated from one another, when many companies were operating near capacity and when marketplace demand was not saturated. It also worked well at a time when media was mostly a one-way street that ran from the company to the customer, never in the other direction. If a company yelled its message into media loudly and often enough, just maybe it could drive consumers to store shelves and cause products to be taken away. At least that's how most marketers seemed to operate as they contemplated metrics such as gross rating points and cost per thousand.

Mass marketing often resulted in mass wastage. Messages were sent to customers for whom the content simply didn't matter, for any number of the many reasons that make individuals different from one another. Just as marketplaces were fragmenting, so too were products and services proliferating. Companies needed to spend more and more on mass media simply to keep the same share they previously held in the customer's mind. And the messages were about as numerous and undifferentiated as grains of sand on the beach. The old marketing math simply didn't work very well anymore and companies trying to operate according to the old rules found that they could never have enough money to make the old rules work for them financially.

Product and service commoditization was compressing margins. So volumes or prices—or both—needed to go up for companies to retain profitability. And, again, commoditization made sure this was unlikely to happen unless some fundamental changes were made in the business model and marketing, specifically.

Along came ever more powerful and less costly new technologies that made accessing individual customers a consideration of economics for many companies. As marketing theory developed in concert with the technology evolution, marketing managers could plan their approach to individual customers strategically and for business advantage. So, at long last, companies could cater to each among their customers uniquely with tailored products, services and communications. Transactions and preferences could be remembered. And the importance of individual customers could be appreciated and recognized without incurring costs in excess of those that previously applied in the era of mass marketing.

While much attention has been paid to the enabling power of technology, customer relationships depend on much more than the artful or thoughtful use of technology. The management of the customer relationship starts with a commitment not to *all* customers but to each chosen one. Every skilled marketer has learned to walk the corridors of his or her customers' minds. Marketers have used cognitive marketing principles to influence the perceptions that drive consumers' attitudes that, in turn, lead to desired behavioral outcomes, such as visiting the store or buying the new product.

Management of individual customer relationships brings with it a new set of tools—those associated with behavioral marketing. The marketer operating according to behavioral principles considers how best to motivate customers' behaviors more directly than the cognitive marketer. Does the name Pavlov ring a bell? According to the Pavlovian stimulus-response model of buyer behavior, customers can be influenced by inducing a purchase response using coupons, price reductions or limited time offers, for example.

And once existing buyers' behaviors are known, marketers can look for customers and potential customers with substantially similar behaviors. This leads to replacement of the market segment as a concept with the "behavioral cluster"—a way of aggregating customers who have behaviors in common rather than those who have similar demographics, attitudes, psychographics or lifestyles, for example. The concept of behavioral clusters alone would be enough to replace traditional marketing principles. But the management of the individual customer goes far beyond this, especially now that communications with customers is bi-directional, now that consumers communicate more with their peers and friends than receiving communications from businesses and now that customers place greater emphasis on learning from one another than from companies. For the most part, companies are now much less relevant to customers than was previously the case, largely because their share of the customer's attention and mind has declined. This decline of "mind share" can be directly associated with a reduced percentage of communications in which customers engage. Those devices in the hands of customers provide conduits to the eyes and ears of the people who matter to them. The companies that supply them with goods and services are almost never among those that matter most. This decline of relevance leads many customers to make their purchase decisions with less input from the corporation for information, guidance and help. Customers rely increasingly on their friends and third parties they are more likely to trust. This challenge is big and it is vital. Now companies must struggle with relevance every hour of every day or risk becoming invisible. And customers don't often buy from invisible companies.

Companies have made themselves and their products more visible by differentiating their customers and treating them unequally according to the value each represents. The saying that "the customer is always right" has been replaced with "the right customer is always right." Just as all customers are not equal, neither are all relationships. Procter & Gamble will place a different value on its end-customer relationship than will marketing management at Ford, the difference being largely associated with a comparison of a lifetime supply of P&G's non-durables compared with vehicle purchases and ongoing service and parts revenues at Ford. Companies such as these will have recognized the importance of relationships to their businesses. Ideally, firms will have currently relevant plans for developing these relationships to create customer and shareholder value (but many firms do not have such plans in place, as will be seen).

A meaningful relationship starts, as in a more private way, when supplier and customer see that it is in their interests to get together for the long term. This means a supplier needs to take stock of the customers it serves and decide which ones will receive special and continuing attention. Which customers are the most profitable now? Which can be made more profitable? Which are very important to the company's future? Which customers should be de-emphasized or even "fired"?[1] Which customers want a relationship and which want to buy on price alone? Relationship management requires that organizations consider issues such as these and choose core customers, develop meaningful insights about them and predict their behaviors, formulate strategies for individual customer relationships and build the abilities within the company to deliver the value each customer wants.

Companies asking themselves these questions may find they have more work to do within the company to assess customers' profitability, strategic value and perceptions of the company and its competitors. Some companies may need to find ways to identify their end-customers in ways they haven't done thus far. Some may want to build better databases about their customers, or create communities or self-serve environments for customers on the Internet, or engage with customers one-on-one, or explore new avenues to be relevant to customers and make meaningful differences in their lives and society more generally. For some companies, opportunities may remain to focus what they do on the customer relationship, in part by placing relationships first and foremost in the company's vision statement, and then making this actionable by, for example, structuring the organization to deliver on the promise of relationships, categorizing and assigning responsibilities for relationships, and integrating people, process, technology and knowledge systems to achieve relationship objectives.

It is management's role to define and shape the basis for the end-customer relationship and to align all aspects of the enterprise with the customer. It is also the purpose of management to recognize and address the importance of the relationships that contribute to the end-customer relationship. For the end-customer relationship to endure, management may often need to rethink aspects about the company's internal and external relationships. For example, are salespeople compensated to be "hunters" or "farmers"? Are call center personnel rewarded for the number of calls they process or the satisfaction of the caller? Does marketing focus on developing new products or on the current and future profitability of its customers? Are investors patient or are they "light switch" investors who believe that money injected yesterday should already have paid them out handsomely today? Senior management might also ask themselves if they model the behaviors they want their internal and external customers to exhibit.

Although the focus of this book is on business, the concepts can also be used by government and not-for-profit organizations, such as charities and foundations, to manage their relationships for mutual advantage with their stakeholders. The concepts can also be deployed by governments, although there is one principle that makes these concepts of selective importance: democratic governments, by their very nature, offer their services equally to all. That is, while relationship management differentiates customers, citizen and public stakeholder engagement is undifferentiated by most governments.

This book discusses a number of considerations for private and public sector organizations to improve customer and stakeholder relationships while incorporating new principles to recognize and adapt to change, plan the management of new arenas and competitive battlegrounds and become an organization to which customers and potential customers can easily relate.

Chapter 1
MANAGING THE NEW CUSTOMER—AND THE NEW CUSTOMER RELATIONSHIP

"All for one, one for all, that is our device."

Alexandre Dumas (1802–1870),
The Three Muskateers

RELATIONSHIPS MATTER

More than the machinery in the factory, more than inventory in the warehouse, more even than people who work for an enterprise, relationships are yet more valuable. While physical assets are a product of a company's past, derived from the resources that created them, relationships are predictive. Relationships suggest the direction in which a company's value will trend. If relationships depreciate, so will the future value of the company. And if relationships grow in value, there will be a commensurate growth in company value. When a company is about to launch a new product, the relationships it already has with its customers could provide an opportunity for testing. Customers will try products such as these if their relationships have built trust in the company. When there is some kind of problem between the company and its customers, it will be relationships that will get it past the bad times as customers remember the good. Relationships stop the unraveling of valuable business connections. Relationships provide a bridge of continuity and an opportunity for companies to develop ongoing revenues from their customers. More generally, relationships help a company reach its potential. And when a company gets weaker, when its products become older, when its competitive advantage declines, when its financial performance deteriorates, when some among its employees or channel intermediaries leave or defect, even then—and perhaps especially then—relationships will still be there to help pick the company up and put it on a successful path again.

So relationships matter. Even more, relationships are vital. Developing relationships and increasing relationship value should be the central strategic focus for every organization. Historically, many companies—especially those driven by mass marketing—sought to convert prospects into current customers using traditional marketing principles and then to cater to them in the usual, transactional way. These well-known marketing principles are no longer of much value if relationships are a fundamental determinant of enterprise value. It is now at least as important for marketers to develop a process for relationship development that comprises relating to existing customers and increasing customer value, and acquiring additional customers by connecting, attracting and converting non-customers into customers.

The first challenge for most companies is to transition their strategies from those based on transactions to relationship-based strategies. The initial focus is on existing customers—especially the ones the company wants most. It is common to build on relationships the company already has with existing customers to acquire new ones. The second challenge is therefore to develop relationships with new customers who may be accessed from existing customer relationships, first by reaching out to these individuals and then causing each to be attracted to the company. There is an important third step that considers customer engagement, the process of engaging with new potential customers—especially social customers—who may not be known to existing customers, engaging with them and then attracting them to the enterprise. Figure 1 describes these various steps with the labels "relate," "connect," "engage" and "attract."

Earlier relationship management principles were concerned mostly with listening to and conversing with existing customers, and developing, sustaining and growing the value of relationships with them. The management of the new customer relationship—the focus of this book—retains a focus on existing customers and their value but goes beyond, to include consideration of new customers and the potential customers who are known to current and new customers.

Figure 1: Moving from Transactions to Relationships and from Current Customers to New Ones

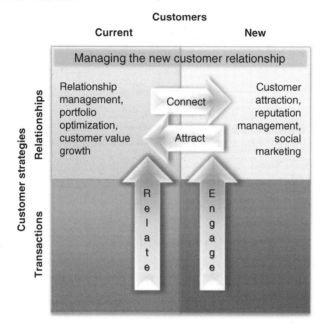

Marketers naturally and generally understand that relationships matter and that relationships are the very essence of most businesses. For some, this understanding leads management to develop IT plans and enhance some relationship aspects of their marketing plans. But customer relationships are much more important than that and merit their own plans from which IT implementations and other tactical considerations can flow. That most companies are still without plans to develop this most important aspect of their business remains a material shortcoming and a gap between intent and execution that needs to be closed. In short, companies need not only marketing plans or IT plans, but plans for customer relationships.

THE OLD RULES OF MARKETING DON'T WORK

It would not be a significant overstatement to pronounce the death of marketing as it once was. It is clear that the traditional marketing principles that focused on standard products, pricing, promotion and distribution for mass markets and market segments is much less important today than was once the case. The importance of marketing has eroded because the nature of markets has changed.

In part the result of product and supplier proliferation, ubiquitous availability and the substitutability of goods and services, most products and services are today much less differentiated than was the case just a few years ago. The consumer's mind is crowded with multiple brands competing for attention and position. When Al Ries and Jack Trout published their influential book *Positioning: The Battle for Your Mind* in 1980, the market was a simpler place.[1] There were relatively few companies and brands competing for rungs on the cerebral brand positioning ladder that Ries and Trout described as occupying the minds of customers. At the time, the financial resources of the companies that owned the brands were unequal and this mattered enormously in an era when purchase behavior required deep pockets to fund the desired communication's reach and frequency. That is, for consumers to hear you, you needed to shout loudly where and when they could hear you, and to do that a fat wallet was of much help. Today you can shout the benefits of your brand until you are hoarse—and broke—and still there is the potential that no one will hear you above the general din of the marketplace. The marketplace is simply too cluttered, resources are much more equal and companies have established more powerful means for communications than simply firing outbound messages using TV that no one watches, radios that no one hears, or newspapers and magazines that no one reads. Okay, perhaps an overstatement—but not vastly so. The digitization and fragmentation of media not only enables a two-way conversation, it demands engagement and two-way communications—a dialog—if companies are to develop progressively deeper bonds with their customers and be in tune with the changing context, needs, wants and feelings of each one.

In the simpler marketplace of the near past, communication was from the enterprise to the customer only. Winners found the best channel and message to motivate purchase. Today this just sounds like noise to most consumers. It doesn't much matter how companies say "buy me, buy me," or how often they say it, because customers pay a lot less attention to what companies communicate than to what their friends say. And when everybody is yelling more or less similarly, the differentiated firm is the one that connects, engages and resonates. While customers might flit from one company to another, they will only form lasting relationships with a few. Those with which customers do form relationships will be on the basis of a trust-building dialog and longitudinal actions that create mutual value—that is, the dialog extends across time to create value from which each individual can benefit.

In social marketplaces, customers serve as the gatekeepers of communications to the potential customers the company does not yet know. These customers serve up messages to their friends. They collectively maintain a repository of marketplace knowledge. They govern the path to a consumer's mind. In this environment, companies have two choices: either be part of the social marketplace in which customers and their friends reside, or compete on transactions, all the while presiding over the declining relevance of their products and services.

Now that "social" governs marketplaces, marketing as it once was is no longer the primary driver or enabler of social acceptance. Marketing has been particularly weak in responding to new technology developments for social media and areas beyond. Bluntly put, the 4Ps of marketing—the core marketing touchstones of product, place, price and promotion—don't work as discrete marketing tools anymore. Technology has digitized the 4Ps of marketing and in the process has enabled an infinite range of possibilities for companies and customers to contemplate more or less equally. Now both are putting practical meaning into the word "custom" that is to be found within the word "customer."

Marketing theory is also not particularly well prepared to provide direction to a number of other technology-enabled changes that govern today's marketplace. These changes include the discrete and interrelated challenges of real-time marketing, local marketing, mobility, context-sensitive marketing, e-learning (and m-learning, which is the e-learning equivalent on mobile devices), teaching customers new behaviors, data mining and much else. For example, marketing theory might frame a customer engagement strategy and consider tactics to execute this strategy. Many of these tactics are driven today by newly emerging technologies. It is common for many companies to have these tactics lead their strategies, in part because marketing personnel are not driving the technology bus and companies cannot wait for strategic oversight to catch up with the enabling capabilities of their technologies. Firms thus have a bias to action and then to corrective action to improve upon their initial thrusts rather than waiting for strategies to frame perfect initial direction. Absent this strategic oversight, new technologies can result in tactics being implemented without a strategic framework to provide focus, clarity or priority. Consider the case of the company that uses geotagging and GPS on mobile devices to determine if its customers are in proximity to one of their stores. They decide to send customers an e-coupon so that they can get a discount on merchandise of a type bought previously. Generally, actions such as these are done without strategic oversight or direction because these strategies usually lag behind the technologies firms have adopted. The result can be the appearance that marketing is more of a hindrance than a help in the generation of new revenues from new technologies or that marketing is simply a service function, operating in support of IT or sales functions.

TECHNOLOGY HAS CHANGED EVERYTHING

The most important enabler of customer relationship development has been the declining cost, increasing performance and, now, growing relevance of technology. Moore's Law, taken to mean the doubling of technological performance every 18 months, continues to underpin the proliferation of increasingly powerful technology infrastructure and the ability of marketers to put it to economical use.[2] Consider where we would be had the price/performance ratios of computer chips not enabled memory, databases, processing, bandwidth, robotics, software, cloud computing (Internet-enabled data storage, processing and communications) and so many other aspects of technology that marketers have put to use. Most notable for marketing is the ability technology provides companies to identify, understand, remember and respond to individual customers, engaging each for mutual benefit. Not only can this engagement be done at lower than mass market costs, it can actually be done at zero marginal cost—that is, virtually free. Since most of the technology infrastructure in a company can be regarded as a fixed cost, the incremental costs associated with customer relationship technologies are minimal. This differs markedly from mass marketing where the variable costs of marketing activities such as advertising are much higher in relation to the fixed costs of marketing.

Although technology has enabled marketers to engage with individual customers at a very low cost, this engagement remains a marketing responsibility and, as such, should still be governed by marketing strategy. Technology without marketing strategy is like a boat without water. It is interesting to behold, it probably won't sink, but it's not going to get you very far either.

THE TRUTH IS VISIBLE

Marketers have long held that positioning is all about what a company does to the mind of the customer rather than what it *actually* does. Charles Revson of Revlon famously said, "In the factory we make cosmetics; in the drugstore we sell hope." Some companies still adhere to the argument that what matters most is what customers believe they do rather than what they actually do. Increasingly, though, companies understand that if they don't really make hope in the factory, they won't be selling much of it in the drugstore. That is, reality is starting to trump perception.

Today, truth will out. What is said behind the walls of the enterprise (and government, as leaks frequently reveal) is soon audible beyond the walls. Today's enterprise is more transparent; in this glass house, more or less everything is visible. If all the resources of the governments very much invested in secrecy can't prevent damaging facts from appearing on the Internet, how is a company to make sure it tells a single story to all and maintains consistent positions using anything other than facts? The truth is evident and customers really *can* tell whether the emperor has any clothes. Promote your vehicle as having a higher gas mileage than it does, and with a few mouse clicks consumers will be aware of the subterfuge. Say that your energy company is concerned about the environment and renewable energy sources, and consumers will remember oil-soaked birds and company-induced disasters. Sell cell phones that irradiate consumers but say nothing of this, and don't expect informed consumers to build trust. Market your "chocolatey" candy bars but avoid mentioning artificial ingredients, and sooner or later customers will wonder what "chocolatey" actually means—and they'll be done with you. Just as with relationships between individuals, relationships between businesses and customers require truth as a starting point for the relationship. Companies ought to conduct themselves as though the truth is visible to customers, because it is.

Truth—unvarnished and naked—is the new positioning. Truth is emotive and it is believable because in the end, truth cannot be challenged. Truth is a touchstone for much about the future of business. Of course, this should be no surprise. The very fact that this matter is raised here suggests a problem in and of itself. Every promise made by a truthful company becomes a foreseeable fact in the minds of customers who trust and believe. Every promise made by a company that is less than truthful is challenged. In this open world of free information flow, anything other than total truth can be more than expensive—it can be a root cause of customer defections and material business damage.

Now this raises a number of other related issues. If there are no secrets, if the truth will out, what ought a company to do about its product development plans, new product launches and other information that has historically been treated as secret? Should a company make all this information available to everybody? Should a company post all its plans on the Internet, for example? Should all employees be empowered to use social media to talk about any-thing they wish? Some would say, "Yes and why not? After all, if everything is known or could be known, if customer attention and bonding is the basis for competitive advantage, then open up." Some would take the reverse position, "Keep secrets secret. After all, there are secrets to be maintained and nothing could be more important to shield from competitors than certain plans that the company has." Yet others say, "Keep secrets secret, but only for a while. Hold onto the new product development plans. Wait to inform customers. Then make a big splash and do so as early as possible before secrets become open ones."

MARKETPLACES ARE SOCIAL

As mentioned, marketplaces are social and social media has become a signifi-cant environment with which consumers connect to, entertain and inform one another, and in which businesses are investing to listen, understand and participate in the conversations. While this phenomenon is generally noticed for its importance, strategies for managing customers in the virtual world of social media have not received much attention.

Customers are increasingly dependent on one another to help inform their product and service purchase decisions, especially where the social risk is high, such as for consumer durables—the case for housing, automobiles, computers, and other capital intensive and infrequently bought items. Social risk can also be high for purchase decisions that demand new information and are no longer as straightforward or routine as before, a frequent case for women's fashion, for example. As customers reach out to one another to make purchase decisions, they become less reliant on traditional media and information channels. In a few short years, consumers who once obtained their product and service information from advertisers, who used one-way communications channels such as print, television and radio, began to use search engines such as Google to get the information they needed and now they also use social media. Friends and respected third-parties have become part of consumers' purchase decisions.

It's hard to overstate the importance of social media to customers as they connect with one another. Social connections are viewed as more important to consumers than are the communications they receive from most compan-ies about most subjects. As a percentage of time spent on media, the voice of companies heard by consumers collectively has declined and the social voice—the amount of time consumers spend chatting to one another—has increased. Social media has trumped traditional media and, because consumers are spending their time there, enterprises ought to consider how best to engage in social spaces.

Marketplaces are becoming *relative* rather than *absolute*—relative in the sense that customers rely on the recommendations of friends and associates for their purchase decisions rather than messages from companies or even facts that may be objectively verifiable. It's no longer just important for marketers to understand what consumers read, hear or see, it's at least as important to know how their impressions have been formed and who helped to shape these perspectives. Companies need to be able to identify these influencers and influence them, too.

As marketplaces become increasingly relative, social context is permeating arenas beyond simple communications like Facebook, for example. Games have already included social context as players compete with one another online. Social context is increasingly to be found in non-traditional areas such as investing, where investors can follow their friends and other investors, and include this insight in their investment decisions.

If companies are to capture opportunities associated with social marketplaces, they need to be heard in the first place. This is no small task, given the increase in the volume of communications occurring among consumers themselves as a percentage of all marketplace communications, as mentioned previously. Marketers can leverage any access the company is able to gain to the eyes, ears and minds of existing customers, not just to create new value with these customers but also to access the people they know and, in so doing, develop entirely new customers. Creative marketers can also engage prospective customers using social media—social prospects—and attract them to doing business with the enterprise. These concepts are the very essence of the new customer relationship.

MARKETING IS SOCIOLOGY

As suggested by Table 1, the nature of marketing has evolved and continues to do so as marketing transitions from a discipline focused on mass and segment-based marketing using the principles of cognitive psychology, to an era in which marketing seeks to cater to individuals by making extensive use of behavioral psychology and, most recently, the application of social psychology and sociology to management of the customer relationship.

Table 1: Marketing Eras and Marketing Theory

Marketing Era	Circa	Predominant Underlying Principles
The era of crafts and cottage industry	Pre–18th century	Limited marketing principles
Industrial revolution	18th to 19th centuries	Limited marketing principles
Mass production	20th century	Production efficiency, e.g., Frederick Winslow Taylor—limited marketing principles
Mass marketing	Mid to late 20th century	Cognitive psychology
Relationship marketing	Last decade of 20th century to present	Behavioral psychology
Managing the new customer relationship and social marketing	Current	Social psychology and sociology

When marketers used cognitive psychology as the model for their marketing, they planned a convoluted marketing process to achieve desired consumer behaviors. Marketers first sought to influence consumers' perceptions so that attitudes would be modified with sufficient importance and urgency that consumers would change their behaviors and make a purchase. This worked well for a time but the era of CRM and one-to-one marketing changed the effectiveness of traditional marketing. In the era of relationship management and one-to-one technologies, marketers could act more directly on consumers' behaviors than in this multi-step cognitive process. Using behavioral psychology, marketers focused on consumers' behaviors more directly, typically using a relevant and timely reward to stimulate purchase, like offering a discount to online visitors who have looked at an item previously but didn't buy then. Marketers connect with individual consumers and sell to each one, this time using a new toolset based on behavioral psychology. While this approach has multiple benefits, such as an ability to measure ROI to assess the success of each program, the downside is that many companies remain focused more on their needs to increase sales than the consumers' needs, either narrowly in the context of the product, or more generally, in the consumer's life. Technology is simply being used as an approach by companies to intervene and come between the company and the customer, disintermediating the selling process to make it both more efficient and effective in a one-to-one marketplace.

Now that markets are both one-to-one and social, marketing requires a greater understanding of the social context of each consumer. Marketing has

Figure 2: Marketing Strategy at the Intersections of Three Branches of Psychology: Cognitive, Behavioral and Social

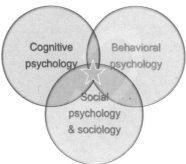

become social psychology and sociology as marketers learn how to apply these principles not just as an overlay on the concepts they have historically used but also as an entirely new discipline to be considered for its marketing impact.

While marketers did pay some attention to social psychology and sociology in earlier eras, the new rules of marketing—the social rules—require deeper insight into the social makeup of markets and for this marketers need to look to social psychology and sociology to develop strategies for influencing social marketplaces. This is not to suggest to marketers that they discard the cognitive and behavioral principles they already know but it is to observe that social psychology and sociology ought to be primary touchstones for marketing strategy. Social psychology and sociology are increasingly important underpinnings for management of the new customer relationship, as suggested by Figure 2.

Given the importance of social psychology and sociology, this book pays much attention to the subject throughout. Before engaging the issue of "social" principles for marketing strategy, core concepts associated with managing the customer relationships are reviewed.

ONE-*THROUGH*-ONE IS MORE IMPORTANT THAN ONE-TO-ONE

Social media invites marketers to capture new opportunities through new strategies. Social media are platforms for engagement through which marketers reach out to their existing customers and an extended network of people to whom they are ready to have a first-order connection—their customers. That is, if existing customers can be considered first-order contacts, then the people to whom they are known become second-order contacts and a

Figure 3: Evolution of Marketing Strategy

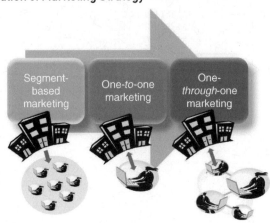

new opportunity for marketers to embrace after building share with their existing customers. This is discussed in greater detail in Chapter 4. For now, let's note that the one-*to*-one strategies companies first deployed when they first pursued relationship marketing had existing customers in mind, while one-*through*-one strategies engage with the customer universe using each customer as a gateway to the next. This evolution of marketing strategy from mass and segment-based marketing to one-through-one marketing is described in Figure 3.

DEFINING THE NEW CUSTOMER RELATIONSHIP

The management principles that underpin customer attraction, reputation management and social marketing in respect of the new customer relationship may be considered both in terms of "new customers" and "new customer relationships." New customers are taken to be those with whom the firm has not historically done business. New customer relationships apply both to existing and new customers and incorporate a series of business strategies for creating and sharing new value with these customers, attracting as customers those people or organizations who are known to existing customers, and engaging each prospect—particularly social prospects—continuously to build relevance and preference over a lifetime of association.

Managing the new customer relationship draws from traditional marketing principles, yet is quite different. Now that every aspect of marketing is digitized, the marketing mix of product, price, promotion and distribution can be configured in almost limitless combinations. Companies that package customer solutions and sell them according to marketing's old rules now have the potential not just to miss the market slightly, but to miss it by a wide margin. Managing the new customer relationship recognizes that each customer differs from the next in terms of his or her needs, influence and value to the enterprise, and that customers ought to be engaged collaboratively to create the value each wants and to engage their friends and colleagues. Taken together, these differences have the potential to transform a company's view of the marketing it undertakes and almost everything about the enterprise, from the work it does to the technology it employs to the products it produces to the structure by which it achieves its objectives.

IMPLICATIONS FOR MANAGING THE NEW CUSTOMER RELATIONSHIP

Management of the new customer relationship includes one-to-one marketing principles and seeks to optimize these. The following are also considered:

- New arenas and networks such as social media and friends of customers
- Ubiquitous and continuous engagement, especially mobile platforms such as smartphones
- Relevance without regard to distance (engagement is with local customers and enterprises as well as distant ones)
- Better customer understanding through customer analytics, and
- New technologies such as the cloud and new apps and platforms.

The definition of the new customer relationship as presented in the preceding section has the following implications:

1. Markets of one—across the entire enterprise

   Markets comprise a collection of individuals and companies ought to recognize and cater to each one uniquely, with strategies that apply to the end-customer and engage the entire business and all its stakeholders. Management of new customer relationships requires that a company, as a consequence of its business strategy and customer focus, design and align its business processes, communications, technology and people in support of the value *individual* customers want—and that it also consider how to engage the people or companies individual customers know.

2. Customer selection

    While all customers are individuals, they are not necessarily equal—some are much more valuable and strategic to the enterprise than are others. It is important for the company to decide which customers will be chosen as the foundation for its future, with whom it will form the deepest and most valuable bonds and which customers will be progressively de-emphasized or even fired, an increasing challenge where customers who are not required have social influence. Customers can be fired politely, proactively or reactively, possibly tacitly discouraged from doing business with the enterprise and some even without knowing that they have indeed been fired. Employing this principle, firms will focus most on those customers who fit their business strategies and business model, and reject others that no longer fit or may represent an opportunity for an alternative business model. This has the potential to produce significant savings from customer investments that would otherwise not produce significant returns.

3. Customer knowledge

    An outgrowth of selecting customers is that companies ought to know much more about their customers, including the following:
    -   Who they are, starting with being able to identify each customer every time he or she connects with the enterprise
    -   How they are linked to one another
    -   How they behave, respond to offers and want to be engaged
    -   How they cluster behaviorally with other customers
    -   What their individual needs are
    -   The value that each customer represents to the enterprise
    -   The potential value of each customer
    -   The influence and thus the leverage each customer has in social media, and
    -   The strategic considerations for doing business with each.

    By exploring issues such as these, the company's core customers can be defined and customer investments made to keep them, grow their value and access their individual social networks as prospective customers.

4. Novelty and mutuality

    As in a more personal way, a relationship is characterized by, and built through, novelty and mutuality. That is, relationships get deeper when something new is done and the value from this novelty is shared. You might go on a trip with a friend to Europe. That's novelty. You might discuss the good times you had every time you see your friend. That's mutuality. And if it stops there, the relationship eventually depreciates. Companies always need to do new things for and with their customers to cause relationships to appreciate.

5. Digital 4Ps

Technology enables companies to atomize markets by connecting with and serving individual customers and then provides for almost infinite variability in customer communications and customization. The challenge for companies is to decide how much variability to actually allow in each aspect of their marketing mix, the 4Ps of marketing: product, price, promotion and placement/distribution. The following considers each of the 4Ps in turn:

- *Product*

Relationship management envisages products being designed, developed, tested, piloted, provided, installed and refined, cooperatively with each individual customer to the extent that this makes economic sense. This is very different from the way products were developed in the past, with the company conceiving concepts, researching these, developing them, and launching completed products some time later. Today's relationship marketer engages the customer in real time as it seeks to move rapidly to meet customer requirements with products that may not be fully finished—at least not in the historical sense. Products are not bundles of tangible and intangible benefits the company assembles because it thinks this is what customers want to buy. Rather, products comprise an aggregation of individual benefits customers have participated in selecting or designing. The customer participates in the assembly of an unbundled series of components or modules that together comprise the product or service. The product resulting from this collaboration may be unique or highly tailored to the requirements of the customer, with much more of their knowledge content incorporated into the product than was previously the case.

- *Price*

Having developed a product, traditional marketing sets a price for it and changes the price from time to time according to changing competitive and demand conditions. About 100 years ago, telephone companies put pairs of twisted copper wires in the ground and decided how to much to charge consumers for the telephone services these wires enabled. Some of these companies still retain prices in regulated environments that values the much depreciated wires in the ground. Today's marketer sets prices for benefits the consumer assembles into a value bundle. So, when customers specify that a product should have specific features and that certain services should be delivered before, during and after the sale, they naturally expect to pay for the value of each component they have chosen to bundle. Relationship management invites customers into the pricing process and all other value-related processes, giving customers an opportunity to make the trade-offs they want and, in so doing, to further develop trust in the relationship.

- *Promotion*

   Traditional marketing was like sending smoke signals to everyone in a specific market segment to see. "Buy me," the signals said to all who could see them. Relationship management instead gives an individual customer an opportunity to decide how each wishes to communicate with the organization, whether by one-way communications or interactively. One-way communications such as mass advertising, promotional offers, manuals, price lists, product literature and warranty response cards have now been largely replaced with two-way communications—dialogs—that involve customers in all matters that affect them. Mass promotion might still be used to provide a branding umbrella under which specific engagement might exist but few relationship managers would use mass promotion as a means to influence purchase directly today. Using Internet-based technologies, call centers, point-of-sale, kiosks, smart cards, e-mail and interactive voice response, companies can now give customers many options to communicate with the company. Opportunities remain for many companies to tie together their various communications channels and customer knowledge systems so that they have a single, real-time view of each customer; in this way, relevant, timely, personalized and customized two-way communication can take place without asking the customer the same question twice.

- *Placement/Distribution*

   Current marketing thinking focuses on distribution channels as the mechanism to transfer a product—or, more accurately, its title—as the goods move from producer to consumer. Relationship management instead considers distribution from the perspective of the customer who decides where, how and when to buy the combination of products and services that comprise the vendor's total offering. Seen this way, distribution is not a channel but a *process*. The process allows customers to choose where and from whom they will obtain the value they want. The customer can choose whether to buy a computer off the shelf from a reseller and take it home immediately, order one that is built to individual preference at the factory and shipped within a week or so, or have one configured in-store and available within a few days. The customer exercises choice with regard to the benefits he or she wants and the location that is best able to provide these benefits.

6. Collaboration

Companies used to think in terms of a "selling cycle" and many still do. This is a clear clue as to the orientation of the company—an orientation toward *self* rather than to *other*—and a cultural legacy that often remains from the command-and-control era of business. It is more helpful for relationship managers to think in terms of a customer-specific purchase cycle as this offers potential for greater organizational empathy and sets the stage for thinking more about how to associate with individual customers over their purchasing lifetimes.

Collaboration starts by thinking, "creating and sharing new value *with*…" rather than "creating and sharing new value *for*…" Managing the customer relationship includes both that which a company does *for* its customers, such as a strategic capability—a website, for example—while paying particular attention to that which a company does collaboratively *with* its customers anywhere in the value chain—from co-design and co-development to customer feedback and all steps in between. After all, customers don't much care how a company organizes to create value. They just care that they receive the benefits they want, and for this they want to be heard and they want to see results. This means the customer's individual voice needs to be injected into value chains if collaboration is to result in benefits the customer can see.

7. Relevance

Companies ought to understand individual customers well enough to be relevant to each. With sufficient customer knowledge, companies can predict what customers are likely to require, often before customers themselves have fully considered their needs. A financial institution example: "Your term investment will come due in two weeks. Should we reinvest it in a similar manner for you, or would you like to review other investment alternatives that could provide a better yield?"

8. Core customers

Existing customers are central to the business; the core customers among them—the ones the company values most—provide the most profitable and secure pathway to the company's future. Companies ought to identify and recognize the role existing customers have in focusing the enterprise and the particular importance of core customers who should receive close attention to ensure ongoing alignment and mutual commitment. A company focused only on its own financial results obviously misses the point that customer relationships are the key enterprise assets to be managed and grown, and that there ought to be an organizational strategy for so doing, starting with core customers.

9. Gateways of influence

Marketers ought to recognize the important role existing customers have to play in opening doors to the people or organizations they know, generally not yet customers for the enterprise. Companies that market goods and services to other businesses have long recognized the potential of existing customers to refer the company to new potential customers—they call these customers "reference accounts." It is less common for companies marketing to individual consumers to seek reference opportunities to customers' friends, colleagues and acquaintances. The preceding statement also recognizes the potential for companies to connect with and engage the customers who may not be known to existing customers—prospective customers who may be accessed, engaged and attracted through social media, more generally. This view requires that marketers not only look past each transaction to understand the value of each customer relationship and the needs of customers, it also requires that marketers understand the impact each customer could have on their business by virtue of their social *influence,* a third dimension of consideration.

10. Now

The time horizon available for marketers to connect with and influence customers has shrunk. Customers expect to have their issues addressed in real time, wherever they may be, using whatever communications channel they wish. Customers expect their issues addressed on their terms, which means now. They want a feedback loop to the product or service originator and a well-functioning mechanism for addressing their questions or concerns. This means companies need to be accessible to the mobile customer, well-informed and well able to address whatever it is that he or she may wish to know or have done. Competing on "now" means that frontline personnel must be able to make decisions on the spot and any support they might need, whether information or approvals, must be similarly real time. In many cases, frontline personnel may not be necessary if business rules can be established and codified for online connection. But those who do reach out for interpersonal connection should find a friend at the other end of the line, someone who really does empathize, listen and assist rather than serve more mechanistically as an instrument of corporate policy, apparently being more focused on transactions than relationships.

11. Anytime, anywhere

The company senses each consumer and understands, interprets and responds to individuals as part of a process of mutual learning. This occurs in real time. The firm is ubiquitously available, however the customer chooses to access the enterprise, using whatever mobile technology he or she chooses. Companies can no longer design their communications and physical distribution channels according to the old rules of marketing that might have considered issues such as density (number of outlets), directness (number of levels in the channel) and so on. Now, companies operate according to the Customer Concept, not the Marketing Concept.[3] They put the needs of each customer at the center of the business and organize engagement and treatment around each individual customer using continuous processes. These organizations pay close attention to openness and customer engagement, on the individual customer's terms.

12. Customer bonding

Once the behaviors of each customer are understood, management ought to identify what behaviors are desired, setting objectives for each customer's behaviors in a progression that leads to the most desirable ones—one step at a time. Imagine a bonding hierarchy on a behavioral ladder that starts with prospects at the bottom rung and advocates at the top. What behaviors should a customer manifest at each rung on this ladder? How does the company elevate the customer one step at a time on the behavioral ladder to achieve the most intense bond possible?

13. Social marketing

Marketers pay close attention to social marketing to engage with existing customers both because of who they are and who they know. In this way, existing customers, especially those most favorably disposed toward the company, often represent an untapped or underutilized asset. These existing customers have the ability to serve as "centers of influence," just as rock stars, sports players, entertainers, media personalities and politicians, to name a few, can influence prospective customers more generally. The social context of marketing is fundamental to managing the new customer relationship and needs to be explored in depth, understood and framed in a strategic response.

14. A chain of stakeholder relationships

Rather than considering supply chains, it is more appropriate for companies to consider how the needs and behaviors of individual customers can drive procurement, production and logistics, among other considerations. For this to work effectively, the firm needs to develop and align a chain of relationships to provide for changing demands, in essence creating a "demand chain" rather than a supply chain. Marketers who focus only on the end-customer relationship will find that such a limitation constrains the results they can achieve because any weak stakeholder relationship can undercut performance overall. The end-customer relationship is only as strong as the weakest link in a chain of relationships the organization uses to create new and mutual value with individual customers. This chain includes the organization and its main stakeholders, including investors, employees, suppliers, distribution channel intermediaries, regulators, governments and even the public at large, a very indirect stakeholder in the enterprise but a category that can impact its very existence on occasion.

15. Structure follows strategy

If relationship management is to be central to the enterprise, as it ought to be, the organization's structure should enable execution of the strategy. Organizational design should thus reflect the relationship objectives of the company and allow strategies to be effectively implemented by ensuring that each of the main processes by which the organization engages with its customers has a process owner. For example, high-level processes (sometimes called mega-processes) such as existing customer management, trade relationship management, new customer acquisition, direct stakeholder management and management of employee relationships could be assigned process owners. Assignment of responsibilities is needed if organizations are to implement and measure the results of their relationship-based strategies.

● ● ●

The emergence of new technologies and evolution of marketing theory has put an end to traditional marketing principles and, in the process, created entirely new opportunities for marketers—this time to serve the individual customer rather than mass markets or market segments. The potential now exists for companies to create new value for and with customers, and to benefit in the sharing of that value. More than that, as companies pursue the potential to engage their current customers as individuals, they might also explore how to capture new business from the customers known to their existing customers and explore the resulting potential of one-*through*-one marketing. Some of this territory is now well known to marketers. Much of this is not. And the fact that many customers in most markets have yet to commit their loyalty suggests that a significant opportunity remains for companies to capture the potential inherent in defining and managing customer relationships. All journeys can be planned and this one is no exception. So, organizations without a plan ought to have one and those that have developed a plan might revisit it, particularly after reading the next chapter that discusses planning in detail.

Chapter 2
STRATEGIES FOR BETTER CUSTOMER RELATIONSHIPS

"Make no little plans; they have no magic to stir men's blood and probably themselves will not be realized."

—Daniel H. Burnham (1846–1912),
in *Daniel H. Burnham: Architect,
Planner of Cities* by Charles Moore

This chapter considers how well positioned a company is at present to develop relationships with its customers and, through a process of self-questioning, suggests possible areas for improvement. The next chapter discusses the planning of relationships with existing customers. The focus here is on the organization as a whole and whether the company is ready to achieve competitively superior stakeholder relationships.

A STRATEGIC CONTEXT FOR RELATIONSHIP MANAGEMENT

Relationships don't just happen, of course. Plans are needed to advance relationships with chosen customers and potential customers, and preparation needs to precede planning. A number of authors have considered what it means to be prepared for relationship management. Some have suggested that companies that are able to identify their customers, differentiate them by need and value, and have the potential to interact with each customer uniquely as an individual, while changing aspects of their products or services to serve individual customers, would provide some evidence of preparation.[1] While appropriately addressing issues such as these would suggest that a company is indeed prepared to launch a relationship management strategy, the starting point for relationship management success is with the CEO, senior management and the organization's board of directors.

Relationship management by its very nature requires more than a near-term orientation and comprises a vision of the organization as it could be. As such, relationship management will require more than passive support from the CEO and board to enable the strategy to be pursued; it will require active involvement. Already many boards are committed to the management of customer relationships and some require that management provide metrics which pay attention to relationships, either as part of a Balanced Scorecard or separately, such as Net Promoter Scores.[2]

If customer relationships are the key assets of the organization to be nurtured and grown, then recognition of this importance ought to be apparent in the vision statement of the organization and its strategic plans. While many leaders know that relationships are important and frequently communicate this importance, their business models and investment plans generally still reflect a focus on transactions. For example, relationship management may require material front-end investments in technology, process redesign and training while financial benefits accrue over time as customers grow more loyal and bring their friends. As a result, many companies do not make all the relationship-related investments they could and should, so they do not fully achieve the benefits of being relationship oriented nor focusing on transactions.

When management does not yet fully embrace relationship management as a strategic focus for the business as a whole, it is incumbent on employees to manage upwards to help ensure a shift in the executives' mindset, attitude and knowledge. Some companies have lunch-and-learn sessions to accomplish this, others circulate articles or books to senior management, and some invite guest speakers to company events, for example.

Locating, connecting and engaging with prospective customers in social spaces require additional commitment to relationships as a basis for the business. The board may ask for the business case for relationship management, whether focused on existing customers, social prospects or both. It is not particularly hard to formulate a compelling business case for relationship management as it is well known that it costs more to obtain new customers than to retain current ones, that current customers offer a wide variety of additional revenue building and cost management opportunities, and that social prospects can be more economically accessed using social media than broadcast media, for example. Business cases can help secure funding but the bigger issue when securing board engagement on relationships is to focus on a vision of the firm where relationships are the essence of the company and, for this, the CEO must be fully and visibly committed.

RELATIONSHIP MANAGEMENT CAPABILITIES

In this world of constant change, capabilities become even more important than strategies because they underpin fluid strategic options and cater to changes that cannot be readily anticipated. Strategies are less dynamic. While strategies typically provide point solutions for single or discrete paths to destinations, capabilities enable strategies—potentially multiple strategies, including strategies already known and those not yet conceived. Capabilities also have the potential to restrict options. As such, strategic capabilities are fundamental touchstones that corporations must get right if they are to achieve their visions because strategies to achieve objectives stem from these. The relatively greater importance of capabilities over point strategies applies equally to relationship management strategy, which requires a number of strategic capabilities to underpin it. These capabilities include the following key elements that ought to be incorporated in an organization's strategic relationship management plan or strategic plan:

1. Culture and values
2. Leadership
3. People
4. Technology
5. Customer analytics, knowledge and insight
6. Process

The goal of relationship management is to align all these aspects of the company—each of these aspects separately—with its chosen customers and social prospects. This is an important observation for it is a rare company that will develop enduring relationships when one or more among these capabilities are not in alignment with its chosen customers. In the extreme, the company coveting relationships with its customers but focused on transactional behavior will not likely achieve the relationships it seeks. The following considers each of the components of relationship management.

Culture and Values

Culture and values underpin and enable stakeholder relationships and organizational differentiation. It is difficult to imagine a company having success with relationship management where the culture and values do not support relationships. Where the culture and values of a company demand maximizing the value of today's transaction and using whatever combination of competence, guile and cunning to achieve its ends, it is unlikely that an enduring relationship can be formed when customers have the choice of doing business with a company geared to building genuine, longer-term value.

Consider for a moment a company that doesn't trust its customers, doesn't listen to its customers, doesn't know what they will do next, and doesn't much care. Obviously, it won't take long before customers understand what employees already know—that companies pursuing profit single-mindedly will face the profit paradox: profit is a byproduct of doing much else right and rarely is achieved when companies focus on profit alone. So take a quick test to reflect on aspects of the relationship-based culture in your own organization. Ten questions are asked in Table 2. Answer "Yes" or "No" to each.

If you scored more than eight "Yes" answers on this quiz, perhaps you should put this book down now and look for ways to improve the environment in which you work as your organization may not yet be ready to compete on relationships. Between six and eight "Yes" answers and your organization may also need material improvement. After you are finished with this book, give it to your boss. Then discuss how you might work together to help create a cultural shift, one executive and function at a time. Leadership creates and shapes cultures—the more urgent the direction from leaders, the quicker the cultural shift. If you scored fewer than six "Yes" answers, your company is culturally ready to embark on a relationship-based enterprise strategy, or to expand the scope of its strategy as it now stands.

The message: the culture and values of the enterprise must be conducive to the formation of an enduring relationship, and should align broadly with the culture and values of the company's chosen customers—the core customers who will take the company into the future.

Leadership

Leadership is an organizational capability that underpins much else and this applies especially to the definition and pursuit of customer-focused

Table 2: A Relationship-Based Culture: 10 Questions

Question	Yes	No
1. Given a choice, our company would prefer a quick win of X dollars today rather than a payout of 2X dollars that might occur over the next few years.		
2. It's common in management meetings to make a joke at someone else's expense, but never at the expense of the most senior person in the room.		
3. We tell our suppliers to freeze their prices or reduce them, or else we'll find someone who will.		
4. When someone goes on sick leave, we think about who will do the job in his or her absence before we think about his or her recovery from sickness.		
5. If our advertising agency were to tell us that they would resign competitive accounts and work only with our firm in this industry if we would give them a long-term contract, we would be more inclined to think about the downsides of a long-term contract with the agency than the upsides of exclusivity.		
6. Our sales force is compensated based on commission calculated on sales alone.		
7. The calculation of executive compensation does not include measures of customer longevity, likelihood-to-recommend or Net Promoter Scores but is closely tied principally to factors such as stock prices, ROI and profitability.		
8. Our organization gives money to charity and hosts and participates in charitable events that are linked in some way to the company's mission or positioning. Donations, when made, are never made anonymously.		
9. There is little evidence of actions that reflect genuine organizational empathy for those who are less fortunate in society.		
10. If a customer wants to return a defective product, customer service first determines the eligibility of the return. The importance of the customer receives secondary attention or no attention at all.		

strategies. It all starts with who leaders are, how they think of themselves and how they institutionalize their values, for it would be the rare organization that would be able to rise far above the people who point the way. For some leaders, relationship management means first unlearning some of the very behaviors that have made them successful. For example, the child who was very protective of toys and had difficulty sharing may become a successful accountant whose Type A and transactional behavior leads to the corner office. The obverse of this is that this same person might also be a demanding and controlling adult who has trouble forging enduring relationships. It is the enduring nature of relationships that leaders need most if they are to see their customers as part of a circular system of value creation in which company and customer must both participate for ongoing value to be unlocked and sustained. The leaders within the organization should be prepared to focus on the mutual interests of the company and its individual customers, employees and other stakeholders. Leadership requires choices, and choices define destinies to be achieved and futures to be forgone. In this case, leadership means choosing customers with whom the company will collaborate most to create mutual value and forgoing certain customers and the possible value they could have created.

One of the largest plastic injection molding companies in the world, Nypro, is a quality focused company determined to bring uniformity to its processes. In 1987, with 800 customers, it did something that would then have been quite controversial: it narrowed its customer base. Over the next 10 years, it jettisoned 750 of these customers, carefully explaining its strategy to these "fired" customers. Nypro wanted to do business with large purchasers that themselves wanted a relationship and valued both quality service and the provision of solutions, rather than just products. By September 1997, Nypro had 65 customers after cutting the rest. Sales had grown from less than $50 million in 1987 to over $450 million a decade later. Only strong leadership could have caused this focusing to be considered and to be implemented successfully. Today this firm's revenues are in excess of $1.1 billion. And it has relationships with more than just its customers: this company is owned by its employees.

More than this, as noted in Chapter 11, companies get the employee and customer behaviors they model and for which they plan. Behaviors that executives demonstrate and that are consistent with relationship management will lead to stronger relationships with stakeholders than companies that talk of the importance of relationships but have leadership that models these behaviors inconsistently.

No organization will be successful implementing a relationship management strategy as long as the leadership in the company views business as a zero-sum game in which winning must be at the expense of others. In some companies, executives try to ensure that they maximize the value of each deal with every customer. In these firms, it is regarded as smart to sweep all the chips to the company's side of the table. Companies trying to forge relationships with this underlying approach to customers will find, for obvious reasons, that customers have no interest in long-term bonding with such suppliers. The opportunity to continuously create new and mutual value over time will go to competitors more amenable to sharing.

Companies with greater bargaining power than their customers and suppliers have a special role to play in the total system of which they are part. These companies have an obligation to lead both their own firm and those of their customers and suppliers to a higher state of relating, one in which new value can be created and shared rather than the more traditional model in which everyone is trying to cut a bigger slice from what they consider to be the same pie.

Take a quick test to consider aspects of your own style in the context of relationships and business leadership. Answer "Yes" or "No" to the questions that follow in Table 3.

On this quick test, too, if you scored more than eight "Yes" answers, the pursuit of relationship management as an enterprise-wide strategy should await your thoughtful reflection on who you are and how you relate, even if you are your own worst enemy when it comes to developing and sustaining relationships. Reach out for coaching or capitalize on your strengths that would not appear to be primarily in the relationship space. If you scored between six and eight "Yes" answers, you know that there are still opportunities for you to improve your relationship orientation, starting with your self-perceptions. You know that you don't have an unshakable focus on the

Table 3: Leadership and Relationships: Assessing Your Style

	Question	Yes	No
1.	When evaluating my skill or expertise as a business developer, people think of me more as a hunter than a farmer—someone who is more likely to bring home a major prize than someone who will plant the seeds of success and nurture it over time.		
2.	In private moments when I reflect on my achievements, I think often of the battles I have waged and won.		
3.	I think more about what others in the company think of me than the empathy I extend to others with whom I deal.		
4.	When I interact with a friend or colleague, I usually think about what he or she could be doing for me.		
5.	I lost interest in former friends or colleagues when I realized that they weren't of much use to me.		
6.	I am much more interested in achieving career and financial success than in the journey that will get me there.		
7.	When I contribute time to pursuits outside of work, I am mindful first about how this involvement can contribute to my career success.		
8.	When I see an overly aggressive employee talking down a co-worker, I am unlikely to counsel him or her about the merits of empathy.		
9.	In most conversations, I want to speak my mind so I don't have to listen to the less thoughtful or less useful ideas of others.		
10.	The world is a harsh place and likely to get harsher. In this world, only the tough survive. Anybody who thinks otherwise is less likely to succeed.		

other in any context—it is mostly about you but if you are committed to change, you know you can. After all, you have made bigger changes before. This book is not about self-help so we will not dwell here except to recognize that if you scored fewer than six "Yes" answers, congratulations. People think of you as a trustworthy person and probably value your friendship. You are ready to lead the charge—and to find like minds among your customers to help secure organizational alignment between their organization or even individual consumers, and your firm.

The message: leaders in organizations should view relationships positively and value sharing as a virtue, not a sign of negotiating weakness. Where companies have bargaining power relative to customers and/or suppliers, it is their role to initiate relationship management in the interests of all and to seek alignment in the total system of supplier-company-customer. Leaders should seek out those among their customers who share relationship-based views that promote value sharing from innovation and mutual success. Good behaviors should be modeled by senior executives so that those who witness the behaviors repeat them in a cycle that radiates to all stakeholders in due course. Customers are watching.

People

People are obviously key to any relationship and a vital organizational capability. Business is still all about people, even in an age where technology disintermediates so many of the processes by which people and companies engage with one another. In an earlier marketing era, market and customer knowledge was centralized and the marketer sought to involve others in the company in strategic marketing programs. Now customer information is pushed to the front line where customers and the company interact. Here, customer-facing personnel have the ability to communicate with customers in a manner that recognizes them, remembers their contact history, understands the current customer issues, predicts anticipated behaviors and suggests appropriate responses, solutions or suggestions. Increasingly, frontline people are becoming consultants, working collaboratively with customers to add value to their company. These roles represent a marked departure from historical practice. Successful realignment of personnel requires that they be recognized and rewarded with incentives that support this redirection, not to mention being enabled by technology, analytics, processes and organizational structure, for example.

When the people serving customers work for third-party organizations and are not directly controlled by the originator of the product or service, human resource systems naturally become more complex. This is the typical case of companies selling their products or services through distribution channel intermediaries, such as retailers and dealers. For example, car companies sell through car dealers, which are somewhat aligned but often not fully so. The profit model of the dealership is quite different from that of the manufacturer, depending more on service, parts and the sale of used vehicles to supplement profits from sales of the manufacturer's new cars and trucks. While there are many reasons the manufacturer usually wants to sustain relationships with the end-customer over his or her purchasing lifetime, the dealer has the potential to amplify or attenuate these ambitions, or even to substantially redirect them to develop its own relationships. To reduce the likelihood of a possible clash of ambitions, car manufacturers have established their own customer databases and provide dealers with access to these data for the dealer to develop relationships and sustain them through better customer service. Go into any Toyota dealership, for example, and the customer service representative will pull up your vehicle history information and be fully prepared to provide service based on this history as well as recommendations generated by software analyzing these data. This is a material change over the last few years when car dealers and car companies used to contest who "owns" the customer relationship.

Many, if not most, people in a company focused on relationship management should move from being functional experts to being process owners for specific categories of relationships. Their role here is to work with others within the company, its customers and suppliers to develop the new value customers want. In the relationship management era, selling, marketing, servicing and supporting customers are integrated processes incorporating relationship management. The process owner must be geared to being the relationship integrator and rewarded and recognized for achieving successful integration.

If rewards are to be geared to this end, people can be measured according to the extent to which they advance the objectives of the firm with each category of customer. As objectives vary, so too do metrics. For example, if the objective is to bond more tightly with customers, specific bonding objectives can be defined and measured.[3] Alternatively, measurements can be focused on long-term revenues and profit, Net Promoter Scores, likelihood-to-recommend scores and so on. Chapter 8 considers metrics and analytics

Table 4: Strategy and Employee Relationships: 10 Questions to Assess the Current State

Question	Yes	No
1. All employees understand who their customers are, whether internal "customers" or customers external to the company, and have performance metrics associated with these customers.		
2. All employees are captains of their own processes for engaging with internal or external customers. This means that they understand those processes and work with others using like processes and more senior process managers to make these processes perform even better.		
3. Performance metrics for internal personnel do not concentrate just on efficiency measures—they pay close attention to the effectiveness of the processes, like generating increased revenues, for example.		
4. Employees know how to listen, having benefited from training in this regard.		
5. Just as customers are categorized according to the value they represent, so too are employees grouped according to the value they create for the enterprise, and employees understand their positioning relative to one another.		
6. Opportunities exist for employees to fulfill their ambitions, whether monetary or otherwise, such as aspects of their personal growth, learning and self-actualization.		
7. People know that relationships are about much more than being nice to one another and understand that trust-based relationships derive in part from mutual respect, meeting promises, no surprises and authentic behavior.		
8. If there were full employment in the job market, people would still be eager to join our firm.		
9. Our firm makes every effort to maintain relationships with people after they have left the organization.		
10. Our firm understands the influencer network within which employees are engaged "outside of work" and enables employees to connect with and engage the networks of which they are part.		

more completely; here it is noted that customer satisfaction measurements should not generally serve as a basis for relationship measurement, since they provide an incomplete view of the customer relationship largely because of the absence of a competitive dimension to it.

See Table 4 for a quick self-test to assess people-related aspects of organizational readiness for relationship management. Reply "Yes" or "No" to each of the questions.

If you scored fewer than six "Yes" answers, it is likely that your firm needs to pay as much attention to its employees as it does to its customers, or perhaps even more so, given that employees may feel somewhat neglected at present. Your firm would not yet be ready for an expansion of relationship management strategies or implementation until it focused more on employees and customers internal to the organization. It is quite likely that a firm with fewer than six "Yes" answers might have a large number of employees who are not just neutral to the organization and its objectives but who are actively antipathetic or even hostile to these objectives. With seven or eight "Yes" answers, the company may be in need of some employee relationship attention and hopefully by the conclusion of this book, some assistance will have been provided in this regard. If you scored more than eight "Yes" answers, your organization treats people very well and probably is among the most highly rated employers in your industry or geography. Congratulations. It is likely, however, that some fine-tuning remains for people-enabled relationships, especially those by which your employees engage with social prospects. For example, are your employees allowed to connect with others using social media at work? Some companies, such as Best Buy, actively harness such employee engagement, which challenges negative assumptions about such a suggestion.

The message: train, develop and grow people into owners of a process that seeks to build customer bonding and achieve other aspects that are specific to individual customers and the process. Everybody has a customer, whether internal or external to the organization. Performance metrics should be geared to the value each process is intended to deliver as part of the overall objective of customer-specific relationship development and value growth.

Technology

Technology has subsumed CRM rather than the other way around. It would have been better strategically for the enterprise if this occurrence had been the reverse, with CRM being the strategic umbrella for customer engagement, including technology. It is hardly surprising that technology has become the focal point for CRM. After all, there have been so many technology vendors saying, "Buy me and you'll have CRM" and their collective voices have overwhelmed the few who have argued that CRM is an enterprise-wide strategy and technology is just one component of implementation.

The challenge for CRM in this context is more serious than a question of definitions, important though this is. It is the uncommon firm that would not perceive more technology as a way to strengthen customer relationships still further. In this context, more technology is better in a sort of virtual arms race with competitors. Give a person a hammer, the saying goes, and every problem looks like a nail. In this case, IT-led technology adoption has the potential to put strategic blinders on the business and focus implementation more on what the technology can do rather than on the organization's object-ive, usually how to increase customer value and earn it out for shareholders.

Technology can serve multiple customer relationship roles within a company and between a company and its customers, including the following:

- External communications
- Internal communications
- Computing (and analytics, discussed in the next section), and
- Content.

The following itemizes selected features and benefits of each of these aspects of technology in the context of relationship management:

External Communications
Technology can help organizations to accomplish the following:

- Facilitate two-way interaction between individual customers and the company about every aspect of their requirements, about interactions and also collaboration between the customer and the company pre-purchase, during purchase and afterwards—the post-purchase experience.
- Provide more rapid or informed communication than was possible with manual intervention.
- Open new communications channels with customers that can provide them with additional benefits, such as increased control over their com-munications or anytime/anywhere access to the company, and may help the company to reduce the cost of customer interaction, increase the effectiveness of the communication and improve the customer experience.
- Communicate more effectively and efficiently with stakeholders (in addition to customers), such as non-customers, investors, the board of directors, employees, management, suppliers and distribution channel intermediaries.

Internal Communications
Within an organization, technology can help enable the following:

- Remove "stovepipe" functionality from the many individual internal processes and technologies that face the customer, including call cen-ters, Internet access, social media, ordering, shipping, billing, field sales forces, dealer sales, direct mail and mass advertising so that the customer relationship can receive clearer attention.

- Tie together diverse communications systems, call centers, communications channels and databases so that the company has the potential to become a more informed and customer-friendly supplier.

Computing

The role of computing in relationship management is to provide organizational memory for customer relationships, a predictive ability to inform these relationships for the relationship manager, and current and timely content needed by relationship managers to add value to the customer or account. Computing is used primarily to facilitate storage and retrieval of huge amounts of data which provide the history of a number of factors important to the advancement of customer relationship and to analyze and interpret these data. Increasingly, computing is being used to accomplish many of the above-mentioned tasks in real time and without human intervention. In one example, Pandora, a supplier of music online, has categorized many thousands of tracks according to categories such as melody, harmony, instrumentation, rhythm, vocals and lyrics, and with this they are able to serve a customized flow of music to individuals that reflects their prior selections or listening behavior. More than simply being pretty nifty, this technology helps to ensure that customers are embraced in a learning relationship that gets progressively deeper and is more scalable, without the organization intervening and increasing their variable costs associated with people, for example.

Cloud Computing

Data are increasingly distributed and networked, and may be resident in the cloud. Previously data resided in closely held data banks or even on desktops accessible to a few who had been with the company long enough or undertook specific functions in the company. Customer and operational data including sales management, for example, is now being gathered, stored, processed, archived and communicated external to the enterprise. Although the specific location of data matters much less than the uses to which data are put, opportunities remain for companies to reconceive their data architecture so that it focuses less on efficiency—the key rationale most companies advance when promoting their cloud-based environments—and more on effectiveness for relationship acquisition, development and management.

Customer knowledge is now distributed, real-time in nature and integrated across channels. Customer knowledge was centralized—such as in research reports and the Marketing Information System, and this knowledge was neither current nor accessible to the people who needed the information, including frontline personnel and management. Now, customer knowledge is potentially open and accessible to those who need it, a major change for some enterprises where information remains closely controlled and access more limited. Chapter 8 discusses technology and its application to customer analytics in more detail.

Content

Content includes a customer profile and related information for each customer. Content also includes the individual customer's context, behaviors such as transactions and interactions with the enterprise, and a customer's needs, profitability and social influence. This information can be used to differentiate customers from one another, to be more relevant to each one, to engage each as he or she wants, and to know which customers can attract additional customers, among other benefits. Each aspect of content is discussed briefly below:

- Customer information includes data describing customer demographics and other profile information, locations, usage patterns, order frequency, favorability toward the organization and the customer's individual preferences.
- Customer context captures information to describe the priorities each customer emphasizes, and is especially relevant for B2B purchasing, describing the purchase decision-making unit, criteria for buying and the purchase process, for example.
- Customer behaviors captures information reflecting interactions before the sale, during the sale and post-sale, the number, nature, scale and profitability of orders, and other behavioral information including response to prior programs and sensitivity to specific media. Many organizations track the scope of customer purchase behavior here, too, in addition to the scale of their transactions with the enterprise. That is, companies often see a relationship to be more valuable and durable when customers buy a range of goods or services from them, rather than purchasing a lot but just of one particular type.
- Customer needs stores individual survey data, sales force input and metadata derived from an assessment of a customer's behaviors to understand individual needs and enable the organization to interpret these needs into appropriate products, services and programs.

- Customer profitability tracks the financial performance of the account or customer with a costing methodology that recognizes all the costs and time associated with selling to, servicing and financing a customer, not just the cost of goods sold.
- Customer social influence is assessed to understand which customers are most likely to attract additional customers and the likely business impacts of this attraction.

Organizations use content such as that described above in many ways to add value to the customer relationship, typically looking to expand the scale or scope of transactions. For example, customized catalogs can have only the categories of goods in which the customer has demonstrated purchase interest, and the goods may even be in colors for which customers have shown a preference. Online vendors such as Amazon track online behaviors and make customized recommendations in real time. Customized newsletters use variable content selected based on matching customer profiles and behaviors to pre-developed content options most likely to resonate with each.

More than simply an enabler of accelerated and high-performance processes to improve the efficiency of the order-shipping-billing cycle, more even than a capability to harness customer information and manage marketing campaigns, technology should be used to disintermediate all customer touch points to achieve a number of important benefits for each customer. Customers will want companies to be able to do the following and technology is likely required to help firms achieve these objectives:

- "Know me all the time, wherever and whenever I interact with your organization."
  Technology enables data integration for cross-channel alignment, mobile access by customers and a single real-time customer view that grows progressively deeper and more insightful.
- "Each time you do something for me, do it better than the last time."
  As the enterprise's view of each customer grows progressively deeper and more insightful, the technology should do something useful with the knowledge that has been developed.
- "Do what I want."
  Technology should create customer-specific value. Companies understand that but many customers continue to perceive that organizations

are not fully focused on the end-customer, placing the firm's priorities and policies above those of the customer to optimize profitability.

- "Speak to me—on my terms."

  Technology should engage individual customers as each wants and most certainly not strictly from the vantage point of what the organization wants to sell.

- "Be relevant to me in the fabric of my life."

  Technology should understand the human and social context of each customer, enabling social connections and, in the process, not only humanizing the enterprise but making it so remarkable that the customer happily makes referrals of the company to peers and other decision makers within his or her spheres of influence.

Today, most organizations understand the importance of technology as a key to their business performance. So if some technology is good, it would stand to reason that management would believe that more technology would be even better. Except that this perspective is not generally true. Consider the many thousands of social media options available to the company. It clearly has to make choices and more social media would not necessarily result in closer customer relationships, especially if all the media are not fully integrated. Choices need to be made because resources are finite, as is management time and attention.

The message: deploy technology to develop a better customer memory. Give customers the communications options they want to help them access and interact with the enterprise, learn, and repeat the purchase experience. Use technology to reach out beyond existing customers to non-customers, including non-customers known to existing customers, using social media. Ensure that the technology leads to memorable experiences—each better than the last—and sufficiently so that customers want to tell their friends and are encouraged and reminded to do so.

See Table 5 for a quick self-test to assess the role of technology in your organization. Reply "Yes" or "No" to each of the questions.

If you scored between eight and ten "No" answers, your organization would appear to embrace the strategic role of technology for relationship management. More likely, your enterprise would have a score of between four and eight "No" answers but if it has less than four and there is no evidence that these numbers will improve anytime soon, the technology orientation might merit a review to ensure more alignment between technology and business strategy, in general, and on relationships, more specifically.

Table 5: Technology: 10 Questions to Assess the Current State

Question	Yes	No
1.	When we analyze our technology investments, much of the ongoing budget goes to ERP-related expenditures (e.g., license fees and modules for SAP) and ongoing operations.[4]		
2.	Of the funds available for new technology investments, most of these go to purchasing upgrades for existing technology infrastructure and new modules to extend functionality of current investments.		
3.	When we invest in technology, the customer experience receives secondary attention while efficiencies gained from the deployment of the technology are uppermost in our minds.		
4.	Our strategic plan for technology investments is not closely integrated with our marketing and customer development plans. (Answer "yes" if the strategic technology plan is not closely integrated with marketing and customer plans.)		
5.	The technologies we are deploying right now to face the customer are not primarily intended to provide customers with anytime/anywhere access to our enterprise.		
6.	We don't benchmark the speed with which we deploy new technologies against our competitors.		
7.	Our technology deployments don't specifically recognize the importance of mobile technologies such as smartphones and tablets in the hands of customers.		
8.	Our cloud strategy is primarily geared to achieve operational efficiencies and performance gains. We have not yet fully considered the opportunities associated with CRM and customer engagement strategies that are cloud enabled.		
9.	The senior executives focused on technology do not always see the connections between technology deployments and usage, and stakeholder relationships.		
10.	It always seems that the priorities of technology investments are based on the "squeaky wheel getting the grease" (i.e., the people who have most influence or complain the most get their way) rather than a coherent series of priorities.		

Customer analytics, Knowledge and Insight

Technology must enable the relationship manager to develop new knowledge and insight about the customer relationship and facilitate action based on the information. Obviously technology must do this cost effectively to achieve the purpose of creating customer value, and the cost effectiveness of technology can be measured channel by channel and initiative by initiative. The starting point for technology is to listen to customer connections and then to inform the customer relationship. As mentioned, it should accomplish these tasks economically, a goal for most firms but particularly for companies with large customer databases and modest margins, the typical case at many mass merchandisers, for example.

Software, modeling, reporting and other tools can help add value to underlying data and even predict what individual customers will do—sometimes in advance of his or her own cognition, helping the marketer to be proactive in the management of the customer relationship. While many relationship managers report significant use of technology tools to help them accomplish these ends, customers often fail to appreciate the benefit. For example, few car owners are in touch with their dealers for other than service requirements during the time they own their vehicle, and even when there is communication initiated by the dealer the interaction is largely inconsequential or not tied closely to most customers' needs, the case of a diligent car salesperson sending out birthday cards, for example. It would be much more helpful to a customer to be provided with information by the service department on the costs of his or her vehicle's maintenance over the past few years and how this is likely to trend based on the service experience of customers with vehicles having a similar mileage. In this way, the customer can make informed decisions about continuing car services and repairs as opposed to purchasing a new one. So the challenge is not just having the right tools to conduct the measurements but to have the feedback processes in place to take corrective actions based on these measurements.

Analytical tools, like all technology, come and go, and there is always a "flavor of the month" effect at work. At the time of writing, the following items that appear in Table 6 are selected tools that many companies are using to track aspects of their customer connections.

See Table 7 for a quick self-test for the reader to assess the company's preparedness to listen to individual customers, store relevant data, interpret these data to develop individual customer knowledge and insight, and take action from the insights gained.

If you have scored fewer than six "Yes" answers, your company has significant opportunities to develop a deeper customer understanding. At present, perhaps your firm is trying to find opportunities without seeing the entire

Table 6: Tools and Customer Analytics

Communications Channels	Selected Tools
Blogs	Google Analytics
Tweets	Seesmic Desktop, TweetDeck, search.twitter.com
Integrated monitoring software	Radian6 Social Marketing Cloud
Video sharing websites such as YouTube	TubeMogul
Web traffic	Google Analytics, Alexa
External links	Google search using "links:www.website.com"
Reputation management	Spyfu.com for pay per click monitoring

Table 7: Customer Analytics, Knowledge and Insight: 10 Questions to Assess the Current State

	Question	Yes	No
1.	Our company listens to the voices of individual customers in every possible channel of communications they may employ, from mail to call centers to click stream analysis to social media.		
2.	The voice of the customer is used not just to assess the effectiveness of individual initiatives or programs but is tied together across multiple channels to provide us with knowledge and/or insight into individual customers and their behaviors.		
3.	We know the ROI of each of the programs we deploy.		
4.	We understand the cost of marketing communications by channel and their relative effectiveness.		
5.	We engage individual customers with need-satisfying solutions, sometimes before they perceive the need for these solutions.		
6.	We monitor our reputation in social media and engage customers and non-customers.		
7.	We view customer data as an essential element of the value we create so that we can sustain an ongoing and valuable relationship with each customer. Customer data is not simply a byproduct of what we do but integral to it.		
8.	We have developed or deployed real-time tools that engage customers in a learning relationship—either directly in the communications channel of their choice, or indirectly, such as when call center personnel are prompted to ask specific questions.		
9.	Our marketing communications channels have budgets that are aligned with one another so that the objectives of the organization can be addressed optimally.		
10.	All our measurements are tied to the customer and his or her value to the organization.		

picture that data development, processing and analysis could reveal. If you scored seven or eight "Yes" answers, your firm is well on its way to engaging individual customers in a learning relationship but be careful that such a relationship does indeed add value to shareholders. With nine or ten "Yes" answers, your analytics are likely outstanding, and your firm may well be a leading practitioner in this space.

A key challenge for the marketer is to secure resources for investment in individual customer knowledge and insight over the longer term. This can be done, even under potentially trying circumstances, as the following example suggests. Founded in 1948, Fingerhut is a direct retailer of many products online and through catalogs sent to customers. The firm has had a succession of owners, including American Can, Federated Department Stores, Petters Group and Bain Capital, and today is owned by Bluestem Brands. It appears the company has been able to sustain customer database investments, a need they recognized early on. In 1997, they already had 6 TB of customer information—very large for the time, and the equivalent of almost 100 pages for each of its customers. Data such as these have enabled the company to have a clear customer focus. It has identified its customer focus as "low to middle income, credit constrained consumers with FICO scores between 500 and 700...those with an annual household income below $75,000..." and noted that the firm has "a deep understanding of [its] customers' merchandise preferences and utilizes [its] extensive marketing experience to develop a tailored message to attract their attention...[It has] developed sophisticated prospect and customer databases that support [its] ability..." The company continues to invest in the development of databases that describe their current and potential customers.[5]

Customer analytics has become an important factor for companies to inform their customer relationships and add value to them. This book devotes Chapter 8 to a more detailed exploration of the subject.

The message: invest in listening to individual customers and the knowledge and insight that can be derived from this listening. Ensure that this insight translates into improved customer experience and, in particular, that the customer thinks a little bit better of the brand, the company and its products each time he or she has anything to do with the enterprise. Maintain the investment through thick and thin, and especially thin!

Process

Although many firms reengineered their business processes some time ago, the individual customer is still not at the center of everything most businesses do. Here is a case in point. Communications processes were originally engineered for mass marketing purposes. With the arrival of customer-specific relationship management, additional processes focused on individuals were grafted onto mass marketing processes. Mass marketing processes continued more or less as before but often with more budget constraints and sometimes less clarity in respect of communications objectives. The following are relevant questions that would suggest opportunities for a new look at communications processes in companies with situations similar to this example:

- Would it be appropriate for an organization to reach out with mass marketing while simultaneously engaging individual customers in a conversation?

- If the answer is "yes," should the nature of mass marketing not be adjusted to integrate the more personal conversation yielded from relationship management processes?
- What should be the nature of packaged, static communications for mass marketing?
- How should these static communications differ from the dimensions and nature of variable content directed to individual customers and how should mass and individual customer communications be integrated?
- When the mass marketing communications model was originally developed, it had no feedback loop other than marketing research. What should the nature and role of feedback be and how should it be undertaken in the context of customer sensing more generally?
- How is the marketing budget to be adjusted to balance broadcast out-reach with interactive connections and interactive communications with existing customers with communications that engage potential customers such as in social media?

In another example, it is still quite common for sales forces to be expected to both create new customers and manage existing ones for increased shareholder value. In the context of relationship management, new customers and current ones require two fundamentally different processes for customer engagement and management, and would thus require separate attention by the sales force—likely with different individuals in the roles of "hunter" (new customer development) and "farmer" (current customer development). It is the rare individual who can function as both hunter and farmer. Most sales personnel have profiles that are much more one than the other—classically trained salespeople are most typically hunters and must learn much—and unlearn even more—if they are to be effective in selling within a relationship management context.

In short—and as painful as it might be to endure a reengineering initiative yet again—it might be appropriate to revisit organizational processes to confirm that they are aligned with relationship management objectives, strategy and structure, and that the individual customer is indeed at the heart of the organization, as the organization would expect him or her to be.

The message: focus processes around individual customers, giving each the value he or she wants. Ensure processes are integrated both operationally and to facilitate an effective customer connection that develops the value individual customers want, and is seen by these customers to be messaging them consistently across communications channels and in real time.

THE CULTURAL IMPERATIVE

A number of questions have been asked in the preceding sections that could evoke in the reader an even longer list of questions, demonstrating the complexity of alignment. It is naturally very challenging to align operational processes throughout a chain of relationships that start with the end-customer, proceed backward through distribution channel intermediaries such as retailers, then through the organization's many processes and backward to suppliers and, potentially, their suppliers too. Difficult though this may be, it is nevertheless possible to do. Companies use technology throughout their value chains to achieve this alignment by facilitating the many dimensions of variability for each category of stakeholder.

As difficult as interorganizational alignment is, internal alignment may prove yet more difficult to accomplish. It is not challenging to chart processes and engineer for alignment but there are non-process issues to be resolved for leadership to orchestrate and many of these come down to culture, attitude and beliefs. Many organizations commit themselves to individual customer relationships but they don't change the culture to match, and results can reflect this lack. Operational alignment requires that companies demonstrate aligned behaviors; on the other hand, cultural change in support of relationship management requires that companies believe something fundamentally different about themselves and what it means to make money.

If money is to be made transaction by transaction and program by program, as many internal metrics and analytics require, then this in itself can represent a strategic blind spot where culture is limiting, often unspoken or unnoticed. Relationship management requires that the customer relationship take precedence over each transaction but there are many situations where this counters the prevailing culture. Accountants like to say that they know nothing unless they have a measurement to inform their knowledge. "You get what you measure," they often say. This raises a challenge for the relationship marketer if the finance department is guided by transactional metrics and these are the same metrics the CEO uses to run the firm. More specifically, where financial measurements sum individual transactions to measure performance such as product line profitability, sales force performance, marketing program ROI and so on, aggregation masks the origination of metrics in transactions, not relationships. That is, when metrics of an aggregated nature are used, the likelihood exists that the organization is being managed according to a transactional focus without even being fully aware of this. In such situations, the knowledge that is being derived would either not encourage relationships or would even be antithetical to attaining relationship objectives. This should serve to illustrate why leadership and culture are so fundamental to an organization seeking to compete on customer relationships. It should also illustrate the importance of at least balancing certain measurements with metrics that derive from and serve to describe relationships.

So how does a firm achieve a relationship-based culture? Or is this cultural change even possible? Cultural change, like any change, starts with recognizing that change is needed. This recognition might involve a comprehensive fishbone (for example) analysis that identifies root causes of financial non-performance that eventually traces these causes back to the underpinning issues, possibly including leadership and culture. For example, this assessment might reveal that the path to power is usually out of a non-marketing function such as accounting in the previous example, that key performance metrics are transactional in nature or that the board of directors, and hence the CEO, don't consider relationship management to be central to attainment of the organization's vision. Alternatively, the assessment might be a simple recognition that the organization is unlikely to achieve its objectives without relationship management. Having identified the importance of customer relationships, it is then up to the CEO to drive a cultural shift that will be supportive of this enterprise-wide strategy.

As the overall champion of relationships in the organization, the CEO him or herself should be widely regarded as a relationship person. A transactionally oriented CEO will send signals—perhaps unknowingly—that transactions trump relationships and will not create the desired cultural change until he or she embraces relationship management in thought as well as deed. Some CEOs have sustained their success by being ever more focused on the profitability and performance of individual transactions but they are nevertheless capable of change. In other cases, the success of transactional CEOs has been cemented by dysfunction that may be evidenced by a projection of power, self-aggrandizement or even narcissism. In cases such as these, cultural change will not be accomplished until the CEOs unlearn some behaviors. Because unlearning is so much harder than learning, without ongoing reinforcement and assistance, experience suggests that there is potential for CEOs to gravitate back to the learned behaviors they already have. If the gravitational pull of prior knowledge, perception, behavior or experience cannot be undone, a relationship-minded CEO may need to be appointed as a replacement. Clearly, this is much harder to do when the CEO is also the founder and owner of the company. In these situations, it is particularly important for the CEO to be self-aware.

BEYOND CULTURE: THE STRATEGIC ENABLERS

How would a firm even know if it needs a makeover of its approach to developing and managing customer relationships? The following reviews selected strategic considerations that precede development of relationship management plans, the subject of Chapter 3.

Relationship-Based Strategy

Relationship-based strategy needs to occur at multiple levels: in terms of strategic capabilities at the organizational level, in terms of market and customer focus at the business unit level, and in terms of specific programs at the product or service line level.

For each level in the organization, strategy should see the customer as genuinely central to the enterprise and everything the company does. While some companies remain locked into the product management era, applying the principles of consumer packaged goods to their companies, in this era of sophisticated customers choosing from products or services that often, in reality, have limited differentiation, product management strategies have less value than strategies geared to creating the value individual customers want. In short, companies with customer-centric strategies are more likely to succeed and endure than companies with product- or service-centric strategies, especially for purchases where there is a risk for consumers.

Product- or service-centric companies may achieve good results and have customer empathy by capturing the essence of the relationship the customer wants in their goods or services alone. This occurs most often for products that have little risk of a bad decision or where the social risk is equally low. Detergents are one such example. In cases such as this, customers do not want customer-specific value. They just want clean clothes and little else. Companies recognize this and put their product or service forward as the embodiment of the relationship they want customers to have with the enterprise. These firms understand that customers are more interested in relating to the outputs of the organization rather than any aspect of the organizational processes, such as communications, collaboration or customization.

By way of contrast, companies would achieve better results by organizing around their customers and providing customer-specific value in situations such as the following:

- When customers see a purchase decision to be risky financially or socially as would be the case when buying a house or set of golf clubs, respectively
- If customers' needs, values or influence are somewhat different from their peers'
- If the information customers seek also is different, and
- Where there is some time-sensitivity or service that enters into the purchase decision.

Strategy also needs to be aligned between the company and its customers to ensure that each understands the direction of the other, enabling each to assess the other in its role as long-term partner, and to create the value each wants. Over time, this means that the supplier must become very familiar with its customer's customer, and be in a position to advance initiatives proactively, perhaps even before its immediate customer appreciates the significance of what the supplier is recommending. This alignment can only take place when there is genuine and near complete sharing of strategic objectives and strategies of both supplier and customer—and company and channel partners—with openness of information sharing that some companies call "open kimono." While this situation applies to relationships between businesses, some would suggest that sharing of objectives and strategies should not occur with consumers. Such a limitation would not be progressive or helpful to the development and maintenance of relationships. Customer alignment in consumer spaces is equally necessary if customers are to be fully engaged, and social prospects are to be converted into best customers. For this, information should be widely shared where it does not put a company's competitive advantage at risk.

The Strategic Value of a Relationship

Relationships can be won one interaction at a time. To do this, the enterprise should make each customer feel better about him or herself, the brand and the customer experience—whether related to a transaction, information or complaint—than was the case prior to the interaction. If customers individually feel better after each interaction with the enterprise than each did beforehand, collectively customers' relationships will grow, as will customer value and shareholder value. So the better the customer feels about him or herself, the more the customer will think well of the enterprise, brand and experience.

The reverse is similarly true. The customer who has a negative interaction with the enterprise, whether through online technology or with a customer service agent, will externalize fault and blame the enterprise and its brand—whether this is reasonable or not.

Just as the very concept of customer strategy needs to be enterprise-wide, so too should the organization seek to win individual customer relationships one step at a time in an integrated way, across all functions, technologies and processes.

Economies of Scope and Data

Companies have long focused on building economies of scale, mostly to drive down their average unit costs. The experience curve effect posits that firms will become better and more cost effective at what they do over time. According to this assumption, total costs decline as cumulative volume—the total number of units ever made by the company—increases. Examples in industries such as chemicals and magnetic tape have been used to show that scale economies and experience curves provide companies with opportunities to spread overheads across a larger volume base and reduce costs in areas apparently unrelated to volume, such as research and development. Now, the rapid lifecycle of products and industries makes experience curves largely an outdated concept. The accelerating pace of change creates substitutes, new entrants and changing industry structures in a much shorter time. Economies continue to exist but now the economies are likely to be found in two other ways, as follows:

- Economies of scope

    Companies with economies of scope provide customers with the goods and services each wants, whether the company makes it or not. As a result, companies compete on relevance and relationships.

- Economies of data

    Companies with economies of data know more and can predict better than competitors. When applied to customer relationships they can be better prepared to sell when customers are most likely to be ready to buy, a competitive advantage that may be very difficult or impossible for competitors to emulate.

    Google's market position is likely unassailable not just because of its algorithms, know-how and giant server farms, although these certainly create barriers to entry. Google simply has more information on each individual than its competitors are ever likely to obtain and Google has been able to monetize this knowledge in increasingly profitable ways. Without these data, even well-heeled competitors such as Microsoft simply cannot compete.

The competitive position of a company and its relative profitability are tied directly to the cumulative volume of data it maintains on its customers, relative to its competitors. The more data companies gather, store, use and share on individual customers, relative to competitors, the more profitable will be their business, again in relation to competitors. Facebook has said as much.[6] The rationale is this: if relationships are the key assets that generate profitability and if relationships are best managed through customer knowledge and insight, then the number of data points tracking individual customer experiences, behaviors, interactions and perspectives, over time, are more likely to reveal truths that can be addressed. The accumulation of massive data is more likely to provide opportunities for timely customer access and management, and possibly even alternative business models and revenue producing opportunities.

Table 8 presents a quick self-test to consider aspects of your organization's strategies in the context of relationships and your firm's preparedness to embark upon or expand its relationship management.

If you scored fewer than five "Yes" answers or found these questions challenging to interpret, it is likely that your company is still at an early stage of its relationship management strategy formulation and perhaps the inception of this focus. Major opportunities in this regard await. Between five and eight "Yes" answers might well suggest that your company has launched relationship management strategies but opportunities still remain to sharpen both the content and process of these plans. If you scored more than eight "Yes" answers, your company is likely well on its way to a relationship management destination. Of course, this little test did not consider whether this is the *right* destination, but it would appear that your organization does have a plan to get there, wherever "there" is!

The message: strategy needs to be customer-centric, with relationship objectives and strategies geared to individual customers both in business-to-business (B2B) and consumer marketplaces. Organizations need relationship management plans or else they have no basis for advancing relationships with customers, channel intermediaries (such as retailers) and others. Relationship managers know that the old adage "If you don't know where you are going, any road will get you there" applies equally to relationship management strategy.[7]

Table 8: Strategy and Relationships: Organizational Preparedness

Question	Yes	No
1. In all our business plans, from the corporate level through the line of business level to the next level—whether product, market or customer—a well-developed relationship planning process exists. As a result, relationship objectives and strategies are articulated, tactics described, and metrics established.		
2. We know who our best customers are—by name—and who our worst customers are—again, by name.		
3. We don't give all customers equal value as this would discriminate against the best and reward the worst, the exact opposite of what we want.		
4. Our company's strategies focus on upgrading our customer portfolio so that we expect to have more good customers over time, and fewer bad ones. Everybody in the company understands these strategies.		
5. We have strategies for either externalizing our worst customers, de-emphasizing them, sending them to competitors, or creating and modifying our business model to serve them profitably.		
6. We have customer-specific strategies for shifting customer share from competitors to our firm so that we get more of our best customers' business and we develop new revenues with these customers.		
7. Our company's strategies focus more on developing progressively deeper relationships with individual customers than on beating specific competitors.		
8. When evaluating people to lead relationship-based strategies, we pay close attention to their personal characteristics as relationship-based leaders.		
9. We categorize customers according to their demonstrated behaviors—such as their communications and purchase histories, and pay more attention to behavioral clustering than customers' demographics when formulating strategy.		
10. When reaching out to prospective social customers, our starting point is our best current customers.		

Relationship management, like all aspects of business, requires thoughtful planning to separate executive vision from wishful intent and to achieve results from relationship management.

Structure

The structure of a company should facilitate its strategy. In fact, one of the easiest ways to see if the company is having problems maintaining a consistent strategy is to review how often reorganization occurs. Companies that reorganize frequently, without strategic context and rationale, often have difficulty defining and implementing a winning strategy.

Relationship management, impacting as it does the entire firm, is a strategy that is enterprise-wide in scope. A company organized according to relationship management principles has managers who each own a specific category of relationship. The following suggests selected relationship categories as examples:

- Current customers overall
- Existing customers clustered into groups to reflect differences in their value, needs, behaviors or influence—or possibly even some aspects of demographics, such as location
- Potential customers such as those who are accessible via social media, and
- Distribution channel intermediaries that might be treated as a category of customer.

So, rather than having a sales and marketing department, for example, a relationship management company may have a department to create new value with current customers while another may be charged with gaining new customers whose profiles match the firm's best customers, for example.

It is no longer uncommon for companies to organize around their customer relationships but it is still uncommon for companies to organize *only* around their customer relationships. The reason for this is the same as the overall challenge for embracing relationship management in the first place. It is all about change management and the willingness of companies to abandon the relative security of the current state for a visionary future state. Existing managers, unable or unwilling to perceive a relationship management future with them in it, often resist structural change in favor of relationship management and senior management may continue to support the current state in whole or in part. This may lead to a hybrid organizational structure with one foot in the camp of transactions and the other in relationship mode. Experience suggests that such cases can result in neither high-performance transactions nor durable and increasingly valuable relationships.

If relationships matter, and they do, and if structure should follow from strategy, and it should, then organizations should organize first around customer relationships, and second around strategic capabilities that are to drive these relationships. That is, a company focused on customer relationships will have both relationship managers and capability managers. The relationship managers will focus on developing and enhancing the asset value of customer relationships, such as by increasing lifetime customer value, while capability managers would seek to create the strategic capabilities that enable customer relationships, people, process, technology and analytics.

Relationships and the Relationship Manager

Relationship managers now face an expanded and refocused role in their enterprises. Table 9 summarizes selected changes in the emerging role of today's relationship managers.

Table 9: Marketers and Relationship Managers

Issue	Traditionally Skilled Marketers	Relationship Managers
Relationship with organization	Motivators and facilitators, seeking to drive product revenue and profitability.	Strategists for, and enablers of, customer profitability. Integrators of customer initiatives with other initiatives internal and external to the enterprise. Managers of processes that touch the customer.
Planning	Market and segment planning in a centralized, research-based, annual planning cycle.	Data-based customer planning that integrates with marketing planning. Often done collaboratively in teams to align with the customer's planning cycle in B2B marketplaces.
Rewards	Based on individuals achieving financial results and share of market expectations for the product.	Based on team and individual metrics for the customer, including peer evaluations within the team, customer evaluations and profitability, Balanced Scorecard measures, Net Promoter Scores and share of customer metrics.
Learning	Typically mass training provided to internal personnel using standardized content.	Learning provided to internal personnel and partners to deliver what customers want. Learning is both team-based and customized to the learning requirements of employees. Learning also serves individual customers so each is more knowledgeable about issues that pertain to their expectations, purchase criteria and other factors the customers consider important. Chapter 9 discusses teaching customers new behaviors.
Management variables	Target market selections and the 4Ps of marketing: product, price, promotion, distribution/placement.	Customer value analysis and selection, strategies for customer engagement to develop competitively superior customer value. Strategies employ methods such as those discussed in Chapter 3.
Innovation	Innovation typically focused on new markets or segments, line extensions and cost management.	Innovation typically focused on enabling benefits that each customer expects. Relationship managers increasingly encourage the enterprise to perform non-traditional tasks, deliver non-traditional services and cater to individual customer needs quite differently than was previously the case when solutions were more highly packaged.

The expectations of relationship managers are clearly different from those that applied in previous eras. More specifically, relationship managers are expected to manage according to different measures of success and use different variables to achieve this success. The measures for the traditional marketer were associated with financial performance and market share. Now, relationship management measures include those that deliver profitable, long-term growth for the company, as was previously the case, but these measures are not focused just internally on the product but also externally on the customer.

Relationship Managers and Mega-Processes

Relationship managers are process owners. They assume responsibility for specific customer-facing processes and seek to optimize these from the perspective of both customer and company. Relationships with specific stakeholders can be categorized as "mega-processes," with sub-processes for specific aspects of relationship formation and management such as the following, for example:

- Current customers
    Engaging current customers in an ongoing dialog, and continuously creating and sharing mutual value with them.

- New customers
    Engaging potential new customers in an ongoing dialog, continuously developing new value to share with them—not just product-related value but value new customers consider to be of importance, such as relevant content.

- Stakeholders
    Managing relationships with stakeholders other than customers, including channel intermediaries, investors and employees.

The implications of defining "mega-processes" in terms of relationships are profound. Each category of relationship manager—such as the person responsible for relationships with current customers—determines on which customers to focus, what products and services to provide and what dimensions of variability to enable, and how to advance the relationship with the chain of personnel and organizations that create the value individual customers want.

In the relationship management organization, the CEO has overall responsibility for the chain of relationships being aligned with business strategy, for arbitrating turf issues that may emerge and for the governance of relationships.

Furthermore, the CEO ensures that the enablers of the relationships are put in place by the company, including technology and various other capabilities needed to deliver on the relationship promise with the end-customer such as R&D and manufacturing excellence. If the focus of the firm is on relationships, all people in the firm will need to be oriented in relationship management *as* their jobs, not simply *in* their jobs.

As noted throughout this book, relationship management is not merely a facet of the company; it is the very core of the company's engagement with those who create the value for which the customer pays and will pay again. Relationship management companies can be very different from their competitors if the relationship and the enablers of the relationship are at the center of everything the company does and if a relationship is *genuinely* viewed as a mutual experience in which value is developed and shared between customers and stakeholders profitably. For many companies, the genuineness of relationships remains uncharted territory.

● ● ●

This chapter discussed key strategic capabilities for the relationship management company to manage if it is to advance its customer strategies. Among the capabilities that were reviewed were technology, process, people and knowledge/insight and it was noted that each of these capabilities changes materially in the relationship management era. With relationship management, the customer integrates with each capability, collaborating in its development and interacting with it to achieve the promise of relationship management: the continuous creation and sharing of mutual value.

The relationship manager has profoundly important roles to play in strategizing for the engagement with each individual customer, optimizing the customer portfolio, managing customer interactions for value creation and driving new profitable net revenue for the enterprise in ways that the corporation will accept and embrace, sometimes in non-traditional ways. Where these tasks are new to a company, the relationship manager may need new skills too. Now, the focus of the relationship manager is primarily on the individual customer rather than the product, on the relationship rather than the transaction, on listening and customer engagement rather than talking and persuading, and operating in real time according to a strategic set of principles that are widely embraced and shared within the company rather than planning in a lengthy research and planning cycle, centralizing information without sharing it, and organizing and controlling point solutions in narrowly based initiatives. If this were not sufficient challenge, the relationship manager also needs to accomplish results in a trustful and friendly manner that is fully and genuinely reflective of the brand's promise and a culture in which relationships take precedence over transactions, trust over expedience, collaboration over individual performance, people over tasks and, as discussed in the next chapter, enterprise-wide customer planning that becomes a fundamental touchstone for the vision of the business.

Chapter 3
PLANNING RELATIONSHIPS WITH EXISTING CUSTOMERS

"'Would you tell me, please, which way I ought to go from here?'
'That depends a good deal on where you want to get to,' said the Cat."
Lewis Carroll (1832–1898),
Alice in Wonderland

The point has been amply made that relationships are important, that they may be the only assets of the enterprise that really matter and that relationships, more than anything else, are predictive of a company's future performance. It should be clear that anything this important ought to have a plan to drive it; the absence of a relationship plan in many organizations is a fundamental shortcoming that this chapter seeks to remedy by discussing such a plan, focusing initially on planning relationships with existing customers.

WHAT'S IN A RELATIONSHIP MANAGEMENT PLAN?

Relationship management plans ought to provide direction to the organization so that the plan answers and addresses the following important questions:[1]

- Customer selection
  On which customers should a company focus its relationship development?

- **R**elationship objectives

  What objectives might be considered with each chosen customer and what type of relationship might the organization seek to develop with these customers?

- Engagement

  How will each chosen customer be accessed, what will be the nature of communications and how will customers be engaged for an ongoing dialog, collaboration, value creation and value sharing?

- Value

  What value will be created *for* and *with* customers? How will this be done proactively and/or collaboratively?

- Innovation

  What processes will be deployed for continuous value creation?

- Teaching

  Are customers to be taught new behaviors? If so, what are these behaviors to be and how is the teaching to be done?

- Sharing

  How will value creation be shared between the organization and its chosen customers?

This model is called the CREVITS model, an acronym comprising the first letter for the keywords mentioned above. The following sections of this chapter discuss each aspect of this model in turn.

CUSTOMER SELECTION

As is abundantly clear to any company, all customers are not equal. The old saw that "the customer is always right" condemns those companies still following this approach to mediocre performance because treating all customers as though each is right allocates the company's resources equally, without selectively focusing on those customers best able to contribute financially and strategically to the enterprise. Companies that operate on the basis of equal treatment for everybody will be unable to achieve results other than those that can be achieved from or with the organization's average customer.

The problem might actually be worse than simply a near-term future of modest results. By treating all customers equally, everyone gets equal value, whether merited or not. That wonderful customer who always gives you lots of business, doesn't complain very much, brings you new customers, makes great suggestions, and leaves behind both profits and a friendly legacy—that customer receives similar treatment to the constant whiner and complainer, the one who returns used merchandise for credit and sometimes sales merchandise for full-value credit, the one who cherry-picks, the one who ties up your salesperson's time without buying anything, the one who is sometimes exceedingly rude, the one who pays bills late. The great customer is penalized at the expense of the bad one. The great customer receives less value than he or she should when the company provides all customers with average value. Over time, the customer portfolio changes to reflect this distortion of reward. Great customers defect in droves. On the other hand, bad customers bring their friends and some of these friends will exhibit the same behaviors as the bad customers. Losing great customers and acquiring more bad ones distorts the customer portfolio and will damage the enterprise.

Only the right customers are always right, and any relationship plan ought to identify who they are and cater to them so they feel increasingly bonded to the enterprise. The firm should identify them by name, know a great deal about them, be able to predict what they will want next, and incorporate the various elements noted in the CREVITS model and thus in the customer's and company's mutual interests.

A company deciding on which customers to focus requires that the following be in place:

- A customer database

    A vital first question is who the company's customers are. The answer to this question requires that companies be able to identify customers by name. For any organization other than very small ones, the firm also needs a customer database to capture this information and relevant transaction and interaction history, among other data that has been gathered or applies to the individual. Then a company can go on to assess customers' relative importance to the enterprise and the reverse, the company's relative importance to each customer.

- Cost-to-serve

    An understanding of the costs of serving each customer with all material customer-facing and engagement processes and cost-of-money considerations included in the calculation (e.g., how much it costs the firm when the customer takes longer to pay).

- Customer profitability

    An individual assessment of customer profitability derived from an allocation of all costs to all customers—not just the cost of goods that they buy but also cost-to-serve and cost-of-money considerations noted above—so that customer profitability can be understood when these costs are deducted from customer revenues.

- Share of customer

    An understanding of share of customer so that the company knows which one of two strategic options applies to each customer: developing new business with a customer (called primary demand development), or shifting customer share from the other companies—the competitors— with which the customer deals.

- Strategic value and influence

    An understanding of strategic value and each customer's influence with other business and social prospects so that the company knows how strategically important each individual customer is. Strategic considerations could include the following:

    - the customer's social network
    - the customer's position in the industry
    - customer referral considerations (e.g., has a customer referred many prospective customers in the past?)
    - innovation opportunities including the new ideas he or she might have brought forward
    - willingness to serve as a test environment for new product or service ideas
    - serving as a reference account, and so on.

    That is, as part of developing an overall understanding of the strategic value of each customer, the company should understand an individual customer's influence so that the enterprise knows which customers have the largest and most important networks.

- Each customer's needs

    An understanding of the needs of individual customers and the alignment of the organization in support of specific categories of needs so that the firm can focus on what it does best and the customers who are most aligned with those capabilities.

Incidentally, the term "customer selection" is preferred over "customer targeting." It is more appropriate to target competitors to gain advantage over them in a variety of ways than it is to target customers. After all, one targets prey and customers are hardly that! This is one instance where a military metaphor is inappropriate.

Customer Database

Relationship management assumes that each customer is discrete and addressable. Unlike the bygone era of mass marketing where it was common for unknown customers to transact with the enterprise, the relationship management-focused company must first know who its customers are before it can plan any aspect of the relationship. Although some companies may open for business each morning not knowing with whom they might interact that day, an increasing percentage of the firm's business should be planned business—from customers it knows something about and learns progressively more about over time. Of course, some business will always be reactive to current and new customers but most interactions—and, from these, transactions—ought to be planned.

So, who are the enterprise's customers? Every customer ought to have his or her own customer information file that describes everything known about the customer, demographically, behaviorally, socially, including what each customer values, their interactions and transactions, and community and household membership, for example. Each customer should have an individual tag that references the customer uniquely. The tag could be a telephone number, an account number, both or something else, such as a loyalty card number. Importantly, each customer should have a unique identifier assigned by the company to the customer. In this way, information about each individual customer can be centralized and aggregated, and manipulations performed to understand each individual (customer analytics) and what he or she might do or purchase next (predictive modeling), and to position the enterprise to sell what the customer wants when each is ready—or can be reasonably encouraged—to buy.

As mentioned, all of this naturally requires that a company first understand who every customer is, by name. After all, how can a company reasonably create a relationship with somebody whose name the company doesn't even know? What sort of relationship would this be? In a more personal way, friends obviously know the names of their friends. So, too, should a company seeking a long-term relationship know the names of its customers, especially the people on whom the company's very future depends.

Given this importance, why do some companies not know customers by name or have detailed customer information files? Some firms put it down to the one-time cost of establishing this and related capabilities. Others consider it too costly to keep data files current. Naturally, the costs and benefits of a relationship management case ought to be developed to inform any business decision but if competitors understand each individual customer by name, companies really have no choice but to ditch the old rules of marketing or risk becoming irrelevant.

Having identified customers uniquely, the next priority could be linking various customer databases so that the firm has a customer-centric view of their business rather than the product- or service-centric approach that has characterized most enterprises. The next challenge is to ensure that this customer-centric database operates in real time and across multiple channels—all those by which the customer can access the enterprise. Now the company has the potential to recognize customers when they return, establish a learning relationship that builds progressively more informed connections based on prior interactions and transactions, and integrate connections without regard to two-way communications and physical distribution channels.

Initially the company may not know every customer by name; this might be an objective. Companies could assess if they have a high percentage of customers under management. Of the total customer base, for how many do they have unique identifiers and customer information files? More than this, companies ought to verify that the data they have on their customers is accurate, recently updated and serves to fully describe and provide a basis for informing customer perspectives. Because the costs of keeping customer data current can be high if the company does this work itself, the firm might consider opportunities for user-generated content—having mechanisms by which the customer can maintain his or her own data, say, on the firm's website. Table 10 describes selected fields that many companies have in their customer information files. Although all companies would generally not have every field, this table suggests selected fields companies might consider adding to their databases.

Cost-to-Serve

To the extent that companies allocate their costs to customers, this is mostly done based on the costs of goods sold or the direct costs of the goods or

Table 10: Fields that May Be Found in the Customer Information File

Identification	Unique customer ID such as account or telephone number Name Telephone number Privacy and data disclosure policies reviewed with customer (Y/N, date and method of review)
Customer value	Customer lifetime value Current position on a relationship ladder or hierarchy of relationships Customer-specific relationship ladder objectives
Demography	Household information Date of birth Geography (home address, business address, shipping address) Income and wealth estimates (based in part on zip code and purchase behavior) Education (highest level attained)
Sociographics[2]	Educational institutions attended Memberships of professional associations Memberships of leisure, community, religious or other personal organizations Memberships of virtual communities, including Facebook and Twitter—number of friends and followers
Interactions	Channels of communications initiated by customer Number of touches of contacts prior to purchases Returns—frequency, nature, tone and manner of customer
Transactions	Consumption habits or preferences (including brands, vacations, reading preferences, demonstrated color preferences, e.g., evidenced from products bought) Responsiveness to offers Sensitivity to different media Recency of last purchase Frequency of purchases over the last year (for example) Monetary value analysis including sales and margin of first purchase, subsequent purchases, last purchase, average Financing and preferred methods of payment
Attitudes	Key vendor and brand selection criteria Positioning of company and brand in respect of criteria Positioning of competitors and their brands in respect of criteria Responses to "golden questions" (the most important questions or the questions a company would ask a customer if it could ask only one or two) Customer satisfaction and likelihood to refer company and products to friends or colleagues Predicted nature, timing, size of next purchase, and contingent variables to be managed (e.g., channels, communications style and content)

Table 10: Fields that May Be Found in the Customer Information File (*continued*)

Influence	Klout Score[3] or other social media metrics from firms such as PeerIndex, Social IQ and Kred that describe how many people a customer reaches, how much each customer influences these people and how influential the customer's network as a whole is. Klout calls these metrics "true reach," "amplification," and "network impact." Some companies also use Facebook "friends" to understand both reach and influence. Twitter communications are similarly included by some firms. Facebook "friends" often more closely resemble known strangers than they do real friends. The difference is a material one because friends are more likely to be open to influence than are known strangers. Facebook does offer an opportunity to discriminate between the two, an increasingly important consideration for many companies.

services customers have bought. According to this approach, companies know the gross margins of customers' purchases and other direct costs but do not have an ability to assess customer profitability until they allocate *all* costs associated with an individual customer. If the customer spends more or less time with a salesperson, the costs of this time ought to be assigned to the customer. If the customer returns goods for store credit, the time associated with receiving the store return, processing it and restocking the item should be notionally allocated to the customer, whether or not the customer is actually expected to reimburse the retailer for these costs. Customers who pay on time obviously have a lower cost-to-serve than those who pay late. A customer who spends time with support personnel to understand how to use an item should receive a different notional cost-to-serve than a customer who does not. And so on. Every aspect of a customer's engagement with the enterprise ought to be assigned to an individual customer, at least to the extent this assignment can be done economically.

It's not hard to calculate cost-to-serve. One approach is to map all the connection points that the customer has with the enterprise and then determine what a unit of time or activity costs. To map all the customer touch points, simulate the customer's interaction—essentially walk through the purchase experience as a customer would—to consider every possible connection the customer might have had with the enterprise pre-purchase (e.g., to gather information), during the purchase (e.g., whether the purchase is made online or in-store) and post-purchase (e.g., in respect of customer support and payment). Identify every connection the customer might have with the enterprise regardless of channel, whether in person, online, by telephone or by mail, for example.

Then identify all the process elements that support a given touch point. For example, what processes enable the restocking of a store return? Time may be spent at the sales counter to communicate with the customer, evaluate the nature of the store return, and make a refund or replacement. The item would need to be handled a second time in-store to assess its appearance and functionality, perhaps. There might be a third touch of the item at a centralized location where the item might be returned to the manufacturer for credit or sent away for upgrade, repackaging or disposal, and so on.

After this, the categories of labor that comprise each process should be established and the hourly rate (fully loaded, including benefits) determined. Then the amount of time that goes into each process ought to be described. To continue the previous example, the time to touch each item as it finds its way back into inventory or disposition would be noted. From this, a calculation can be made as to how much a specific customer process would cost the company. The company can establish metrics to elevate or reduce cost elements where there are material departures from the norm, such as when a customer acts far outside the parameters used for costing. One example would be a customer who spends far more than average time talking with customer support. Figure 4 describes an approach to assessing cost-to-serve.

Figure 4: Calculating Cost-to-Serve

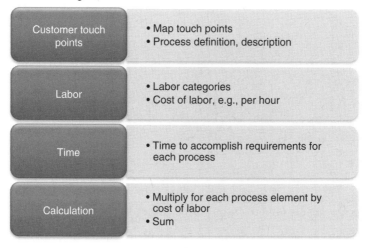

Customer touch points	• Map touch points • Process definition, description
Labor	• Labor categories • Cost of labor, e.g., per hour
Time	• Time to accomplish requirements for each process
Calculation	• Multiply for each process element by cost of labor • Sum

Customer Profitability

Once cost-to-serve is known, and because a company already knows revenues by customer from its customer transaction database, a calculation can be made of customer profitability. That is, a company would deduct from the total of revenues for each of its customers over a specific period the costs of the goods or services bought and then also deduct the costs of serving each specific customer that were not previously allocated on a customer-by-customer basis. While most companies already understand customer profitability at the gross margin line, it is still atypical for companies to allocate all their costs to specific customers. It's not hard to do, of course—it's just time consuming to do the first time.

Once customer profitability is understood for each customer, companies can project the cash flows from each customer over an extended period and discount these cash flows to the present using the firm's cost of capital or hurdle rate of return as the basis for discounting. This results in what is called the customer lifetime value. That is, the lifetime value of a customer is simply a projection of all the expenditures each customer makes with the firm minus the company's costs of producing the product, communicating, educating, serving and supporting each customer. A brief example for a putative car company follows, after which more general concepts are explored.

Over a 40-year purchasing lifetime, a typical customer who buys a car for, say, $20,000 (in constant dollars) every three years will buy 13 cars, spending a total of $260,000, assuming this customer buys a similar car each time. If the dealer margin for each car is projected to be 12 percent (or $31,200) on average over this time, the car company will derive $228,800 in revenues from this customer. In addition, parts revenues may be estimated at a further 20 percent of sales (or $45,760) that accrue to the car company, bringing total revenues to $274,560 for the car company.[4] From these revenues, the car company must net all the costs of attracting, retaining and providing for the customer's requirements. Table 11 provides additional detail.

There are a number of possible questions that can arise from the calculation of customer lifetime value. In the hypothetical example presented above, the following questions might be asked:

- If each customer matching this customer's profile is worth approximately $55,000 to a car company, how would a company make sure it does in fact realize this amount over the period projected for the customer's lifetime revenue stream? That is, how would a company maintain the customer

Table 11: Example of Customer Lifetime Value: Hypothetical Car Company

Revenues (Cars and parts)	$274,560
Less direct costs:	
Cost of vehicles produced (13 @ $12,000)	$156,000
Less cost of parts produced (45% of $45,760)	$20,592
Cost of warranty work reimbursed to dealer (13 @ $1,000)	$13,000
Less costs of financing customer	Nil
Less relationship costs:	
Time to manage customer feedback and restitution—low involvement customer	$5,000
Depreciation of customer's portion of communication capabilities (e.g., call center, Internet site)	$5,000
Amortization of customer's share of relevant capabilities such as a customer database and dealer access and training in the use of the database	$5,000
Cost of communicating with the customer directly and through the dealer	$5,000
Less other costs directly attributable to the customer relationship	$10,000
Net lifetime value of relationship (in constant dollars)	$54,968

for the desired duration (20 years, in this example) if this was the prediction horizon used for the calculation? In the auto industry, actually having a customer for his or her lifetime would be an extremely challenging objective indeed based on today's business models and approach to business conduct. But companies seeking to achieve this—those who really do want customers for life—might be prompted to reimagine their business models, which in turn might lead them to innovative solutions for being more relevant to today's consumer, such as providing customers with cars for life. For example, a new car could be provided every three years to those customers who commit to such an evergreen program, presumably at a substantial discount to existing pricing.

- How much might a car company be prepared to spend to attract a customer matching the desired customer profile at the outset of his or her spending lifetime, while recognizing that it may take some time before the investment in the customer relationship breaks even?

- How should the car company reward a lifetime customer and what should the financial and other arrangements be for a customer not as tightly bonded with the firm? How might a company distinguish among the alternative forms of reward, including but not just limited to financial incentives? That is, do some of the best customers of the company want financial inducements while others might prefer something else, such as distinctive vehicles, an ability to preview and drive new models before the neighbors do or other forms of recognition, such as preferential service, loaner vehicles and promotional merchandise? What approaches might be adopted to recognize preferred customers? For example, would some of the best customers like to collaborate in new vehicle exterior and interior design or service improvement concepts? Would they like to join with other best customers in a bonding experience, say, at a company-sponsored event such as at the Indianapolis 500? In short, customers who are bonded more tightly to a company should be treated quite differently than those who are less loyal.

There are a number of necessary preconditions for a company to be able to calculate the lifetime value of each of its customers. Some of these comments link back to earlier sections in this chapter but are repeated here for completeness. The preconditions include the following:

- Single, real-time view
  The need for a single, real-time customer information file providing a comprehensive view and integrated profile on each customer.

- End-customer line of sight
  A detailed information profile of their end-customers—that is, the customers of their customers. While many companies have interaction and transaction data informing them of retailers' or distribution channel intermediaries' purchases, they often have little information about the end-customers who buy from retailers.

- Customer analytics
  An ability to mine the data to understand customer behaviors uniquely, to track this over time, predict future behaviors and develop strategies to intercede with each customer to sell when each is most ready to buy. What has been the annual purchase volume of this customer from all companies in your industry each year? What have been the purchases of this customer with your company? This yields a calculation of customer share, a most important measure for a relationship manager.

- Projections and predictive modeling
  An ability to project expenditures and replacement rates of each customer, based upon the demonstrated behavior of each individual or

business. This is linked to the previous point and includes consideration of predictive modeling.

- Purchasing lifetime

    An assessment of a customer's reasonable purchasing lifetime. This could include consideration of issues such as the lifetime of the company itself, the longevity of the company's purchase processes or other factors. Many companies use 10 years as a lifetime for purchasing expectations from most customers. It might be appropriate for a specific company to look at its history with its most loyal customers, however customer loyalty is defined, and assess from these data what a reasonable projection could be for customer lifetimes.

- Customer profitability

    An understanding of the profitability of the customer, for all the products and services each buys from your firm. That is, how much did this customer contribute financially to the company last year?

    Cost projections

    In industries where prices and costs are volatile or changing (which means most industries), an ability to project prices and costs forward over the effective lifetime of the customer. As most companies face fluctuations in areas such as energy, currency and interest rates, it may be better to consider projections in constant dollars based on the current year with some judgmental overlay as to margin trends, industry competitiveness, dealer industry structure, competitive position and other factors that can be projected with some assurance. This also leads to a sensitivity analysis, allowing the company to estimate ranges within which its costs may fall so that it can bring into sharper focus the key customer success factors upon which it needs to act.

    Cost of capital

    An understanding of the cost of money or the rate of return expected for new investments—also called "the hurdle rate of return"—in the enterprise. Some companies may choose to assess customer lifetime value in inflated dollars, in which case the firm will need to apply an average weighted cost of capital or the hurdle rates of return employed for capital purchases to discount the profitability of the financial flows to the present.

Share of Customer

Marketers have long used market share metrics to keep track of their market-place success relative to competition. When companies focus on individual customer relationships, they ought to replace or complement market share metrics with customer share metrics. By aggregating customer share and weighting it for each customer, companies can calculate market share. Customer share is important especially for the company's best customers because it helps the firm understand how important it is to its customers. A company might perceive itself as satisfying its customers but share of customer considerations provides evidence of the company's actual standing. For example, a charity might enjoy significant gifts from a major donor but perhaps this donor might also be giving to other charities and the charity would only know how important it is when comparing the donations it receives to all donations made by the benefactor. It is quite common for companies to say that share of customer metrics are simply too hard to determine and this may indeed be the case in some industries. There are many situations, however, where companies haven't asked salespeople to pose the following question of their best customers: "How much did your firm spend with all companies over the last 12 months for products similar to the ones we supply to you?"

Customer Strategic Value

As companies examine their customer portfolio and consider each individual customer, one dimension of categorization that has been discussed is customer lifetime value, a measure of the importance of the customer to the enterprise. Another dimension is the importance of the company to the customer, such as the share of customer metric just discussed. A third dimension for consideration is strategic value, how much a customer can contribute in tangible and less tangible ways to the future of the business.

Customers are more or less strategic to the enterprise according to the extent to which each helps the organization achieve its objectives. So, different companies will consider the strategic value for customers differently. The following are among the important considerations for categorization here:

- Community

  If this customer is part of a community—either a virtual network or one in the physical world—say, a member of Rotary, the United Way, a political party or a religion, then that customer's strategic value would be enhanced according to the nature of the network to which the customer belongs, the number of people in it and the customer's role in influencing it (see the discussion on "Position" shortly).

- Connections

    If an individual has a large number of connections, then his or her strategic value would naturally be increased. The reverse is equally true. If a company makes a mistake with someone who has limited voice or sway, this mistake will not be amplified and the company's future prospects will be less affected. On the other hand, no company can afford to turn off customers who have significant standing within a community of some kind. This consideration obviously and particularly includes online social communities, such as Facebook friends. As mentioned previously, companies often use the Klout Score, PeerIndex, SocialIQ or Kred as a metric for assessing customer influence in respect of customer reach, individual influence and community influence. Salesforce has introduced functionality that allows its customers to engage customers differently according to their Klout Scores. One hotel reportedly upgraded their customers to better rooms based on those customers' Klout Scores. Until recently, the only person who reportedly had a perfect 100 Klout Score was singer/entertainer Justin Bieber.[5] His Klout Score was higher than Lady Gaga's or Barack Obama's.[6] Recent updates to Klout algorithms seemingly now account for the real world and have elevated the President above Justin, now discriminating between influence in a cultural setting and influence that can change the world![7]

- Position

    If this person is an opinion leader within the community—such as the president of an industry association or someone who leads opinions on blogs, for example—strategic value ought to be recognized. The company needs to be able to listen to customers and prospects in the physical world and online to identify opinion leaders. This is discussed shortly in terms of customer sensing.

- Referrals

    How often are referrals to potential customers expected to be made? How valuable are these referrals expected to be? How much time is expected to be saved by virtue of the referrals? In other words, referrals can take much cost and time out of the business development process while simultaneously accelerating revenues significantly and customers who make referrals ought to be recognized for their strategic value.

- Collaboration

    Customers who collaborate with the company should be recognized for their contribution to the organization's strategic value. These customers might help the enterprise by suggesting new product or service concepts, by collaborating to streamline joint processes or by making marketplace success more likely by offering to serve as a site to try out new ideas, for example.

- Reputation

    This category deals with customers who aid a company's marketplace and customer-specific positioning by lending their reputation to the enterprise. Customers who enable the enterprise to leverage his or her reputation and relationships to improve marketplace positioning more generally, perhaps to accelerate or facilitate marketplace updates for the company's products and services, naturally ought to be accorded a higher strategic value than those who don't.

- Competition

    This category considers the contribution a customer makes to the competitive advantage of a company. It includes the extent to which a customer helps the company improve its value proposition, learn more about competitive activity or promote its products to colleagues or more generally in the marketplace.

As mentioned, organizations ought to have an ability to categorize individual customers according to the strategic value each represents to the enterprise. Companies marketing goods and services to other businesses or institutions naturally have an ability to listen to individual customers and categorize each account appropriately. This would apply equally to categorization of the strategic value of distribution channel intermediaries—those companies that take title to goods as products find their way to market. Consumers are naturally harder to categorize strategically in part because companies often don't know their place in social communities, whether online or more conventionally. Categorizing customers according to the strategic value each represents therefore requires that companies have an ability to listen to individual consumers and this, in turn, requires that they have appropriate technologies and processes for what might be termed "customer sensing"—listening to customers' conversations, interpreting them and acting upon them as they occur or as near to in real time as possible.

The categories mentioned above, supplemented by those that are specific to an individual company's business strategies, should be weighted according to their relative importance and then customers can be rated according to their performance in respect of each strategic value category. By multiplying weightings by ratings, an aggregate score can be established for each individual customer. Naturally, this is easier to do for B2B customers although the complexity of the purchase decision-making unit, decision influencers, backers and blockers (those who are supportive and those who are against your enterprise in an account) make this categorization more difficult than it appears on its face. Still, assessing consumers for their strategic value is important and merits the creative use of technology support both to listen to customers and to establish business rules to assign customers to each element of strategic value and to calculate strategic value scores.

Customer Alignment

It has been noted that, while traditional marketing principles take the view that the customer is always right, relationship management offers an alternative perspective, one that recognizes only the right customers as always being right and that other customers may or may not be right, depending upon a variety of circumstances and considerations. An organization ought to build its capabilities around the so-called right customers so that it is best able to cater to their requirements. If this is done well—so that the right customers receive competitively superior customer value from the enterprise—the company enjoys a competitive advantage in return. Organizational alignment in support of the right customers requires that the organization be able to distinguish customers from one another according to their needs, map these needs to organizational capabilities, and develop excellence in respect of these capabilities so that organizational alignment is complete. Figure 5 provides an illustration in the case of one customer need—price—being mapped to factors the organization can influence, both in terms of reality and perception, such as costs and margin expectations, and the communications of competitively superior value.

Much of the preceding discussion seeks to identify right customers according to their value to the enterprise. This identifies the right customers today. Tomorrow's right customers are best identified according to their future

Figure 5: Mapping Customers' Needs to Internal Factors the Organization Can Influence

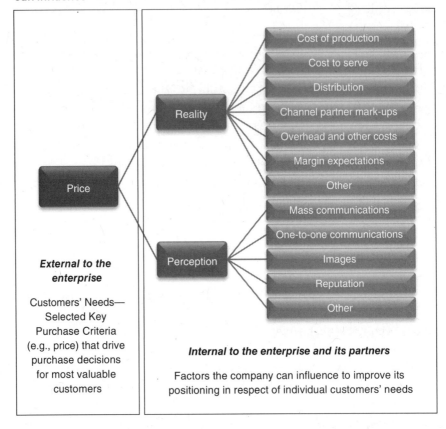

External to the enterprise

Customers' Needs—
Selected Key
Purchase Criteria
(e.g., price) that drive
purchase decisions
for most valuable
customers

Internal to the enterprise and its partners

Factors the company can influence to improve its
positioning in respect of individual customers' needs

value, calculated as customer lifetime value—as noted above—and enhanced through organizational alignment to drive efficiency and effectiveness, which will result in a further increase of customer lifetime value.

It is common for companies to distinguish among its customers by categorizing them simply as "Best," "Average" and "Worst" customers. This is called customer triage, in much the same way that hospitals triage patients and cater to them quite differently. Figure 6 describes this graphically, using a pyramid for representation. The shape of the customer portfolio will differ according to the criteria used to determine best, average or worst customers and so the shape of the portfolio for a given company may be other than pyramidal. In this example, the best customers are smaller in number than customers categorized as average, and both of these are less numerous than worst customers. A

Figure 6: Customer Triage

portfolio such as this would obviously lead the company to consider whether or not it should reduce the number of its worst customers, how it might do so and even whether or not customers such as these might represent an opportunity for an alternative business model. Consider the customer who goes to Starbucks and wants quick service, a capability for which Starbucks' processes were not originally designed. Might Starbucks modify their customer service practices and processes, might they create an alternative approach to serve the quick in-and-out customers, or, in the extreme, might they find a way to focus only on their best customers?

Having identified which customers fall into the best, average and worst categories, a company can decide what to do with this mix of customers to improve the customer portfolio. What value will be created for and with the best customers? How much will these customers be rewarded? Which customers are to be core to the organization's future and which are to be peripheral to it? Core customers take the company into the future while peripheral ones who are still among the company's best customers may be additive but not necessarily strategic.

To distinguish core customers from the others, and to choose which customers are really the best for the enterprise, an organization may categorize the customer portfolio using a method similar to that presented in Figure 7. Here, the customer is right for the enterprise when he or she is profitable and/ or strategic in the near or mid-term future. The calculation of customer profitability can be performed based in part on today's profitability with projections associated with cost-to-serve and other considerations, as discussed previously. Having categorized customers in this way, the company can make a decision as

Figure 7: Lifetime Profitability/Value and Strategic Value

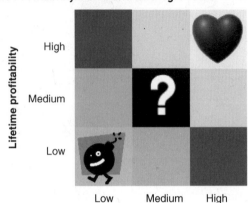

to which customers merit the most investment for retention and value creation, and how to prioritize everything it does—technology, process and people—to align with the best customers.

Some organizations consider whether they should continue to do business with customers who are presently unprofitable and will remain so. By no longer catering to these customers, an organization has the potential to improve profitability while affecting their competitors' profitability negatively. On the other hand, in a world of social media, companies have to be very careful when they fire customers. Rejected customers are likely to tell many of their friends, potentially influencing good customers in the process.

RELATIONSHIP OBJECTIVES

Categorizing Relationship Objectives

At this point in the process of planning customer relationships, the relationship marketer has selected customers for priority treatment. The firm has described the current state of its customer portfolio. The challenge is now to establish relationship objectives for each customer so that the company can describe what needs to be done to achieve each objective to advance individual customer relationships and, in so doing, improve relationships for the firm's customer portfolio as a whole.

Companies set behavioral objectives for their customers. That is, they examine what behaviors customers currently exhibit and then identify what

Figure 8: Relationship Ladder

- Advocates
- Patrons
- Accounts
- Shoppers
- Testers
- Prospects

behaviors they want from their customers. A behavioral objective is something that the organization wants the customer to do—a measurable action. Behavioral objectives can be measured in the following ways, for example: the frequency or nature of interactions, the level of purchases or the types of goods or services bought.

It is common for companies to consider the relationships they have with their customers as a continuum, from those customers who hardly know the enterprise to those who are deeply engaged and interested in the company's success. This continuum might be likened to a ladder on which each rung represents a progressively greater relationship intensity that serves to bond a company with its customers. At the lowest rung of the ladder is the non-customer and at the highest rung is the advocate who really appreciates the enterprise and is willing to communicate this appreciation. In a sense, the bonding ladder can be compared with the evolution of a serious personal relationship, from the "I hardly know you" stage, to "I have some interest," to "crush," "casual dating," "serious dating," "newlyweds," and then "long-term marriage or commitment." Figure 8 describes the customer relationship in terms of a bonding ladder of progressively escalating relationship intensity as follows for customers who are:

- Prospects
- Testers of the product, experience and company
- Shoppers who buy on occasion
- Accounts that demonstrate loyal behaviors

- Patrons who are frequent and broad-spectrum buyers who engage often with the business, and
- Advocates who demonstrate all the preceding behaviors and also promote the company.

Relationship ladders are important because companies rarely develop immediately loyal customers or advocates. Rather, as in a more personal way, relationships develop one step at a time. The ladder reflects increasing behavioral loyalty toward the enterprise.

Relationships, if they are to create new shareholder value, must be behavioral in nature (at least in part) because an enterprise needs transactions to make money. A customer who thinks well of an enterprise but never spends money with it (transactions) and never tells anyone about his or her thoughts (interactions) might be well intentioned, but intentions are not sufficient. Only behaviors create enterprise value and this is usually done through transactions either by a current customer or, as an offset, by people in his or her network. That is, while companies might want to orient themselves away from simply considering transactions to a business built on relationships, they still need the transactions that relationships foster.

Behavioral Clusters

Some companies, working with their customer data, may determine that customers fall into groups within which certain behaviors are common. These are behavioral clusters and some firms consider that all customers within a cluster may be treated similarly so that the company need not incur the costs of catering to individual customers. For example, a company making laundry detergent might decide to treat its major retailers as important individual customers because of their economic and strategic value. On the other hand, individual end-customers and some smaller retailers may not be perceived to merit such individual treatment. It may be appropriate for companies to cluster some among their customers into groups that have similar behavioral characteristics and then to act on each cluster as though it were an individual customer. For example, smaller retailers might be clustered according to the dollar level of their purchases and the scope of products bought from the enterprise, with customers in each cluster receiving standard pricing and service levels, and a specific level of organizational support, such as an assigned account manager. As customers migrate from

Figure 9: Achieving Customer-Specific Relationship Objectives

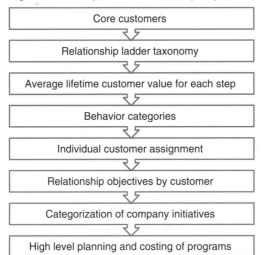

one cluster to another—as their relationship intensity increases—they would receive increased value from the enterprise.

Whether it is acting on individuals or clusters, the objective is to advance the customer along a relationship continuum such as that described by the relationship ladder. That is, relationships should be conceived as bonding strategies to manage behaviors so that each customer moves progressively toward the highest rung—and most valuable position—on the relationship ladder. This suggests that companies might approach customer-specific relationship planning in the sequence suggested by Figure 9 and discussed thereafter.

As described in Figure 9, companies could develop and achieve relationship objectives for each individual customer by following the sequence of steps described below. This description is intended to be indicative of the kinds of activities many companies use when planning relationships. The relative importance of specific steps will depend upon a number of circumstances for an individual firm. The following are the steps:

1. Confirm the list of selected customers as described in the previous sections.
2. Establish a relationship ladder and taxonomy of terms—a hierarchy of classifications describing types and subtypes of relationships. The categorization described in Figure 8 might be used here.

3. For each rung on the relationship ladder, describe the average lifetime value of customers based on the company's own assessment of the average value that customers represent on each rung of the ladder.

4. Identify the behaviors applicable to each step on the ladder. Examples of behaviors are described in Table 12. The reader might tailor these examples to his or her own requirements. However described, the categories should be mutually exclusive and collectively exhaustive to fully describe the range of behavioral options being examined or the business rules that are needed to distinguish among behavioral options for cases not covered in the table. An example would be where a customer buys infrequently but spends a considerable amount each time. Note that each of the identified behaviors do not include what the company has done to motivate the behaviors—just the customers' own behaviors.

5. Assign each individual customer a position on a rung of the relationship ladder described above according to demonstrated behaviors. Customer relationship value for each customer should then be summed to determine aggregate customer relationship value for every rung on the ladder. In this way the organization can establish a shape for the relationships on its relationship ladder, as suggested by Figure 10. The organization depicted hypothetically on Ladder 1 has much of its customer value on the ladder rung described as "Shoppers." Assuming that customer value rises for each rung on the ladder, it is appropriate that the organization consider how to change customers' behaviors so that they migrate up

Table 12: Customers' Demonstrated Behaviors on Each Relationship Ladder Rung

Rungs on the Relationship Ladder	Average Lifetime Value of Customers	Customers' Demonstrated Behaviors Applicable to Each Rung				
		Interaction frequency	Channels	Transaction frequency	Transaction volume	Referrals
Advocates	***	>15/year	1–2	6–10/year	>$500/year	>5/year
Patrons	***	10–15/year	1–2	6–10/year	>$500/year	2–5/year
Accounts	***	10–15/year	1–2	6–10/year	$101–$500/year	1/year
Shoppers	***	10–15/year	1–2	3–5/year	$50–100/year	0
Testers	***	5–10/year	1	1–2/year	<$50/year	0
Prospects	0	<5/year	1	None	$0	0
Non-customers	0	No behavioral expectations				

[*** refers to the specific calculation of the average lifetime value of customers on each step of the ladder]

Figure 10: Planning Customer Behaviors Using the Relationship Ladder

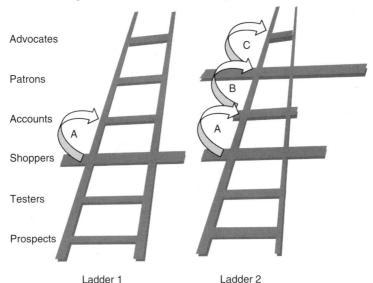

Advocates

Patrons

Accounts

Shoppers

Testers

Prospects

Ladder 1   Ladder 2

the ladder, as suggested by arrow A. The organization with relationships described as Ladder 2 (a ladder with a broad base, rungs of uneven value and a narrow top step) is likely to have different strategies from the firm represented by Ladder 1, in this case a series of strategies described by arrows A, B and C as the organization manages customer behaviors upward and creates new customer value for the enterprise with the altered shape of its relationship ladder.

6. Establish relationship objectives for each individual customer. This assessment would be based largely upon the average lifetime value of customers on each step of the ladder. For example, it may be evident that by elevating customers from one rung to another a significant average increase is possible in customer lifetime value, as mentioned previously when discussing Figure 8. Alternatively, it may be appropriate to keep some customers within an existing category while advancing others. Or a firm may decide to focus only on those customers that are on a specific step on the ladder, say, the Patrons that are to be converted into Advocates.

Determine the categories of activity that are to advance the behaviors of each individual customer according to his or her relationship objectives. For example, a firm may formulate programs to address specific aspects of relationship activity noted in the behavioral ladder table,

Table 12. That is, there might be a program for interaction frequency, say a reach-out program encouraging prospects to interact more often and thereby receive a benefit, perhaps of an information, financial or social nature.

7. Plan the deployment of specific programs at a high level and associate costs with each program. Detailed program planning can follow as discussed in subsequent sections. Once compared to the potential gains associated with achieving customer-specific objectives, the costs of specific programs can lead to a calculation of return on investment. That is, the firm should be in a position to assess whether the program costs have merit by comparing the investment to be made in each individual customer relationship and then examining whether the likely aggregated return on that investment merits the initiative. This calculation should satisfy most CFOs and help the relationship management initiative achieve internal legitimacy and support.

The preceding discussion has focused on establishing relationship objectives for each individual customer or logical cluster or grouping among the firm's existing customers. Some companies might be tempted to consider market segments here. The temptation should be resisted. The focus should instead be on customers aggregated according to their behaviors and the value of their behaviors to the enterprise. Typically customers on a given relationship ladder rung are quite different from one another demographically. It is quite common for a mix of older and young people, the wealthy and less affluent, educated and less educated and so on, all to be on a specific relationship ladder rung. They co-exist on the rung because of their behaviors, not their demographics. The realization that customers can be demographically different from one another while still behaving somewhat similarly is starkly evident when one conducts focus groups to explore ways to change behaviors and increase customer value, and sees customers with a variety of different demographics in the same room.

Relationship Objectives to Optimize the Customer Portfolio

Having selected individual customers the company considers to be right for it, and having clustered these customers according to criteria such as lifetime and strategic value, a company may elect to aggregate customers further and then change the resultant customer portfolio in order to improve profitability. Just as every company has a portfolio of products or services, firms have a portfolio of customers; while many companies pay attention to upgrading the profitability of their product or service portfolios, few pay as much attention to improving their customer portfolios. Companies can migrate the mix of their customers just as they do with their products or services. This may be done more or less proactively with the chosen approach depending on a variety of factors. For example, when survival is threatened, companies are typically more willing to optimize their customer mix, which was the case when GM, near bankruptcy, shuttered Saturn and Pontiac divisions and sold off Hummer and Saab, likely losing some customers in the process.

The prevailing use of social media has resulted in many companies choosing to manage their customer portfolios gently, adjusting the customer mix carefully in response to specific circumstances rather than firing customers outright. For example, companies manage their customer portfolios by increasing their focus on desirable customers rather than focusing on the undesirables. Most firms pursue prospective customers who match the profile of their most valuable and strategic customers and retain their best customers rather than marching their least attractive customers to the door. Companies typically adjust their investment of customer time and attention to manage their customer portfolios. Over time, customers who receive less attention or investment than they feel are due to them are likely to find the value they want by migrating to competitors and this has the dual benefit of improving a firm's customer portfolio while potentially damaging a competitor's—not an altogether bad thing.

It is appropriate for a company to map customers into groups or clusters determined by their customer value and strategic value and then to identify the cluster (or clusters) of customers on which it chooses to focus. This could mean fundamentally reshaping the customer portfolio to build the longer-term profitability of the company and then pursuing specific types of relationships with priority customers to achieve the relationship management objectives set for each.

More specifically, companies have four main options when managing their customer mixes to improve the overall portfolio. These options are as follows:

- Reward and Invest
- Manage
- Discipline, and
- Fire.

Reward and Invest

Today's ideal customers—customers with high customer and strategic value—naturally merit reward by the company. Reward can take many forms, including investment by the company in its customers on terms that matter to each customer. This may mean assigning the firm's best staff to serving priority accounts, giving customers access to the company's technologies, investing time with key customers, recognizing their importance in material and face-enhancing ways (such as awards dinners), providing priority access to innovation or fashion (such as launch galas) and rewarding them financially for their loyalty, or some combination. One company offers its best customers a secret 1–800 number through which they receive top priority service and support.

McDonald's has found that 77 percent of its sales are attributable to typically male customers aged 18 to 34 who eat at McDonald's three to five times a week.[8] Perhaps tongue in cheek, McDonald's has referred to these customers as "superheavy"[9] users or "heavy hitters"[10] and was concerned that ending sales of supersized fries and drinks would affect retention of these important customers, although it's not clear if this actually happened.

Manage

Some customers need to be managed if they have high customer value but low strategic value. The company can then help to create strategic value that will enhance the business prospects for both the company and the customer. If the reason for low strategic lifetime value has to do with the outlook of their industry sector, the company may work with the customer to identify growth opportunities that often exist even where the future looks negative. In another example, supplier and customer could explore the outlook for one another's businesses in joint planning sessions and then work to advance their mutual interests.

Remember those vacuum tubes in old TVs and radios that would get red hot? Before it was generally known that the outlook was bleak for these devices, tube retailers continued to view their future as closely tied to the tube manufacturers because they profited from sales of replacement tubes and appliance repair. Manufacturers knew that the tube industry would never revive as they themselves were driving the change, engineering transistors into devices to replace vacuum tubes. Companies such as RCA and Motorola understood—before their channel intermediaries did—that the manufacturer-retailer relationship was about to undergo significant change and would need to be managed. Intermediaries would have to change their business models. Some would go into the business of retailing transistorized devices, others into servicing this equipment, yet others would become service operations for the tube devices that remained in consumers' homes and some went out of business when they couldn't adapt.

Discipline

It is common that between 30 and 40 percent of a company's revenue base is generated by customers who have low lifetime profitability but may be made into medium- or even high-value customers. There are two main ways of doing this. One is to change and/or cost-reduce the processes that are employed by the company to market, sell, serve, support and manage the account. Another is to charge customers in this category a fee for not conforming to the company's "rules of engagement" as a "best customer." For example, banks prefer their average consumers to use automated teller machines (ATMs) for routine transactions, an area in which banks have made major investments. Teller services are retained for consumers not willing to use ATMs and for processes that require human intervention rather than the routine, rules-based processes for which banks' technologies are well suited. So banks charge consumers who use teller services for routine transactions. These customers are, in essence, being disciplined.

Fire

Some customers are unprofitable today, will be unprofitable tomorrow, have low strategic value and do not merit further attention by the company. Companies may choose to let them become someone else's problem or opportunity—although, as noted, one has to be careful about how one de-emphasizes undesirables or risk some among these customers, especially those with social media clout, creating bad word of mouth. Nevertheless, the customer portfolio still needs to be managed and this can be done by managing communications effectively. Terminated customers, like terminated employees, should leave feeling good about the relationship in which both have invested but which, for whatever reason, no longer creates targeted value.

Although not all customers merit continuance by the firm, this doesn't necessarily mean the "wrong" customers ought to be shown the door. Some may be asked to leave but others may simply choose to go if and when they find a better value proposition elsewhere. That is, firing can be proactive or passive. In either case, it is appropriate that companies consider who among their current customer base merits a continued relationship, size and align the business in accordance with the mix of customers on which the firm has chosen to focus and then pay relatively less attention to the others.

ENGAGEMENT

Before considering customer engagement today, consider how marketers used to engage their customers. Broadcasting was a mass marketing channel that productized communications for delivery and consumption by everyone. Communications vehicles included TV, radio, newspapers and outdoor media, all of which were one-way in nature: from the sender to the recipient, with no feedback loop, no listening and no connection with individuals at any stage in the purchase process. As markets fragmented into smaller and smaller submarkets, the promotional channels also became narrower and more highly targeted, and remained one-way in nature—a monolog. These channels included specialized and trade magazines, advertising on everything from park benches to ski chairlifts, and unaddressed admail (junk mail). Broadcasting—"one to many" communication—first became "narrowcasting" (outbound communications to a segment of customers), and then "pointcasting" (addressing a single customer with an outbound message such as using e-mail). Pointcasting was a precursor for a customer dialog and a genuine conversation. Whether in real time or near real time, this was the first time a connection was made with individual customers and set the stage for engagement in a continuous process for mutual value creation. When pointcasting became interactive and real time, it evolved into a conversation where there was little or no lag between messages sent and received.

Conversation now occurs at the initiation of either sender or receiver and can involve a wide array of social media and more traditional technologies such as call centers, e-mail or interactive voice response, and perhaps several technologies at once. A stockbroker, while speaking with a key client, may simultaneously e-mail a research report and debate the relative merits of an investment with the client using the document now in the client's hands to advance the discussion. Other forms of interactive communication include interactive telephone-based communication, using the call center for so-called telemarketing or telesales, and communication over the Internet that offers an opportunity to engage the supplier.

It is increasingly common for organizations to engage customers in real time by sensing what they are saying—say, using social media—and then

Figure 11: Communications Become Interactive and Real-Time

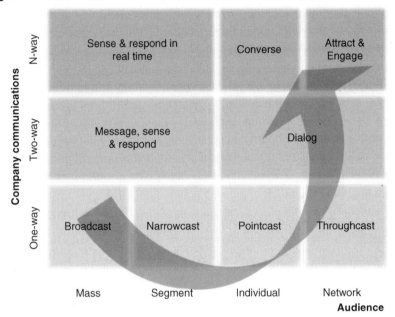

respond right away so that customers are engaged instantaneously and any concerns they have may be immediately addressed. These alternatives are described in Figure 11. Communications *through* existing customers to their networks is also referenced in this diagram and is discussed in Chapter 4.

Sensing and responding isn't the same as engaging. Examples of sensing include observing, measuring and listening. Sensing occurs now—in the present tense. One listens to a customer (say, on Twitter), understands and interprets the conversation (say, a service complaint) and responds appropriately (say, offering some sort of assistance). Engagement, on the other hand, is forward looking. It seeks to involve the customer in a collaborative exploration of some kind to which there is commitment to an outcome, such as knowledge gained (say, what the customer will teach the company and vice versa), a purchase made (say, a customized product or service) or a friend helped (the case when a client might introduce a new account to the law firm, for example). To confirm this point: engagement seeks some evidence of commitment and investment, whether time, money or knowledge, or something else of value, such as referrals or guidance. With commitment comes an opportunity to create future and mutual value, and thus some indication that the relationship will grow over time.

It is common for companies to say that they cannot understand the needs of each individual customer economically and without this understanding, they perceive that they cannot relate effectively to specific customers. It is naturally very hard to treat customers uniquely if one does not know very much about them. On the other hand, customer understanding need not be ruinously expensive to develop. Companies can use simple ways to identify customers uniquely, some as simple as asking the name of customers or offering a benefit in exchange for providing customer information, such as special offers to those who do.

Learning Relationships

Companies that have capabilities to track the interactions and transactions of individual customers can learn progressively more about each customer every time they connect and this learning can be applied for mutual benefit. One approach to gaining this deeper understanding includes asking customers a deeply insightful question—a single question intended to help the organization understand much more about an important aspect of the customer. For example, a pet food company seeking indulgent pet owners who might potentially be interested in a new premium pet food could be asked for the names of their pets, a seemingly innocuous question. But the name of the pet can be deeply revealing. Research suggests that anthropomorphic pet owners—those who treat their pets as though they are people, perhaps as friends or even surrogate children—often give their pets a human name. Understanding that a pet is named Max would enable a pet food company to understand and engage this pet owner quite differently from the owner who calls his dog Spot, for example.

Many companies seek a learning relationship and, in some cases, customers voluntarily give a company an opportunity to learn more about themselves—what has come to be known as permission marketing. Naturally, companies would like nothing more than to have customers seek the engagement that the company also wants. By checking a permission box online, customers may be saying to the company something as narrow as "please send me relevant offers of a certain nature at a certain time," or something as broad as "please learn more about me so you can be more relevant to me." It is this learning that is at the heart of a learning relationship and, in some ways, is central to what a relationship really means. Imagine a personal situation where you might ask a friend repeatedly what he or she did on the weekend. At some point the friend will surely say, "I told you already. Are you not listening?" Yet it is common for companies to ask customers the same question repeatedly and then wonder why customers perceive suppliers to be undifferentiated. Examples of apparently deaf companies are not hard to find. Consider the last time you went to get money out of the bank's ATM. Did you receive the same menu of options as the previous time and the time before that, even though your transaction is always the same? Or perhaps you called your local cable company or telephone company and were automatically prompted to type in a 10-digit telephone number before proceeding. As soon as a customer support person came on the line, guess what question you were asked? What is your telephone number, of course! One clue as to whether or not a company is deaf to its customers is whether it asks customers the same question twice.

Communications Channels and Customer-Specific Objectives

Communications methods ought to be selected according to the customer-specific objectives the organization is seeking to accomplish. Most companies should want to engage their most valuable customers in a conversation in order to understand the uniqueness of each individual customer, then reward and recognize them appropriately and manage their behaviors. Technology might be used to aid the conversation but high-value conversations generally benefit from personal touch. In these cases, organizations might consider how best to engage individuals in real time with relatively less technology disintermediation. For example, a fashion store might invite its most valuable customers to a showing of its new fashions for the season. A restaurant might welcome a new sommelier by inviting its most valuable customers to a wine tasting evening. More generally, customers ought to be engaged using communications channels that reflect customer-specific objectives. In turn, customer-specific objectives are achieved by managing customers' behaviors so that each is moved up a rung on the relationship ladder—or maintained at the very top of it.

Technology for Disintermediation of Communications

Communications investments should reflect the value of the behavioral change that the organization is seeking to accomplish overall and for each customer. Generally this means that companies might use personal touch to engage high-value customers while using technology to disintermediate relationships with customers of more modest value. For example, charities might assign their executives to engage with major donors while using technology

Figure 12: High Tech vs. High Touch

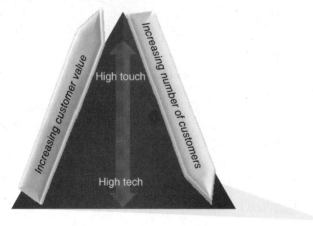

to communicate with donors of lesser means or charitable intent. Figure 12 illustrates this point.

Intelligent Engagement

Virtual communications requires mastery of a compendium of communications options by which to engage customers as each wants, ubiquitously and seamlessly without dropped messages, missed communications or evidence that the customer has not been fully heard. More than this, the company needs to demonstrate an ability to reach out intelligently to each customer when the customer needs assistance. A customer may require help immediately as a direct result of product or service usage—e.g., "My hard drive just crashed." Or a customer may have a need that can be inferred, something the company discovers from an inbound call or by listening to social media. A need may have surfaced when a customer said something on social media like "I'm thinking of buying a new computer. What would you suggest?" This sets up an opportunity for the company to respond immediately and really shine because of the unexpected nature of the assistance.

Customer "Stickiness"

Engagement usually results in increased customer value and customer "stickiness"—the time period during which the customer is willing to interact and transact with the enterprise before he or she loses interest or defects. The longer a customer remains engaged, the higher the associated profitability and/or customer value so it is clearly in the company's interest to seek an increase in customer stickiness.[11]

Multichannel Integration

The processes for multichannel integration and a seamless customer experience are complex but this does not reduce the need for the company to understand and integrate all customer touch points. Customers expect this integration so the company needs to ensure that a customer is able to access the enterprise through whichever window he or she chooses, whenever he or she wants, to accomplish whatever he or she has in mind. Regardless of how complex it is, it should not matter to the customer that the company faces a challenge in integrating technologies and processes in mobile, social and online channels of communications with bricks-and-mortar facilities, for example.

Touch Maps

Many companies use a touch map to identify every point of contact and the nature of connections and to help plan communications integration. For example, an airline might have the following touch points with its customers: sales offices, airport counters, Internet access, telephone access, e-mail communications, personal communications at the gate and onboard, communications by partners (such as car rental companies and hotels) and so on. The airline would seek to knit the customer experience into a unified whole by integrating communications across all the service touch points, with all their solutions talking to one another. The solutions might include a loyalty system, a reservation system, a central guest repository, a rewards program system, campaign management, salesforce automation, airline operations solutions and CRM software. By integrating across the various touch points, a company has the potential to be more relevant to customers by providing meaningful information said in the right way through the right channels at the right time to the right people.

Customer-Specific Positioning

In addition to finding ways to access the customer, communicate with him or her, and engage the customer in an ongoing dialog to create mutual value, technology can play important roles in assisting the company to position itself with each customer. In traditional marketing, marketers often partitioned their markets and developed different products and messages for different audiences or distribution channels. For example, some manufacturers of white goods such as ranges and dishwashers made different SKUs (stock keeping units) for specific retail chains. This let each chain position the product differently in the marketplace—on price, service, quality or other factors, for example. Similarly, relationship management technologies enable companies to partition customers and engage each on his or her terms, possibly positioning the company uniquely and in context. This situation applies equally in the B2B marketplace. For example, major management consultancies maintain client service teams that differentiate individual accounts according to need and value, and engage each account uniquely.

VALUE

At this stage in the relationship management plan, companies have selected customers, decided on relationship objectives with each one and determined how they will engage each customer in an individual conversation that will become progressively more meaningful to both company and customer over time. Now the enterprise ought to establish what value it will create for and with individual customers. And it needs to establish how this will be done proactively and collaboratively. This section reviews selected considerations for developing proactive and customer-specific value—what it means to give each customer the value he or she wants.

Differences among customers do not require that companies necessarily cater to each customer uniquely if no incremental shareholder value results. Shareholder value derives from new customer behaviors, changes that cause customers to do something they did not do previously such as rejecting a competitor in favor of the company, accelerating a deferred purchase or purchasing many things instead of a few, such as an integrated solution instead of a specific product or service. Companies ought to understand what behavioral changes they want, what it will cost them to secure these changes and what the resulting financial gains will be. From this, firms can assess whether to change customers' behaviors before they determine how best to do so.

Changed behaviors derive from a number of things and the most important of these is competitively superior value that customers readily perceive to be better than competitors or their current solution. If an enterprise is to change behaviors it needs a number of strategic capabilities such as the ability to sense and understand each customer and deepen customer-specific knowledge and insight over time. The firm needs to be able to connect with and engage each customer and to collaborate one customer at a time. The following section discusses customer sensing, what it means to understand an individual customer, to connect with him or her, and then act with and for each.

Customer Sensing

Customer sensing is the process by which an enterprise adds to what it knows about each customer. Sensing tells the organization what changes are occurring in its customer environment—one customer at a time—in much the same way as a person's five senses provide sensory feedback and interpretation of the physical environment. Sensing also tells the organization how customers respond to specific outputs of the organization so that changes can be made to specific programs, initiatives, products or solutions to accomplish the desired results and behavioral changes. That is, sensing is an integral element of the feedback loop that connects with, listens to, and embraces the customer for primary, remedial and secondary[12] value creation, as suggested by Figure 13.

Organizational listening[13] is an important component of sensing but not the only component. Listening implies that the voice of the customer is being heard and, to that extent, the concepts of listening and sensing conflate. In addition to listening, sensing also includes customer observation,

Figure 13: Organizational Sensing, Understanding, Interpreting and Responding for Customer Engagement

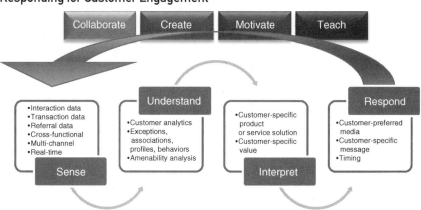

experimentation, and customer data acquisition of many kinds and from many sources, including, but not limited to, the customer him or herself. Sensing seeks to acquire customer data at every touch point, whenever the customer interacts with the enterprise and whenever the customer buys something. As will be discussed in the next chapter, sensing goes beyond this and seeks to understand what customers are saying and not just when they are in direct contact with the enterprise.

Customer Understanding

Having sensed what a customer is thinking, what he or she is saying and what is changing in a customer's personal environment that may reasonably affect the organizational relationship (without being overly intrusive), a company can examine the data to develop a deeper understanding of the individual customer and insight upon which the company can act. This understanding is developed using customer analytics, a subject discussed in Chapter 8. Companies may examine the data to understand what has changed in the customer's behaviors and communications, i.e., departures from the customer's norm. The data can also be examined to understand differences among customers, between an individual customer and prepared customer profiles, and to understand linkages between specific observed or demonstrated behaviors, among other areas of understanding.

Customer Amenability

One of the most important issues to be explored and understood for customer insight is that of customer amenability, an indication of the interest a customer has in a relationship on terms important to the customer. After all, no one has ever formed a durable relationship with someone who didn't want this too. This means that the customer must be amenable to a relationship for it to last. And the customer must become progressively more amenable for the relationship to deepen. Thus, an organization ought to have an ability to understand customer amenability. Amenability can be gauged in many ways, from listening to what customers are saying in cyberspace to asking them periodically and from this developing a Net Promoter Score as discussed in Chapter 8.

Developing Customer Understanding

Knowledge and insight come from data on customer interactions, transactions and manifested behaviors, including purchase, service and return activity. This, in turn, means that the capability of knowledge development is very closely tied into the underlying technologies that can help develop customer knowledge, including the data warehousing, data mining and predictive modeling technologies that allow an enterprise to forecast customer behaviors and ask "what if" questions at the individual customer level so that they can deepen their understanding one step at a time as they build a learning relationship.

Learning relationships depend on giving the customer an opportunity to teach the organization well enough that the organization is able to cater to the individual customer better each time. Learning relationships depend on the underlying strategies, capabilities, people and processes that convert better customer understanding into more meaningful outputs, such as products, services and communications. Organizational sensing, memory, knowledge and insight about each customer are central to the underlying capabilities that enable learning relationships. If the company has learned well enough and to the extent that the company recognizes the importance of teaching, the firm may have an opportunity to develop a highly differentiated position in the mind of each customer, one that helps customers learn why they should engage in new behaviors and how to do so. Chapter 9 discusses this subject.

Real-Time Integration

Real-time customer understanding creates additional opportunities to engage and influence customers. A supplier of engineered aluminum castings to the automobile industry bids on contract opportunities according to a well-defined set of specificatins from the auto companies. Unlike their competitors, the company has improved its chances of winning each contract by having more customer knowledge than its competitors. With the consent of the auto company, it places staff full-time in the customers' premises and collaborates with the customer's staff with product conceptualization, design and planning, blurring the line between where the supplier ends and the customer begins. This castings company has grown rapidly in a very competitive industry, one contract at a time, through improved customer knowledge and a learning relationship.

Interpretation

Having understood each individual customer, an organization now needs to convert this understanding into customer-specific solutions. In a process of interpretation, an organization develops clarity as to what elements of its products, services and even communications will be standard and what will be customizable, changed to meet the needs of individual customers. The organization arranges the customizable components together with the standard ones in an appropriate combination in order to provide each individual with the customer-specific value that he or she wants from the enterprise. This issue is discussed in the next section.

With customer understanding and interpretation in place, the organization can now respond to what it has sensed, acting to give the individual customer what he or she seeks, whether or not the customer proactively sought that from the enterprise in the first place. That is, the response is generated with respect to what the organization has sensed, not necessarily what the customer has specifically said, although much response will be as a result of customers initiating a request for information, guidance, a unique purchase or something else. In reaching out to an individual customer, the organization will use the customer's preferred channels of communications, with a customized message framed in a way that will be most sensitive to the customer's needs and feelings, and style of communication.

Response

The organization's response ought to not only deal with the customer's issues, whether current, pending or inferred from data, but should also consider how and when to motivate each customer to a changed state of behavior or attitude that is more supportive of long-term, mutual value creation, ideally consistent with the customer-specific objective the company has for an individual. More than this, the enterprise should consider how to create the value the customer wants, and welcome and manage the collaborative participation of each individual customer in the company's processes for value creation, such as fixing the general conditions that led to the issue being reviewed, giving the customer choice and control over processes for the customer values, and possibly other issues of both an operational and strategic nature, such as process improvements, new products, line extensions, packaging and so on.

An effective process for organizational sensing, understanding, interpreting and responding to individual customers' explicit and implicit requirements has the potential to make the customer feel genuinely heard. Companies looking to accelerate customer engagement and relevance might reexamine whether their sensing, understanding, interpreting and responding processes, technologies and people are doing what ought to be done: handling repetitive customer-specific tasks efficiently and managing adaptive tasks—those that require some departure from usual routines—creatively and effectively. Naturally, the customer should be engaged to understand if the enterprise is indeed being effective, rather than having the company itself arrive at this conclusion independent of customer input.

Customer-Specific Value

Customer-specific value derives from knowledge and insight into each individual customer. If companies are to establish definitively what each customer wants, they need to know each customer's key purchase criteria and the relative importance of these criteria. Although this can be established one customer at a time, the cost of doing this comprehensively usually only makes sense for B2B marketers. Table 13 provides an example to illustrate the development of customer-specific value. This table assesses what each customer wants with respect to selection criteria, and the positioning of a company in respect of those criteria. The diagram could be further extended to understand how each customer considers competitors as substitutes, an often overlooked or

Table 13: Customer-Specific Value

Decision-Making Criteria	Weighting of Importance	Rating of Performance (1=Very Poor and 10=Excellent)		
		Company	Competitor A	Competitor B
First price and cost in use	25	7	6	5
Information systems, reporting	5	5	5	6
Collaboration and joint planning	8	4	5	6
E-business capability	5	3	6	6
Service quality, responsiveness	15	5	6	5
Customer acceptance	10	8	9	4
Product conformance to specifications	20	8	8	8
Delivery	5	8	6	5
Returns policy	2	7	5	8
Financing, payment terms	5	5	3	8
Weighted total	100	641	640	589
Percentage of needs being met		64.1%	64.0%	58.9%
Value of company compared to competitors A and B			+0.2%	+8.8%

insufficiently considered aspect of this assessment. After all, who the company considers to be its competitors does not much matter, but which company a customer thinks could be a replacement is vital. This table shows ratings of the importance of purchase criteria and the rankings of the performance of a company relative to two competitors. When rankings are multiplied by ratings and the result totaled, the company is able to compare the value it delivers to the customer with that of competitors, one customer at a time.

A further refinement for B2B marketers is to identify criteria in the minds of each purchase decision maker in the customer's decision-making unit and then to weight these scores by the relative importance of specific decision makers. For reasons of simplicity, this multidimensional view is not presented here but the reader should consider undertaking this more comprehensive analysis to understand better where and how to manage each business account and to what purpose.

Although this assessment would make most sense for B2B marketers to consider for each customer, it is possible to complete this analysis for every consumer—either directly, online or through inference—based on customers' demonstrated behaviors when engaging in interactions with the firm, their transactions and their social communications.

If a table such as Table 13 were actually to have resulted from a customer listening exercise, a number of possibilities remain to be examined in order for the company to have a comprehensive understanding of its position at the specific account. For example, the company in this example provides less than two-thirds of the value that is possible (64.1 percent) and the company might reasonably explore what it might do to elevate its performance with respect to the attributes that the customer values most, in this case first price and cost in use, the conformance of the product to specifications, and service quality and responsiveness.

Again, on the assumption that the preceding table is the actual result of customer-specific listening, these data suggest that the company has something to learn from Competitor A with respect to those attributes where Competitor A has scored higher. There are also some purchase criteria where Competitor B has scored higher and, even though this company has a lower overall weighted customer-specific performance, it still has something to teach the company about improving the value it delivers to this specific account.

Had a company been through a listening exercise such as the preceding, it should have an ability to understand the needs, expectations and preferences of each of the individual customers it chooses to serve, whether they are individual businesses or consumers. With such data in hand, the company may be in a position to allow customers more choice, to give each the value he or she wants and to enable decisions in real time. This leads into a discussion of mass customization, the subject of Chapter 7.

Customer understanding generally requires thoughtful application of technology to customer databases, developing analytical insight from a wide variety of data points. Chapter 8 reviews this in a discussion of customer analytics.

INNOVATION

While customers appreciate it when companies develop solutions *for* them, this typically has less impact on the durability of a relationship than would be the case if customers were involved in the process of designing or developing solutions. Relationships deepen most profoundly when customers have a chance to collaborate *with* the enterprise to create the value they want. Customer collaboration is all about innovation, one customer at time.

Collaborative Innovation

A relationship based on collaborative innovation benefits from and requires mutual learning, with the enterprise developing increasingly relevant and timely customer knowledge and insight. Companies now recognize that they should work with their customers in joint knowledge-creating processes to develop customer-specific knowledge and a more informed capability to respond to, and shape events with, the customer. While this is most typically done B2B, there are many illustrations of customer-specific innovation occurring in business-to-consumer spaces. Of course, many of these examples can be drawn from online retailing where customers give companies an opportunity to learn about themselves, use this learning to advantage and give back increased value, the case for Amazon making suggestions based on prior inquiries or purchases—for example. There are also examples of business-to-consumer enterprises engaging with customers in processes that are not just enabled by the Internet. To illustrate, Streamline, a pioneering Boston-based virtual grocery retailer, visited customers in their homes with bar-code readers and took inventory of each customer's kitchen cupboards. When a customer ordered pretzels from the Streamline website, the company knew what brand that customer preferred and could suggest this type and size first. If the customer chose another, the database was updated.[14] Examples such as this have informed the practices of, and paved the way for, other online retailers, including Peapod, which acquired Streamline.

The development of a learning relationship with customers provides side benefits in addition to knowledge creation. Companies marketing to other companies find that inter-enterprise teams that solve problems together will remain bonded, even after the problems are solved. Companies in the business-to-consumer space find that customers who have been collaboratively engaged are more likely to be forgiving in the event of a mistake by the organization.

Multiple Levels of Engagement

Companies may consider engaging individual customers at multiple levels in the company because customer-specific innovation benefits from customer engagement throughout the value chain. At the highest level, this may mean customer advisory groups guiding senior executives and perhaps having a customer representative on the board of directors. Operationally, this customer collaboration may involve customer service teams planning together and executing those plans in areas such as product development, logistics, communications, end-customer promotion and customer service. This is described more generally using a manufacturing enterprise's processes as an example in Figure 14.

The more points of engagement, the more durable will be the relationship. This occurs because a customer feels that his or her voice is being heard in multiple ways and at several touch points, and the customer perceives he or she has influence to impact outcomes. Such a customer is more likely to value not only the resulting product or service but the processes that created

Figure 14: Customer-Specific Innovation

| Customer | | | | | | | | |
| Conceive | Design | Develop | Procure | Produce | Sell | Install | Service | Support |

| Marketing |
| Human resources |
| Information technology |
| Finance |

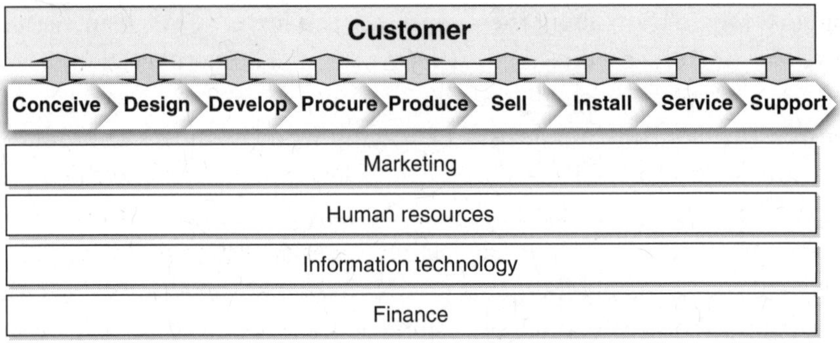

it. Figure 14 suggests that there can be opportunities to engage a customer at many stages where value is created, possibly including conception of the offering or solution, to the design and development of it, right through to the product support. There may even be additional points for customer engagement and collaboration, such as in respect of co-marketing and collaborative finance arrangements. Co-marketing occurs when a customer and the company engage in joint marketing efforts for mutual benefit, such as when they both might leverage one another's reputation. Procter & Gamble included Scope mouthwash in some of its Crest toothpaste formulations and advertised both brands on packages and in marketing communications. Collaborative financing occurs in many permutations and combinations, such as when customers provide financial support to suppliers by making milestone and other accelerated progress payments rather than waiting to pay until the end of contracts, which defense contractors are now doing with some of their suppliers.

Relevant Technologies

Real-time and other technologies can provide capabilities to serve an individual consumer that competitors cannot duplicate with equal relevance if customers are not engaged equally with the organization and its processes. Consider this example: Your washing machine breaks down and you call the service department of the manufacturer to remedy the problem. The call-center operator says the service technician will be at your home within four hours. You wait. After four hours, you call again to find out why the service person is not at your home. Your call comes into the call center where hundreds of employees are taking calls. Your call is identified and routed to the operator who told you that the technician would be there by now. The operator is best placed to handle the problem and finds the answer instantly by contacting the service person by cell or seeing status updates via GPS and online reporting. Technology has been applied in meaningful ways to help the company learn from prior interactions and ensure that you are treated uniquely and appropriately by the person best positioned to help you.

Competing on Scope

Relationship management has led many companies to compete on scope, becoming more of a "one stop shop" for its customers with a broader product and service assortment. Consider the case of Lear. Lear is a supplier of seating and electrical power management systems to the auto manufacturing industry. Lear spent heavily to acquire companies such as Masland, a manufacturer of auto carpets, and the seating businesses of Fiat, Ford, Saab and Volvo, as it built its vehicle interiors business. Why? Major parts companies know they need to become integrators of subassemblies rather than simply providers of point solutions, which many firms have focused on in the past. They need to become what the auto industry calls Tier 1 suppliers because car companies have narrowed the number of suppliers with which they want to deal and they expect Tier 1 parts companies to deal with smaller suppliers to integrate the value they want. This dramatically expands suppliers' range of services and geographic scope as they cater to customers globally. Lear, for example, provides parts for more than 300 vehicle nameplates worldwide.[15]

TEACHING

The penultimate component of the CREVITS model is Teaching. The art and science of teaching customers new behaviors is a vital and often overlooked aspect of creating new customer-specific value because relationships only create additional stakeholder value when there is a change of behaviors. This change often starts with customers learning something new. To date, much of the focus on changing behaviors has been within the enterprise as it seeks to modify its processes, incorporate new technologies, identify motivating marketing or pricing offers and train its staff, for example. But there are even bigger yields to be obtained by finding ways to teach customers new behaviors to accelerate adoption of new products and to advance customers up the rungs of the relationship ladder. As such, teaching customers merits its own chapter and is discussed in Chapter 9.

SHARING

The final component of the CREVITS model for planning relationships with existing customers is Sharing. For new value to contribute to relationships, it must be mutual—both parties must benefit—and shared between customer and supplier. The mutuality of value creation has been previously noted but it is as yet uncommon for companies to approach the customer relationship as an opportunity to *share* the benefits of new value creation.

Certainly, companies do give customers a chance to assemble the value they individually want, such as by choosing how fast they want goods to be delivered and, in the process, place a price on shipping speed. By charging different amounts for different speeds, a company can share in the benefits of the delivery option chosen by the customer. Examples such as this occur frequently in online businesses where customers build the value they want after the company has unbundled many of the individual elements of value that it used to sell previously as an integrated, bundled solution or product. Dell pioneered this approach when mass customizing computers and now a wide variety of online and offline companies allows customers to select the aspects they want from services (such as cable or telephone service) or products (such as eyeglasses).

Unbundling

B2B companies used to show B2C companies how to listen deeply to their customers and assemble the value that individual customers want. Management consulting firms are such a B2B example. Now online businesses have demonstrated that, by systematizing rebundling of the unbundled parts of goods and services, they can create customer collaboration, engagement and mutual learning in areas that were not possible in the era of mass production, distribution and marketing. In the process, these online companies have made themselves more or less impervious to competitors because customers are simply further down a mutual learning curve and that makes it very inconvenient and sometimes more costly to switch suppliers.

Companies ought to unbundle as many components of the value they presently provide as can economically be done. If firms have enough information to cost a component of the value they provide and track this throughout their enterprise, they surely have enough information to unbundle. Bundling is typically an attempt by an enterprise to simplify what it does, not to give each customer what it is that he or she wants. So when a cable company bundles channels to offer tiers of service, they are paid for channels few people watch. They are reluctant to unbundle and offer customers channel choice although they could clearly do that. Their reason for this is likely that they perceive their profits would decline when customers stop choosing marginal channels. So rather than being fully transparent, cable companies reveal their lack of genuine relationship orientation and mask underperforming products by cramming product bundles to dwindling audiences. Is it any wonder that their customers are increasingly defecting to other forms of information and entertainment, including the Internet and video games?

Fair Sharing of Value

Now online companies have something to teach goods producers and service firms. While it is still common for B2B firms to mass customize for their major and midsize accounts, they are often unwilling to provide a full range of unbundled options so that smaller accounts can assemble the value each wants. The message here is this: companies ought to plan the sharing of new value creation with their customers. It is not simply good enough for companies to price their goods or services based on margins that escalate as customers add more options. Companies ought to have plans to share fairly new value created for their customers according to the value individual customers choose. The sharing of this new value ought to reflect relationship objectives and these in turn ought to link to the value of the customer and the value of the pending transaction, and most certainly not just the cost of the input and escalating margin expectations, as is most frequently the case at present.

If new value is to be shared fairly, a reasonable question to ask is this: What value should be shared? Should it be the incremental value of the unbundled components only for a specific transaction, the margin on the rebundled components of the transaction, the incremental value of the customer as a whole, all of this or some other combination? When relationship objectives were established earlier, the company placed a value on the outcomes of specific behaviors. It is now appropriate to share the value achieved by the accomplishment of these behaviors. That is, if customers have moved up the relationship ladder, they ought to share fairly according to the mutual value they have created both for themselves and the enterprise, just as the company ought to benefit from this value creation. So if the objective was to move customers from buying an average of three items to four per month, to buy from more than one department, and to escalate spending levels by 50 percent annually, this had a definable profit impact and this profit can be related back to specific transactions in ways that are more or less complicated, depending in large measure on the industry within which the company participates. In summary, it may be appropriate for companies to unbundle their goods and services, allowing customers to rebundle them as they choose, and then to share value with each customer according to the relationship objectives that individuals attain.

●   ●   ●

While all companies have financial plans and most have marketing plans, not all companies have relationship plans to guide the appreciation and management of this most important asset, even though almost everyone now acknowledges the importance of customer relationships. Companies do have CRM plans—by which they usually mean plans for the deployment of CRM technology—and some of these plans are growing a little dusty now that the technologies have been implemented. To help remedy this shortcoming and bring focus back to where it ought to be—on the customer relationship—this chapter has provided and illustrated a framework for planning relationships with existing customers.

This chapter noted that there are a number of models for planning customer relationships, including the widely used IDIC Model.[16] This chapter offered an alternative, comprehensive model, CREVITS, for planning relationships with existing customers. CREVITS is an acronym for Customer selection, Relationship objectives, Engaging individual customers, Value for each customer, Innovating and collaborating with individual customers, Teaching customers new behaviors and Sharing with individual customers any new value that is created with them. Whichever model companies adopt, a plan is needed to guide the direction of relationship acquisition, maintenance and development.

The focus of this chapter has been on the management of relationships with current customers. The following chapter explores the development of relationships with people and companies that are known to these customers, with particular focus on social spaces.

Chapter 4
ONE-*THROUGH*-ONE: ENGAGING SOCIAL CUSTOMERS

"Get someone else to blow your own horn and the sound will carry twice as far."

Will Rogers (1879–1935)

This chapter discusses the development of relationships with potential customers who are known to existing customers as well as those people and organizations who might reasonably be engaged using social media. This chapter is entitled "One-*Through*-One" because, in this discussion, the company looks to sustain relationships not only with its existing customers but also to access and then develop relationships with the connections these people know. As customers and potential customers converse, the enterprise seeks to become part of the conversation, engaging in communications and progressively deeper dialog that leads to more meaningful interactions and, in due course, transactions. The company seeks to use existing customers as a gateway to reach their individual networks, associations and connections. This gated access is termed "one-*through*-one," in that the company looks at, through and beyond existing customers to bridge to, and connect with, those they influence. This is more than simple word of mouth or even what might be termed "word of mouse," the online equivalent. While word of mouth is about facilitating the proliferation of information from customer to contact, one-through-one seeks to engage each individual customer uniquely with a tailored message best suited to his or her prior interactions, transactions, context and profile, and specifically geared to facilitating pass-through of communications to that customer's contacts.

In this chapter, we go beyond the simple observation that social media is important. That much is generally known, of course. This chapter also avoids a discussion of every conceivable social media technology or point solution, although it does mention several. The proliferation and rapid growth of the number of options would make an attempt at comprehensive coverage rapidly obsolete. There is also the risk that an in-depth and complete review of the many technology options available and emerging could obscure the very landscape that is to be understood and managed—that of people and their relationships with the enterprise and especially with one another.

THE "PEOPLESCAPE" OF SOCIAL MEDIA

The focus of this chapter is on social media as an enabler of a flexible, customizable connection to engage customers and create a more durable and valuable relationship with them. More than the long-held intent of marketers to create positive word of mouth, social media creates new opportunities for companies to find new customers through their customers' existing networks. Because social media has become a key means by which people connect with one another, it is appropriate for the enterprise to master this channel of communication and do this not just to keep its existing customers and create new value for them, although that might indeed be part of the goal. In addition, the focus here is on understanding each individual customer's network.

The organization needs strategic capabilities by which potential social customers can engage the enterprise and proactively reach out to become part of the social media universe to which everyone who knows the enterprise would generally connect. In much the same way as a hiker considers the terrain ahead of him or her as the landscape he or she must master to get to his or her destination, so too must the enterprise become proficient in navigating the people who form the landscape to be navigated by the enterprise. This terrain is called the peoplescape of social media.

Customers are not equally important to the enterprise and, similarly, prospective customers who might be engaged using social media are also not all of equal importance. The company seeks to identify and selectively engage its customers and prospective social customers as it receives direct customer communications and listens to conversations, tries to make sense of them and do something meaningful—something customers and potential customers will value—with what has been learned. The organization treats each customer and connection as a center of influence—a gateway to new connections beyond a specific person. This approach creates a different basis for selecting customers than in the case of existing customers discussed in the previous chapter. Here the focus is on the number of people each person has access to, the quality of those connections (including the revenue potential of those people and the networks they have), the standing and reputation of the person among those to whom he or she is known and the ability of a person to influence others. A person with an ability to influence and who knows the right number of the right people becomes very important to an enterprise seeking to build its reputation and access to potential customers. A number of social media companies have recognized the importance of accessing the right networks. For example, Facebook's Graph maps connections between people and their friends, enabling developers focused on the Facebook platform to identify target audiences, deploy networks effectively and improve the user experience.

THE COMPANY IS NO LONGER CENTER STAGE

In the past era of mass marketing and segment-based marketing, all the world was a stage and companies were the stars of their own dramas as they performed for their audiences and gave their best performances: their products and services, and their advertisements. In this world of marketplace entertainment, the company really was master of its own universe.

Extending this entertainment metaphor, one-to-one marketing might be likened to street art. Here the company engages in micro-plays, each one for just a few people or even just one. There is audience engagement, there is an interplay of content, reaction, listening and speaking as the actor performs and the mini-audience responds in ways big or small—but respond they usually do, even if the response is a negative one.

Now, in this age of social media and one-*through*-one marketing, the world is no longer a stage and street art is no longer an appropriate analogy for today's marketing. Today, it might be more appropriate to think of the company sitting among the very audience it seeks to influence. Members of the audience go up on stage to perform every once in a while. They act however they wish, say whatever they want, convey as much or as little meaning as they choose, do so for as long as they want and then sit down, to start again at a time they select. All the while, another person may be on the same stage too, acting on his or her own terms. The company sits among the audience as it listens or does not, reaches out to the audience or not, and perhaps takes the stage once in a while. This may sound chaotic, and it is, but that is the reality of the company's social media setting today. In this arena, the marketer doesn't own the stage but has occasional access to it. Today's play is in a democratized communications environment where content originates with others and is co-created collaboratively between the enterprise and the customer or prospect. The marketer may seek a role in the plays of others. If the marketer plays this role well, the firm will be sought out. If the audience ignores the company, well, the marketer might come to know what it means to be an out-of-work actor.

THE CUSTOMER IS SPEAKING

Companies have a dwindling aggregate share of marketplace voice—the firm's share of the total communications occurring between marketplace participants, including customers and companies—than was the case when mass media prevailed. Given the declining share of corporate voice, companies cannot expect to influence customers as they did in the mass-marketing era. Broadcast is no longer central to the firm's marketing communications mix. For purposes of acquiring customers, one-to-one marketing is also less important than was previously the case because customers are less influenced by what the corporation says than by what their friends say and do. This makes marketing a relative activity—a process of continuous engagement with a network—where peers determine relevance and influence purchase more than an enterprise is able to do with its traditional command-and-control approach to marketplace influence.

In this post-broadcast era, the individual voice of each customer matters as people connect with one another's friends, associates and a network of connections. Companies can seek to engage the people known to their existing customers and thereby extend the reach of the company's communications through each of their individual customers. When such an approach is formalized, this might be termed "throughcasting." Examples of throughcasting include reaching out to existing customers and asking them to forward the company's e-mail to their friends and family to get a discount, or the actions recipients take independently when they forward or "retweet" communications they have received on Twitter, for example.

LISTEN

If the enterprise's communications are less important to customers than what friends say, the firm ought to be listening to that which impacts the organization by customers and others. Dell understands the importance of listening to social media conversations in order to respond effectively and in real time. Dell monitors Facebook, LinkedIn, Twitter and blogs (through Google Alerts) because this enables brand defense and the provision of answers and stops misinformation before it damages the brand.[1] Dell's Social Media Listening Command Center in Round Rock, Texas, listens in many languages to tens of thousands of posts, blogs and microblogs—upwards of 25,000—that mention Dell and then manages the communications to ensure rapid and appropriate response as indicated, presumably balancing intrusiveness with the benefits of helpfulness. The information Dell gathers can be examined according to categories such as topics and subjects of conversation, sentiment, share of voice, geography and trends.[2] PepsiCo's Gatorade division established a similar capability to that of Dell. The Gatorade Mission Control Center in Chicago monitors real-time social media conversations and tracks their top-performing pages to ensure that followers are directed to the best ones. Like Dell, Gatorade also uses Salesforce's Radian6 Social Marketing Cloud as one of its technology solutions.[3]

Of course, social media listening and all the associated expenditures on technologies, processes and people only matter if the customer is genuinely heard, if the information is put to use while it is still fresh and when a response can make a difference, and if the information can be aggregated and examined for trends, problems and opportunities. Many companies say they understand that listening to customers in social media spaces is important but still customers feel unheard and unappreciated. This feeling provides companies with an opportunity to close gaps between what the company hears compared to what customers have said, what the company acts upon and what actions customers perceive to have occurred. Figure 15 illustrates these potential gaps.

A number of companies use technology platforms and point solutions to help them listen to, and engage with, customers and others in their markets. They try to do this in real time because customers are more likely to be managed if their perceptions, attitudes and behaviors are dealt with when it matters—right now. Many companies are used to searching traditional search engines such as Google. Social search may in many ways be more important

Figure 15: Listening and Hearing—Closing the Gaps

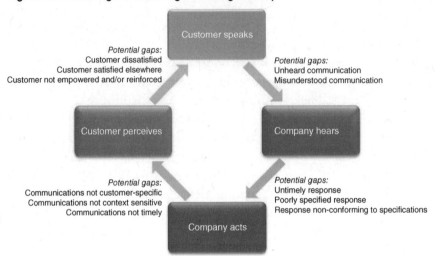

because social search pays more attention to relationships and social search engines are used for interpersonal engagement, the essence of what the company seeks to unlock. Unlike the dominance of Google in traditional search, social search comprises many different engines such as Facebook, Twitter, LinkedIn, YouTube, Yelp and Data.com within Salesforce.

Real-time search polls social media sites such as Facebook and streams content in real time. In this, the real-time social search engines differ from conventional search because these search engines don't conduct periodic, indexed searches that are stored and presented based on selected features.[4] They stream the results of their polling for companies to hear in a variety of ways. Listening for tactical customer engagement can include social media monitoring and search, analytics (discussed in greater detail in Chapter 8), and other features and benefits from companies such as those mentioned in Table 14.

In addition to listening to the social communications of customers about the company, firms ought also to listen to conversations that affect their competitors in social spaces. This can provide helpful competitive intelligence on what they say, how they say it and where they say it, potentially leading to a change in the company's own social media strategy, messaging and approach to customer listening and engagement.[5]

Table 14: Selected Companies and Solutions Related to Aspects of Social Media

Company/solution	Description
Alterian (by SDL)	Social media monitoring tools as well as campaign management, Web content management and e-mail.
Boardreader	A free search of, for example, posts, microblogs, videos, movies, news, press releases, articles, websites, domains, etc.
Citizennet	Demographic and behavioral mapping specific to Facebook.
Collective Intellect (by Oracle)	Real-time market intelligence.
Crimson Hexagon	Monitoring and analysis of insights from user-generated content in social media.
CoTweet (by ExactTarget)	Social media, campaign and conversation management.
Google Alerts	A free tool that listens for references to you and your firm.
HootSuite	Manages multiple social profiles, schedules messages and tweets, tracks brand mentions and analyzes social media traffic. Supports Twitter, Facebook, LinkedIn, Ping, WordPress, Foursquare, for example.
Linkfluence	Reputation management, community identification and conversation analysis.
Radian6 Social Marketing Cloud (by Salesforce)	Widely used social media monitoring tools, e.g., the Dell and Gatorade examples discussed previously.
SAP Sentiment Intelligence	Social media monitoring, analytics and insight.
Seesmic	Connectivity platform for managing social connections, Twitter streams and Facebook feeds, mobile apps, web-based services.
Social Mention	Real-time social media search.
Symphony Social Media	Social media management.
Trendrr	Popularity and awareness tracking of social networks, buzz, videos, etc.
Twitter Search	Free tool from Twitter.
Twitter TweetDeck	For heavier users of Twitter to listen in, arrange feeds with customizable columns, filter data and schedule tweets. Downloadable app.
Visible Technologies	Social media monitoring, analytics and engagement.
WhosTalkin	Conversation search.

SOCIAL MEDIA TAXONOMY

Before considering how to use social media to engage new potential customers through the enterprise's existing customers, it is appropriate to first review the landscape of social media by exploring a taxonomy or classification scheme for the many categories of options and solutions.

Just as there is a proliferation of social media solutions, there are many social media taxonomies.[6] These typically group social media solutions into categories of content, such as blogs, photos and videos. An alternative to a feature-driven approach such as this is to categorize content according to the intent of the content from both the perspective of the content provider and the content consumer, both of which are required for social media to be a conversation. Content and the associated technologies on which it resides may have one or several purposes. The intent could be to enable the providers to inform, educate, communicate, entertain, collaborate or engage in a transaction, for example.

The processes by which content is developed and shared facilitates social media categorization. Taking these considerations together on two axes of a diagram, with "content intent" on the X-axis and "content sharing" on the Y-axis, yields a perspective of social media taxonomy as described in Figure 16. Content sharing as described in this diagram considers time as a discriminant for content generation, consumption and regeneration. Where content is generated, consumed or regenerated in more or less concurrent communications, this is termed "synchronous." "Asynchronous" communications occur where there is a time delay between content being developed and consumed, and possibly regenerated as a communications response. Synchronous content can be a higher involvement experience for users because,

Figure 16: Social Media Taxonomy

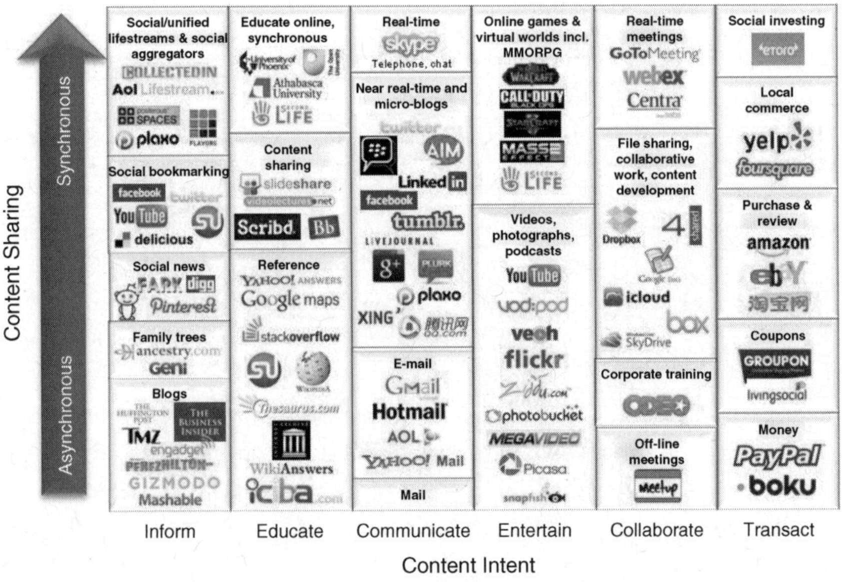

by its very nature, it requires engagement and near instantaneous response whereas asynchronous communications does not expect this. An example of synchronous communications is MMORPG, an acronym that describes the playing of role player games by mass audiences online.[7] At the other end of the spectrum, asynchronous content may be lower involvement by both generators and consumers. As an example, blogs have lower involvement than role player games for those engaged by the content.

The taxonomy provided in Figure 16 serves to illustrate how the connections between people and organizations can be intermediated and classified. Any attempt to provide a fully exhaustive social media typology must necessarily fall short, given the arrival and departures of companies, technologies and platforms, and the sheer number of entrants. Figure 16 should be seen for its intent: as an illustrative—and necessarily partial—taxonomy of the kinds of solutions that facilitate synchronous and asynchronous connections. The examples displayed in Figure 16 illustrate the kinds of sites that might be assigned to each social media category and have been chosen in part based on general marketplace awareness and in part on Alexa mentions and rankings. The allocation and order of sites as presented should also be regarded as illustrative, since rank order is out of date shortly after categorization, as indeed may occur for specific solutions and even, in some cases, the companies themselves.

SOCIAL MEDIA OBJECTIVES

For reasons suggested previously and especially because of the need to communicate with customers and potential customers where they are, companies naturally ought to consider social media as part of their communications mix; most already do, of course. Mention social media and companies often think "Facebook" or "Twitter." But as described in the taxonomy of Figure 16, there are many more social media options than these two firms, significant though they are. In fact, there are too many options for any organization to fully adopt all or even most of them. Choices must be made principally because resources need to be allocated to be active across multiple platforms and solutions.

As social conversations are occurring with or without the direct presence of the company, it doesn't matter as much to customers or potential customers if the company is present or not but it could matter a great deal to the firm if it was not aware of conversations that could impact them if they do not respond in a timely way. There are many examples of issues that grew more problematic over time because the company didn't engage customers and attend to their concerns. Perhaps the reader, like over 11 million others, has seen the YouTube video that tells the story of a traveler whose guitar was apparently broken by United Airlines—a public relations disaster that could have been avoided had United been listening more actively and engaging customers more effectively in near real time.[8] Once the video went viral, United still had an opportunity to apologize and provide some restitution.

Companies could have three principal social media objectives that are overlapping in nature, rather than mutually exclusive, as follows:

1. Reputation management—sustaining and enhancing the brand and reputation of the company.
2. Customer management—building bonds with current customers.
3. Customer acquisition—enabling the acquisition and retention of new customers.

The first objective speaks to the issue of enhancing the general value of the brand and reputation of the company in social spaces as well as the amelioration of problems before they become major, to reduce the amplitude and proliferation of negative messaging that threatens to reduce the value of the brand and creates cognitive dissonance among existing customers. Even someone who does not have a guitar can surely empathize with the poor traveler's guitar story mentioned previously or the hapless fellow whose computer monitor was thrown over a fence by a FedEx delivery person in another YouTube video (this one watched over 8 million times). To show that no one courier company has a monopoly on occasional and weirdly bad customer service, in yet another YouTube video, a USPS postal worker is shown lobbing a boxed antique cuckoo clock. Instances such as these may be unusual but this visual evidence of poor customer service seems to resonate with customers and depreciates the value of the brands. Most companies now listen to their customers closely, carefully and in real time to avoid similar or repeat occurrences.

As noted previously, Dell's Social Media Listening Command Center listens to customer sentiment and communications, tracks conversations across the Web and routes specific issues requiring resolution to Dell employees for handling. In this way, even smaller issues—what Dell calls issues in the "long tail"—are dealt with effectively and before visibility and intensity escalate in social media or more generally. Dell engages with customers in the languages they speak, with as many as 11 languages being

Figure 17: Social Media Objectives

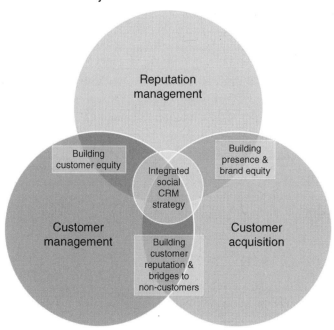

used in the monitor center to respond to more than 22,000 daily topic posts related to Dell as well as mentions of Dell on Twitter. The information can be analyzed based on topics and subjects of conversation, sentiment, share of voice, geography and trends.[9]

The three objectives of reputation management, customer management and customer acquisition are depicted graphically in Figure 17. This graphic suggests that there are a number of important sub-objectives at each intersection of the Venn diagram. At the intersection of reputation management and customer management, the company's social media objective is to build customer equity and bonds. At the intersection of reputation management and customer acquisition, the social media objective is to build company social media presence and the equity of its brands. Where customer management and customer acquisition intersect, the social media objective is to enhance the relationships customers have with the people they know and to enable bridges to be built from existing customers to potential customers. The company's integrated social media strategy for creating a sustaining ecosystem that facilitates ongoing engagement with existing customers and potential customers is at the heart of the Venn diagram. This is where all three circles intersect.

SOCIAL MEDIA PLANNING

So back to the earlier question: how to choose among social media options in the context of the business objectives a company is trying to accomplish? As with any plan, the starting point is the objective—what is it that the company seeks to accomplish? More specifically, the starting point is not in technology, such as identifying a particular technology, community or solution that the company feels it ought to develop. While it sounds obvious that any plan, including the social media one, ought to have a clear objective statement, perhaps surprisingly it is not uncommon for companies to give limited attention to their objective statement.

After establishing objectives, the next activity is to develop an analysis of the company's current state in social media, especially its readiness to engage customers and potential customers in social media.

Then the company might consider its social media future state by defining what the company's position in social spaces should be. This might be when the company considers its technology options, among much else.

The final activity is to develop a transitioning plan that will describe how the company should move from where it is today to where it wants to be tomorrow. Figure 18 notes this sequence and selected activities that might reasonably be considered for each component of the plan.

Figure 18: Social Media Planning

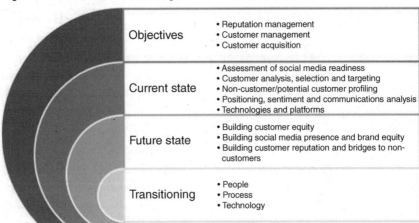

Objectives	• Reputation management • Customer management • Customer acquisition
Current state	• Assessment of social media readiness • Customer analysis, selection and targeting • Non-customer/potential customer profiling • Positioning, sentiment and communications analysis • Technologies and platforms
Future state	• Building customer equity • Building social media presence and brand equity • Building customer reputation and bridges to non-customers
Transitioning	• People • Process • Technology

Setting Objectives

Social media objectives are often stated in terms that are directional and aspirational, and sometimes not easily measurable. So it wouldn't be uncommon for a company to articulate a social media objective such as "increasing customer engagement," "talking more with our biggest customers," "building brand sentiment," or "engaging customers in an ongoing dialog," etc.

Sometimes companies state their social media objectives in a more tactical way, such as by outlining the specific technologies they plan to use, communities with which they intend to engage, or more specific benefits or results they seek to achieve. These outcomes could include enabling user-generated content (e.g., customers posting their observations, videos and photographs), obtaining rapid customer feedback, or receiving input in the design or development of goods and services.

While statements of objectives such as these are typically measurable and may resonate internally within the company, setting tactical objectives suggests an approach to social media that is focused more on execution and less on strategy. As such, this is often the reverse order for approaching objective setting. If the tactical objectives are successful, a subsequent review may be required to retrofit social media strategy in a more comprehensive and high-level manner. Social media statements of objective ought to achieve the following:

- Integrate with and resolve a material gap in the company's communications mix and/or relationship marketing strategy.
- Address the three categories of objectives as noted previously: reputation management, customer management and customer acquisition. Each of these objectives will likely have a number of sub-objectives that ought to be identified, particularly the desired attitudinal and behavioral changes that the company is seeking to achieve.
- Enable subsequent measurement of success, both in terms of accomplishing the objectives and the timeline.

Current State Analysis

The current state analysis is the starting point for the organization's assessment of its readiness to engage its customers and potential customers. This review could include a consideration of the customers and potential customers with whom the company seeks to engage, the positioning and sentiment the company has with these customers and potential customers, a communications review—including, for example, where customers and potential customers are to be found in virtual spaces, what the company does to engage with them at present, and what metrics inform the company's current results from these efforts.

Customers and Prospects

The first component of the current state analysis deals with customers, who they are, how much they are worth, to what networks they belong, who they influence or how influential they might be. Customer valuation was discussed in Chapter 3. This serves as a basis for customer triage into best, average and worst, or other methods for customer differentiation as previously discussed. Marketers naturally want to identify the most influential customers because these offer the greatest opportunity for seeding markets with information and creating new customers from among the customers' contacts, and treating these contacts as prospects.

The objective to identify the people with whom to connect and engage can be addressed in many ways, starting from the company's own databases to yield target profiles. Companies such as Facebook offer target profiles too, and make outreach to these profiles practicable. But this tends to put the technology before the strategy—a common shortcoming of companies' social media planning.

The concept of a network has changed materially with the advent of social media. Marketers previously viewed themselves at the center of information flow, with customers being at the end of spokes, much like a bicycle wheel with hub and spokes. Marketers knew that customers were in contact with one another, of course, and viewed this communication as important but not central to the purchase decision. Many marketers considered customer-to-customer communications as peripheral and secondary to enterprise-to-customer communications, but still an important component of reducing buyer's remorse or generally creating a supportive environment within which to market.

Customers' connections one to another are today considered more important. Rather than seeing a network as a series of hubs and spokes, marketers today consider a network to be more like epidemiology. They think of communications progressing in much the same way that a disease would—although without the pejorative context, of course!

Figure 19: Hub and Spoke vs. One-Through-One

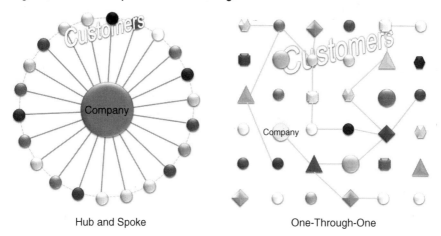

Hub and Spoke   One-Through-One

The difference between these two categories of networks is shown in Figure 19. As suggested by the diagram for one-through-one, the company is part of a fabric of a network within which communications are occurring whether the company knows this or not, or participates in the communications or not. In the network as described, every person is different, every connection is different, and the strengths of ties are usually different too, with some individuals being more influential over others on occasion or generally.

Influencers

In Chapter 3, key influencers were discussed, as were mechanisms for identifying the most influential people (Klout Scores being one example). Companies typically try to understand the reach of each of their customers and prospects in the network, individual influence and community influence. One way of assessing reach is to understand the number of connections each individual has to others in the network, a simple arithmetical process once the network is understood. Certainly, the number of connections a person has is an important—but not sufficient—consideration for assessing a potential ambassador or promoter of an idea or product. After all, every marketer would want to leverage the connections of individuals who know many people within the network. Unfortunately, the number of connections an individual has is an insufficient basis to determine his or her relative influence. We all know people who have hundreds or perhaps thousands of social media connections without any real influence over them. So, while reach is important, the influence a person has in a community and in respect of specific individuals may be more so. The former is easier to identify as companies can readily assess who the opinion leaders are, such as authors of blogs, for example. By paying attention to the structure of their networks and isolating the centers of influence and key decision makers within them, companies can readily identify whom they should seek to influence most based on their specific communications objectives.

Decision influencers in social media are people a customer does not know. For example, many people take a look at the recommendations of others who have bought a given product before deciding whether or not to proceed with the purchase. Marketers can stimulate the purchase decision by matching customers with similar interaction and transaction histories. It is a simple matter to cluster customers by behavior rather than demographically—as mentioned previously, relationship management requires that behavioral clustering receive more attention than demographic segmentation—and to pass along recommendations to an individual based on the behaviors of others in the cluster.

Location

Marketers need to know where the people they want to communicate with are to be found. People may be information seekers or information sharers, or both, depending on the context. A customer wanting to know the departure time of an aircraft is an information seeker. The same customer who sends the departure information to friends and family is an information sharer. Customers and prospective customers may "hang out" in different places, sometimes simultaneously. They may be on Facebook at the same time as they are streaming a YouTube video or collaborating on a Prezi presentation. They may even be virtually and physically in the same place right now, having signed in to a store they are visiting using Foursquare, for example. Social media planning requires that one knows where customers who match the desired profiles are to be found, an important aspect of a communications objective. If customers are watching YouTube and a firm's objective is to introduce a new product's features, the company may decide to bypass dominant social media platforms such as Facebook and Twitter, and focus on YouTube instead.

As should be apparent by now, it is not appropriate to choose a platform like Facebook or Twitter and *then* design the communications strategy.

Table 15: Social Media Objectives and Process Taxonomy

	Reputation management	Customer management	Customer acquisition
Inform			
Educate			
Communicate			
Entertain			
Collaborate			
Transact			

Some companies might say otherwise, since firms such as Facebook and Twitter obviously have enormous membership and many capabilities for the enterprise to consider. However, choosing the platform ahead of the customer has the potential to focus an organization on point solutions rather than its own objectives, and may even distort or redirect the objectives of the company.

An alternative to choosing the best known platforms to engage customers and potential customers is illustrated in Table 15—a matrix of the organization's three categories of objectives and the social media taxonomy explored in Figure 16 earlier. A company might consider how each of the IECECT taxonomy options (or just those that are particularly important to the enterprise)—Inform, Educate, Communicate, Entertain, Collaborate, Transact—affect or contribute to the firm's management of its reputation, customers and new customers. This prioritization may well lead the company to pay less attention to certain options and instead consider, for example, how best to acquire potential customers by educating them. This in turn can lead to identification of communications and technology options best suited to this purpose. In the end—in the future state analysis—the company may decide to court, influence and engage using one of the options mentioned earlier, say, Facebook, but this would not be the starting point for an objective assessment of the current state. As a result, the selected approach would have offered the company an opportunity to consider a broader range of options and be objective in the ones it selected. This approach also offers the marketer an opportunity to shield communications strategy from top-of-mind distraction, such as the boss who wanders into the marketer's office and recommends a new app he just heard about from his kid!

Future State Analysis

At this stage, the company will have completed a current state map of its social media objectives in the context of the social media taxonomy and its process alternatives for customer engagement, as presented in Figure 16 previously. Each of the key intersections in the map contains social media choices the company has made. The company then assesses and prioritizes the current state intersections in the matrix of Table 15 and considers whether the solutions it has adopted for social media are the "best" ones to help it achieve its social media objectives.

Social Media Performance

The company makes the determination of what is best for it by examining whether the customers and potential customers it seeks are best engaged using the current state media choices. It may be helpful for a company to review the social media performance of the company and its competitors, and the social media alternatives and options available to a firm by reviewing information available from organizations and websites such as AdGooroo, Alexa, Communispace, Compete, comScore, Cymfony, Experian Hitwise, Nielsen Online BuzzMetrics, Quantcast, Ranking.com and Socialbakers, and then evaluate selected options.

There are many approaches for measurement (discussed in Chapter 8 and therefore not discussed at length here) that can be used to inform aspects of social media options; it remains important to focus on key variables that are specific to an organization's own objectives, such as how many of its current and potential customers are accessible using each of the social media options, how many of these customers and potential customers are accessible every day on these media, which media key decision influencers use (i.e., those influencers who might be engaged or co-opted to influence customers and potential customers), and how communications and engagement costs would likely vary according to the media chosen.

Niche and Mass Social Media

Facebook has 845 million unique visits per month with 425 million people visiting on a mobile device and 483 million visiting Facebook each day.[10] Given the sheer scale of Facebook—about 12 percent of planet Earth visits it at least once a month—and the frequency of visits, some companies may reasonably take the view that Facebook must be central to any social media strategy but the bigger issue might be whether or not their specific customers and the customers they covet are indeed on Facebook.

As a simple illustration, there are about 700,000 Facebook users in China at time of writing—a small fraction of the approximately 300 million Internet users in that country.[11] A company might be wasting its marketing efforts if China was important to its marketing success and it used Facebook exclusively. In China, a firm might choose to use an alternative social media platform such as Renren, Sina, Tencent or a focused solution instead of, or together with, Facebook. That is, a company might want to engage with people who are focused more specifically than Facebook contacts, perhaps on a subject matter such as sports, for example. Numerous social media environments are emerging to cater to niches within social media spaces, such as JockTalk, which focuses on followers of professional sports athletes, and DineMates, a food social network catering to Asian food lovers.

The niches for social media are called Vertical Social Platforms (VSPs) and can get very specific. Consider the site StachePassions, which is for singles who like mustaches and VampireFreaks for people who associate with "dark, alternative culture," according to the organization's website. Some of these networks come and go. ZiiTrend was a social media platform for people who predict the future (sounds like social media for social mediums) but apparently not the demise of the site itself, as it is now, perhaps predictably, silent.

Social Media Engagement

Not all content producers are equally valuable. They differ according to the value of their audience. This audience value may be calculated according to the number of connections multiplied by the average annual expenditure of each connection on the product or service category being considered.

The spectrum of social media engagement is described in Figure 20 and is as follows, in order of decreasing value and desirability from the company's point of view:

1. High volume and influential social media content producers, gauged both by the number of followers they have and the intensity of their following
2. Those who participate to some extent in social media
3. People who present themselves in social media but do not generate much content or following

Figure 20: Customers and Social Media Engagement

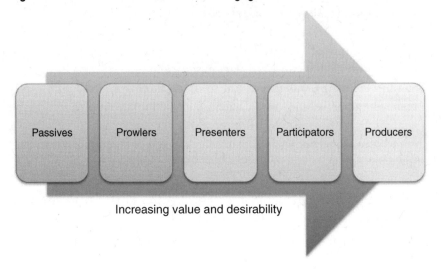

Passives   Prowlers   Presenters   Participators   Producers

Increasing value and desirability

4. The social media prowlers who scavenge and absorb content but don't produce it
5. Those people who are mostly passive in social media, inert and non-participative

The outgrowth of this review will be a new or newly affirmed social media map that aligns the organization's social media objectives with social media it has selected. This assessment may prove to have been the easy part of the consideration. The more challenging issue of transitioning, and related tactical considerations, is discussed next.

Transitioning

It is difficult to unwind those processes and technologies that pertain to social media choices that are now unwieldy or inappropriate for the organization to pursue for strategy, cost or other reasons. Consider a company that once embraced Myspace and now wishes to refocus resources to concentrate on, say, Twitter. Myspace began in 2003 and was the most popular of social media for a time. Myspace's former success has receded into history so any organization that once focused its social media efforts principally on Myspace would need to redeploy to connect with customers and potential customers using another social media option.

Multiple Platforms

To help avoid future difficulties associated with moving from one social media platform to another, an enterprise could use one of a variety of social media listening platforms to listen to customers and a communications engine to simplify and cost-reduce the management of social media across multiple platforms.[12] This multiplatform communications integration has the additional benefit of providing cross-platform message consistency while also lessening the firm's dependence on specific point solutions which may be here today but gone tomorrow. As the Myspace example suggests, even powerful social media platforms are not invulnerable to shifts in consumer preference.

Gaps in Maps

Companies need to ensure that their message is consistent across platforms and that they manage and update their communications effectively, regardless of the social media platform they are using at the time. For example, a company using Facebook for social media in North America, Europe, India, Indonesia, Brazil, Mexico and Turkey[13] may supplement the gaps in its social media maps with platforms such as, for example, Orkut (Brazil), Renren, Sina or Tencent (China), Mixi (Japan), Cyworld (Korea), and VKontakte (Russia), where these organizations have strong social media positions.

Centers of Influence

One way of influencing customers and/or potential customers is to create awareness and interest among those with the potential to influence them, such as bloggers and micro-bloggers with significant networks—most especially including the customers of the enterprise as well as those to whom they look as trustworthy resources. In addition to understanding the networks of their own customers, some companies use Technorati's Blog Directory to understand what the most influential blogs are, among other purposes. Technorati catalogs approximately 1.3 million blogs, the top three of which at time of writing were The Huffington Post, Mashable and Gizmodo.

Ketel One vodka initially built its brand principally through word-of-mouth, facilitated in part by bartenders who made recommendations to customers in bars and lounges where Ketel One was sold. One of Ketel One Wordwide's owners, Diageo, educated these bartenders to better understand differentiating factors in the Ketel One vodka.[14] Diageo identified and ranked bloggers according to their influence based on the number of site visits. Bloggers were educated about the brand and some were given product sample kits.

The result was an increase in favorable communication to Ketel One's target audience, with over 120,000 readers reached through the blog postings and a significant increase in sales.[15]

Pass-Through Stimulus-Response

Marketers have long recognized the importance of stimulating response. The stimulus-response model of buyer behavior is most widely adopted to influence buyers by providing a short-term reward in order to change, modify or accelerate a purchase decision. Examples include using a coupon code to obtain a discount or simply clicking on a link, such as in a shopping basket where companies such as Szul, an online jewelry retailer, makes reduced-price product recommendations based on observing click-through behavior of customers. A number of online retailers encourage their customers to make product referrals to their friends by providing discounts to both new customers and the people who make referrals, thus rewarding communicators and receivers of the communication.

Facebook's "Like" and "Timeline"

Perhaps the most significant of social media communication pass-throughs is Facebook's "Like" function, which allows visitors to websites other than Facebook to post to their profiles, communicating to friends and contacts that they like products, services or content, and facilitate display of this information in friends' newsfeeds. Facebook's social plug-ins, Facebook Connect and Open Graph social media map, provide developers with an opportunity to create personalized and customized visitor experiences and leverage the information learned on one website to another, in a new, more relevant way to each individual person, which further increases the likelihood of people communicating their praise and preference to others.[16] In a manner such as this, a customer visiting the online music website Pandora without first liking specific music on it may receive a customized playlist based on prior likes on other websites while also communicating music choices to his or her network and receiving playlists from others in the network with similar likes.

Facebook has a number of other capabilities that enable a company to market to its customers and through them to their connections. These capabilities include the "Like" box, the "Comments" button that allows users to comment on any content on a site, and the Timeline. The Facebook Like box is applied on the company's own website to, for example, enable promotion of a Facebook page, provide information on how many people—and their friends—have liked the page, feature recent posts and make it easier to like the page. The Facebook Share Link function was made obsolete by the Like button but the Share Link function allowed messages to be added to Likes, enabling explanation or other information to be provided, and thus remains a benefit, one that can be implemented on websites nonetheless. Facebook's additional social media plug-ins include the following: the Send button that enables visitors to a site to send content to friends, the Subscribe button that lets visitors subscribe to other Facebook users without logging into Facebook, the Activity Feed plug-in that describes users' site-specific likes and comments to their friends, the Registration plug-in that enables visitors to register for a company's website using Facebook accounts, the Facepile plug-in that provides pictures of people who have liked or registered, and the Livestream plug-in that provides an opportunity for users to interact in real-time.[17]

The Timeline allows users to add data to their updates according to life events. These data provide Facebook with much insight into each person as users populate what amounts to their autobiographies.[18] Customer analytics provides Facebook with an ability to help marketers find the right customers.

Twitter's Retweet

The microblogging website Twitter enables users to send—or "tweet" in Twitter-speak—messages of up to 140 characters. Twitter handles hundreds of millions of tweets per day and many of these are communications that are forwarded from receivers to new recipients in much the same way that e-mails are forwarded. Twitter calls this forwarding "retweeting." Companies stimulate retweeting by providing information more likely to be passed along to friends and other connections. This information may be thoughtful or interesting tweets, information that is time sensitive, or offers of economic incentives such as daily deals. Retweeting can also be encouraged by simply asking followers to do so, using hashtags to reach out to non-followers, providing a URL in the message to offer more information than would normally be available in 140 characters, and communicating directly with those who retweet most often, identified from, for example, retweetist.com. Twitter offers a number of other ways for customers to connect with their constituencies, such as sharing a link, following people already on Twitter, using hashtags and mentioning. By using the hashtag "#" (the number sign or pound symbol) before keywords in a tweet, tweets can be searched and accessed more easily by non-followers. For example, by clicking on a word that is preceded by a hashtag, other tweets in that category are displayed. Twitter categorizes people by their usernames "@username" and any mention in a tweet that contains such a reference are captured and communicated by Twitter to users' personal Mentions tab.

Other Opportunities to Encourage Content Sharing

A number of other companies provide opportunities to share social media content with their friends and connections. These include the LinkedIn Share button,[19] which is similar in intent to Like and Tweet buttons from Facebook and Twitter respectively. LinkedIn's Product Recommend button enables visitors to recommend a company's products and services and keeps count of these recommendations for the company, enabling subsequent marketing as evidence of social support. Google+ has some capabilities similar to those of Facebook, such as their +1 button which is the Google+ version of the Like button, and the Google+ Share Link button, similar to that described previously for Facebook.

A number of other social media sites provide opportunities for a company to broaden its reach and to market through existing customers to their connections. These sites include content aggregators such as Digg and Reddit, social bookmarkers such as Delicious and StumbleUpon, social media sites with entertainment or other differentiated focuses such as Bebo (formerly owned by AOL), Buzznet (music community and pop culture), Club Penguin (Disney, for kids), Flickr (photo sharing), Friendster (social games), Hi5 (social games), MyLife (formerly Reunion.com, for connecting with former classmates), PerfSpot (locating friends), Photobucket (photo and video sharing), Pinterest (online pinboard), Plaxo (address book), Polyvore (sets of things that go together), Second Life (virtual world for play and education), Spoke (business information), Svpply (social shopping), YouTube (video sharing), ZoomInfo (business information and directory) and, of course, many, many others. Figure 16 provided a partial indication of the range of solutions and options according to their main objectives or the primary benefits they deliver.[20] Some firms also layer intelligence on top of social media connections consumers already have. For example, Meeteor searches through an individual's social network to identify people outside his or her network with whom a person should connect and why this ought to be done.[21]

In addition or as an alternative to using the solutions of others, companies such as Ning enable companies and individuals to create their own websites for social communities.

Discussion forums and sites that feature customer reviews also provide opportunities for a company to hear what customers are saying about their brands and to comment in response.

INDIVIDUAL CUSTOMER ENGAGEMENT

While it is true that companies cannot control social media conversations, that is not to say that they cannot influence these communications. Every conversation requires that both parties to the conversation have the ability to initiate discourse, speak, be heard, and terminate the discussion as they would using a telephone. In this situation, as in any conversation, one party to the discussion has no more or less opportunity to command or control than does the other. When customers are engaged in their own communities and networks independently of the company, the company would be an interloper in discourse and would need to manage a number of things deftly in order to have the customer enhance the company's reputation with his or her own connections. These challenges start with having customer-specific objectives for each interaction before considering issues such as how to connect with each customer and whether to ask, remind, persuade or inform.

Customer-Specific Communications Objectives

Figure 21 describes the four categories of customer-specific communications objectives to be considered prior to engaging each individual in a conversation, whether initiated by a customer, the company or a third party, such as a social media "friend." The objectives a company may have will depend on whether or not—and how—the company seeks to accomplish the following:

- Behaviors
   Modify or influence the actions and behaviors of its customers or potential customers; the desired actions or behaviors likely link back to the relationship ladder and the customer-specific objectives that the company is trying to accomplish by having customers modify their behaviors and act differently in both their interests and those of the company.

- Attitudes
   Cause an attitudinal shift such as by influencing the perceptions that drive customers' attitudes

Figure 21: Customer-Specific Communications Objectives

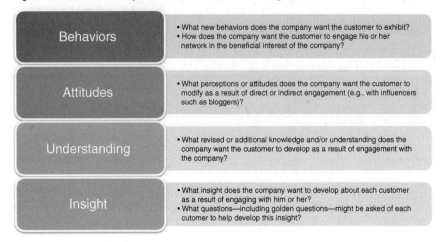

- Understanding

   Create new knowledge or understanding in customers' cognitive processes, and

- Insight

   Develop new insight into each individual customer, such as their purchase decision-making processes, purchase decision-making criteria, purchase decision influencers, likelihood to recommend the company to friends and colleagues, purchase or defection intent, and so on.

The company's social media employees who engage customers in social spaces ought to be trained in establishing customer-specific objectives and then framing approaches for customer engagement. These employees might also be supported with technology platforms that help them set these objectives and track customers' progress toward achieving the objectives.

Persuading Individuals

Organizations seek to influence individuals once they have set customer-specific objectives and have plans for action. Principles are well established for one-way communications with customers in advertising and direct mail, for example, but the principles for two-way customer engagement are less well developed. Companies are increasingly using social psychology to achieve positive outcomes from their customer connections. This raises the issue of social psychology, one of the key platforms for bringing about customer compliance. Positive outcomes from one-to-one communication can be achieved in six main, often interrelated, ways: reciprocity, consistency, social validation, liking, authority, scarcity and selective disclosure. The following briefly illustrates each point:[22]

- Reciprocity

  When a company gives something, it's more likely to get something in return. When a survey company encloses a free pen with a survey, it is more likely to get an increased survey response rate. Chapter 11 takes this discussion further and argues that a company might give much more of itself without necessarily an expectation of immediate benefit but, in return, be well perceived and gain from stronger reputations and relationships.

- Consistency

  When people publicly commit to something, they generally follow through. Restaurants lose revenues when customers don't show up to reserved tables. Some restaurants have cut the number of instances where customers did not appear by simply asking the person making a reservation if he or she would kindly call should plans change—and then waiting for the customer to respond to the question. It is the public articulation of a commitment that leads people to do what they said they would.

- Social validation

  Donors are more likely to be motivated to give to charity if they are presented with a list of people they know who have already done so. People comply when there is evidence of compliance by others and the more people there are to validate an individual's actions, and the closer these people are to the social circles of the individual, the more likely it is that a person will behave as the group does.

- Liking

  People say yes to people they like. Tupperware built its business on home-based social "parties" where friends would get together for in-home demonstrations and where the importance of the social group would play into purchase decisions. In much the same way, companies use attractive spokespeople (even though most people say they would never be influenced by this, many are) and seek to develop rapport in a sales setting, trying to find common ground as an initial basis for getting to yes. Customer data accelerates the customer connection because the common ground can be rapidly known or inferred from prior interactions and transactions.

- Authority

  People are more likely to follow others they perceive to be authorities. Companies that use survey results suggesting a high percentage of medical practitioners recommend Product X are invoking authority. With social media, authority is often demonstrated through knowledge but authority may also be increased by having many followers or social media friends.

- Scarcity

  Items and opportunities become more desirable when their supply is rationed. That is, when consumers perceive that there aren't enough goods or services to go round, an item would appear to be better than in the case of surplus supply.

- Selective disclosure

  Information, like goods and services, can also be rationed, directed and can serve to influence individuals who perceive they are receiving special treatment when indeed they are. Importers frequently call their best customers when they become aware that a given product will soon be in short supply and want their customers to take advantage of existing availability, for example. Recommendation engines on websites do much the same when they provide mass-customized and tailored communications to individuals.

Encouraging Communications Pass-Through

When Facebook's president, Mark Zuckerberg, wanted to use his company's platform to increase organ donor registrations, "users were given an opportunity to click a box on their Timeline pages to signal that they were registered donors, which triggered a notification to their friends."[23] The new features resulted in an increase of organ donor enrollment by a factor of 23 across 44 U.S. states.[24] Like the creation of social pressure illustrated here, there are a number of other practical tips associated with encouraging and facilitating the pass-through of communications from one person to another. For communications to be retweeted or otherwise passed through with the comment and tacit endorsement the originator seeks, communications ought to have one or more of the following attributes (in fact, the more the better):

1. Simple

   If customers are going to communicate features and benefits to others they know, the company's value proposition will need to be clear, demonstrable, understandable, simple, differentiated and novel in one or more respects—and ideally "cool," an elusive and fast-moving target for most firms. Without most of these attributes in place, the company will need to rely on ancillary value, like helpful communications, good advice, quick response or loyalty programs. It would be better for enterprise and customer alike if the company did not seek to create value in parallel value systems like loyalty cards and points programs, as these have the potential to distract customers and may only be needed when the firm has not been able to stand out and be remark-able.

2. Remark-able

   For communications to be remarked upon, it must stand out from all other communications that the customer receives and be perceived to be, well, remark-able. Remark-able communications are noticed, remarked upon, serve to stimulate further customer communications and are sent on their way to be consumed by the next potential customer. Viral communications have at least one thing in common: they stimulate an emotion and, as such, they are remark-able. Communications that appeal to logic—i.e., only to the left side of the brain—are generally not likely to be remarked upon. For total engagement, a company ought to engage both hemispheres of the recipient's brain. This means using appropriately emotive content as well as rational appeals. How much emotion to use will depend on the specific recipient. One would expect that typical communications with customers at an accounting firm will be different than with customers in an ad agency or digital media firm. The key is to know what makes communications remark-able from the perspective of the customer. The communications will need to reflect what matters most to him or her, communicate in an outstanding way and engage out-of-the-ordinary content to respond to each customer's communications and present relevant ideas and concepts.

3. Repute-able

   Communications that enhance the reputation of the customer are more likely to be passed along. If the re-sender thinks that the final recipient will benefit from the company's communications, direct more business to the customer's enterprise or otherwise create customer value, the communications are likely to be passed into the customer's network or to specific individuals, providing the company with an opportunity to broaden its reach and ultimately create new leads for its sales funnel.

4. Novelty

For a new relationship to be built, new content ought to be communicated. Relationship innovation depends on the company's communications bringing innovative content to the customer—content that matters, stimulates new customer ideas, thoughts and opportunities to create new business value or solve challenges of some kind for the customer and the possible recipient of the communication. Nobody wants to be barraged with company propaganda such as product literature, PR notices, executive announcements or even recent acquisition information. None of the company's communications matters if it doesn't matter in the customer's context, which raises the next point.

5. Context

Companies have long focused their communications on *what* they say—i.e., content. It is time to take a closer look at *context*. Social media requires that this be done or else the company risks being considered a social media stalker—a firm that is perpetually following customers around while shouting its message to more or less deaf ears. In social media, context trumps content—communication ought to have more context within which it will be consumed. Companies ought to reflect upon prior communications with individuals, the responses of customers to previous offers, transaction histories, interactions across multiple channels, and other aspects of the learning they have developed about each customer. Generalized customer profiles can be developed as a starting point for situating new prospects and these profiles can guide communications and then be modified as the company learns more about each person. For example, if a new prospect's business is a start-up, the communications should be tailored to the dynamic that customer would likely face. If the business is struggling, communications should demonstrate sensitivity and empathy. If the customer is a large enterprise, communications should reflect this very different context. And so on.

6. Variety

Variety matters because no firm wants to be a one-trick-pony when it comes to communications—or anything else, for that matter. Customers are easily bored when they perceive a company's communications to be a variant of what has been said previously, particularly if those communications are personalized. The firm's communications should recognize the history of prior communications with the customer, knowledge gained from those communications and get progressively deeper and more insightful about context and innovative insight, as mentioned before, as well as providing a variety of perspectives. This is the essence of a learning relationship, but it's also more than that. Take a learning relationship, add context, innovation and variety, and customers will be more receptive and ready to pass the communications on to the next recipient.

7. Right-size communication

Just as customers don't want to be bombarded with irrelevant information, they don't want to receive more communication than is absolutely necessary. If one is going to err, it is better to communicate well and less often than to be in touch more frequently than the customer wants. Over-communication applies in two main ways: the number of messages from the company to the customer, and the amount of content in each message. Over-communication in either way will saturate interest and customers will turn off. And turned-off customers are naturally marketing dead ends, not only for current business but for the leverage potential each one represents.

8. The right time for specific channels

Many customers are accessible in many different ways but their interest and response varies according to the time when communication takes place. If one is talking with a customer at his or her desk during the day, they may engage business topics but are less likely to do so when they return home, when customers generally want to relax and deal with more personal matters.

9. Benefits, not features

Marketing communications should focus more on product, brand or company benefits than the features they provide. That much is well known. So why do so many companies communicate what their products and services do rather than how these products and services can make the customer's business more profitable, faster, less costly, more controllable, and so on?

10. Communities

Trust is built when companies provide customers with opportunities to talk to the enterprise and one another in a company-owned but customer-supported environment, such as the firm's own website.[25] This trust leads to more communications and greater information sharing. Some companies go beyond this asynchronous environment to create synchronous communities, such as hosting customer events online or in person. Of course, these events will need to be oriented from the customer's point of view, such as learning something that matters to them. There is no need to manage what customers say to one another. They always discuss the firm and invariably find some nice things to say. As a result, companies invite prospects to these events, whether physical or virtual.

11. Passionate ambassadors

The development and use of passionate ambassadors is more likely to result in effective customer engagement and the pass-through of information. These ambassadors can be created or may pre-exist among the firm's existing stakeholders—not just customers. Who would be more passionate about the enterprise than its own employees, for example? Best Buy's very successful Twelpforce initiative for employee engagement has resulted in tens of thousands of Twitter inquiries being answered with timely and knowledgeable responses by the firm's own employees, resulting in higher levels of employee engagement and customer satisfaction with their responses.[26]

12. Social pressure and "the ask"

As in the Facebook example discussed at the beginning of this section, customers are more likely to make referrals or pass information along if there is an easy mechanism for doing this (it is a small request, after all) and if they are indeed asked. When the ask is infrequent, comes from a trustworthy source, follows a prior situation that created value for the customer or user and enhances the reputation of the re-sender, the customer is more likely to comply with the request. The last-mentioned factor—the enhancement of re-sender reputation and personal brand equity—is a most important one. Additionally, when the asker is able to create social pressure, users or customers are more likely to re-send communications. This social pressure may be achieved by creating cognitive tension between a person's self-concept and the reputation-enhancing actions of their friends. In the Facebook example discussed earlier, non-donors likely perceive that friends are completing organ donor registrations, and this gap between an ideal self-concept and the perceived actions of friends is likely to drive request compliance, behavioral change and program participation.

• • •

This chapter discussed how an enterprise might not only connect with existing customers but also reach the people who are known to them using one-through-one marketing principles to access each individual customer as a gateway to his or her network. This discussion noted that an enterprise ought to become part of the "peoplescape," in which prospective customers who might be engaged are identified according to their importance and potential, and not necessarily treated equally. As with any communication, companies ought to listen before speaking, and to sense what customers are thinking, feeling and talking to one another about, in real time and especially in respect of their use of social media. When it is time for the firm to speak, companies ought to communicate to one customer at a time using customer-specific, context-sensitive and timely communications. Were it to do otherwise, the company would run the risk that communications will be noise in the customer's already over-communicated universe. Customers block out noise, of course.

Social media is vital to today's enterprise and its relationships so enterprises ought to pay significant attention to this category of communications and plan accordingly. Firms should start by considering social media objectives and plans and, most emphatically, not constrain their thinking by simply asking themselves how best to anticipate on any specific platform such as Facebook or Twitter, for example. There will be opportunities for companies to consider channels and solutions such as these as they explore options for accomplishing their objectives and other important issues such as multichannel customer engagement, the role of social media and that of mass media.

Companies consider three principal social media objectives when developing plans for an integrated social customer management strategy. These objectives are reputation management, customer management and customer acquisition. This chapter discussed how to establish objectives in these three regards as companies contemplate how to accomplish such important tasks as informing, educating, communicating, entertaining, collaborating and enabling transactions with customers.

The four key communications objectives to be considered prior to engaging each individual in a conversation, whether initiated by a customer, the company or a third party (such as a social media "friend") are Behaviors, Attitudes, Understanding and Insight. Communications objectives should be established for each individual to guide the focus of communications and to align it with the firm's relationship ladder where appropriate, particularly for objectives that focus on behaviors.

Chapter 5
B2B RELATIONSHIPS

"Coming together is a beginning.
Keeping together is progress.
Working together is success."

Henry Ford (1863–1947)

This chapter contrasts and discusses relationships that companies have with businesses and consumers. As customers, businesses differ from consumers in many ways so relationships companies form with businesses naturally differ from those they have with consumers too. It is the rare company whose future depends on winning and keeping one or even a few consumers. For example, while an airline may be eager to develop and maintain a relationship with each of its passengers, it would probably survive even if some stopped flying with them. But it is different for businesses catering to other businesses. In some cases, the defection of a single major customer could damage a company beyond repair and unfortunately this scenario happens all too often.

This chapter explores selected differences between relationships formed and maintained with businesses and consumers and the implications for the marketer building B2B relationships. For businesses, the reader may substitute another concentration of market demand such as governments (federal, state, and local), institutions (schools, hospitals and prisons), industrial manufacturers and service providers (financial institutions, advertising agencies and accounting firms).

Many aspects of the previous chapter apply here as well, including how businesses can connect with their customers using social media. This chapter considers selected aspects of the preceding chapter in respect of social media as well as the use of social media within the enterprise so that employees can connect with one another and with customers, too.

CONSUMER AND BUSINESS-TO-BUSINESS RELATIONSHIPS

Relationships with consumers and business customers can differ markedly. Many factors may influence the nature of these differences, including the specific industry the company is in, the business issues the company faces, its mix of customers and its chosen strategies, among much else. The most important factor affecting customer relationships is the significant difference that exists in respect of end-user demand. In consumer marketplaces end-user demand is typically more fragmented among a large number of customers than is the case for B2B marketplaces where, because of their relatively greater scale and concentration, business customers assume particular importance to a supplier. Table 16 summarizes some of the relationship differences between a company catering to consumers as opposed to business customers. A description of each of the differences follows this summary.

Table 16: Consumers, B2B Customers and Relationships

Consumer Marketplaces	Business-to-Business Marketplaces
Goods and Services	
Convenience, shopping and specialty goods and services necessitate different categories of relationships, ranging from relationships that are more product- or brand-centric, or comprise more ephemeral variables—the case for convenience goods—to relationships that focus more heavily on benefits, intangibles, social, contextual and longitudinal variables—the case for specialty goods.	B2B goods and services can vary significantly according to whether or not they are associated with near-term consumption—in which case they have elements more similar in nature to convenience goods in consumer marketplaces (e.g., cleaning supplies)—or are at the strategic heart of the value the company delivers, such as the glass Apple uses in its iPods and iPads—in which case relationships become more complex and mutual planning becomes more important.
Marketplace Structure	
Demand is typically fragmented among large numbers of customers, making it especially important to triage customers so that the enterprise knows who is best, average and worst in the context of profit expectations, strategies and capabilities.	Demand is more concentrated among fewer customers, making it especially important to understand each individual business customer as a separate and distinct market.

Distribution Channels	
Companies marketing to consumers often go through multiple layers of distribution as the channel intermediaries such as wholesalers, dealers and retailers perform various intermediary functions such as breaking bulk (buying in quantity and selling in more modest volume), consumer financing, delivery, installation and after-sales support, for example. E-marketing has served to de-layer distribution channels so that consumers have the option of buying goods more directly than previously, although perishables and some other goods continue to go through multiple layers of channel intermediaries out of necessity. Suppliers of consumer goods often have two categories of relationships that must be developed and sustained: relationships with channel intermediaries and relationships with the end-buyer or consumer (e.g., where buyer and consumer may be different—as in the case of children's clothing).	B2B marketplaces have typically had shorter distribution channels than consumer markets although e-marketing has shortened channels for consumer goods, too. Major accounts such as those the company has with its global or national customers continue to have short distribution channels as goods and services are marketed directly to customers such as these.

Purchase Decision-Making Unit	
The consumer purchase decision-making unit comprises fewer decision makers than that of business decision making. The number of decision influencers has increased significantly in social media and makes consumer purchase decision making increasingly resemble the complexity of business-to-business.	The B2B purchase decision-making unit typically comprises more decision makers, influencers (other than social media) and users than that of consumer decision making, making the purchase decision-making process complex.

Purchase Decision-Making Criteria	
Purchase decision making can comprise a greater range of criteria, especially those of a non-functional nature, such as emotional benefits.	Purchase decision making is more highly specified and may comprise a narrower spectrum of criteria, typically focused on functional attributes such as dimensions of quality, delivery and service, and value, including initial cost and lifetime or lifecycle cost and benefits.

Purchase Decision-Making Process	
Customers may make decisions independently or be influenced by one another. Social media helps customers influence one another's purchasing decisions.	Customers have always been influenced by one another's peer groups when validating suppliers and making purchase decisions.

Communications Channels	
Customers can be reached through multiple channels, making the mix of mass and two-way customer communications more complex and the integration of communications across platforms and communications channels a challenge.	Customers can be reached through a more limited range of communications channels but, because business customers are inundated through these channels, it is difficult for enterprises to gain and retain customer access.

Goods and Services

The nature of goods and services impacts the kinds of relationships that organizations have with their customers. The following briefly discusses the difference between goods and services marketed to consumers and business-to-business.

Consumer goods and services may be classified according to the level of effort consumers expend in the search for them. Consumer goods and services are usually categorized as either convenience, shopping or specialty goods. Consumers are typically not willing to spend much time to find convenience goods or services, as the name suggests. A newspaper (remember them?) is a good example of such a product. At the other end of the spectrum, specialty goods are those for which consumers are prepared to spend considerable time and effort to make the right selection decision, often because the wrong choice can be financially, socially or personally risky. A house, car and the services of a criminal or divorce lawyer fall into this category. Shopping goods fall somewhere in between convenience and specialty. Most clothing and financial services can be exemplified in this way. The value a consumer derives from each type of good or service differs. Convenience goods have short consumption time horizons within which the consumer achieves the desired benefit. A newspaper is read, a chocolate bar is consumed, the pet has its fill of food. Convenience goods also have less social context than do shopping and specialty goods. In part, this is the result of convenience goods not often being seen and thus not often evaluated by peers in public. On the other hand, specialty and some shopping goods must often help the purchaser manage financial risk and, in all likelihood, also mitigate social risk.

In one of the more interesting paradoxes of human behavior, people want to simultaneously stand out and fit in, and specialty goods and services are often selected in part for this reason. A house in the trendy part of town says the owner fits in. The specific house and its furnishings say the owner stands out. A baseball hat suggests peer group acceptance is being sought while the wearing of game-worn or other labels implies the wearer wants to stand out from the reference group, too.

Specialty goods have much longer horizons over which the consumer derives utility. When the consumer makes such a purchase, a psychological contract with the purchaser is initiated that says, in effect, "I will give you my money now and will then consume this product or service over a fairly long time. By giving you this money, I am also providing you with my good faith and trust. If your product or service fails to meet my expectations over the consumption horizon, you will be in default of my trust. And for that, you will pay a price. Perhaps you will incur higher costs satisfying me, by listening to me, fixing the problems, providing me with replacement or loaner units and otherwise bearing the costs of poor quality. Also, I may tell my friends about the experience. I may never give you my trust again, even if you do make it right again."

The value the marketer of convenience goods seeks to co-create with the consumer may be quite different than value co-developed for specialty goods. Taking the case of a newspaper, a marketer may provide the consumer with the ability to assemble the news each wants rather than the news the paper chooses to provide. Many companies now have Web portals and apps to facilitate this, using technology as a key component of mass customizing news.

For a specialty good, the marketer will have a complex interplay of initiatives that create value and engage the consumer. For example, a car company must have people, processes, customer knowledge and technologies that converse with and involve the customer before, when and after they buy, and then throughout the ownership experience of each. This complexity is similar to the relationships businesses develop with their business customers.

B2B products and services may be categorized as described in Table 17.

Table 17: B2B Products and Services

Product or Service	Description
Process infrastructure and installations	Enable the business processes of the company, such as computers, networks and production equipment.
Accessory equipment	Ancillary to the main business of the company, such as fire extinguishers, intrusion alarms and exit signs.
Component parts and subassemblies	Integrated into the higher value offering, such as spark plugs used in a car engine and automotive interior subassemblies incorporated in the vehicle.
Process materials	Inputs to the production process without being identified as parts. Products such as plastics and resins extruded in the fabrication of plastic toys and water pipes are examples.
Raw materials	Constituent components transformed in the process of production, such as ingredients for pharmaceuticals and chemicals.
Consumables	Examples include Maintenance, Repair and Overhaul (MRO) supplies used in production operations to ensure the continued operation of the plant, packaging, pallets, etc.
Services	Services supplied to businesses such as environmental management and accounting services, for example.

Product and service categories such as those mentioned in Table 17 typically have different buyers within a company and will be bought for different reasons, in varying amounts and with varying frequency. The relationship expectations of each of the product categories would also be expected to vary according to factors such as the strategic importance of the product or service category, the substitutability of the vendors and the level of expenditures that are made. However, there are few products or services that cannot be made more strategic to business customers. Those suppliers competing on operational considerations, such as product or service functionality and price, while selling to the purchasing managers, for example, may well be missing important opportunities to differentiate and elevate strategic importance through bonding, find new business opportunities and become more relevant to business customers. With relevance comes the potential for more business and possibly higher margins. Consider a company providing lawn maintenance services to corporate customers. Is the firm selling closely cropped, well-manicured lawns as part of an annual maintenance agreement, or is the company enhancing the personality of the customer in its physical environment? If the latter, perhaps they could also be maintaining other components of the exterior of the building, providing landscaping, painting, sign and sign light maintenance, window cleaning, snow removal, parking-lot maintenance, flagpole maintenance, flag replacement and other services. In short, relationships lead to opportunities.

Market Structure

B2B markets tend to have more concentrated end-user demand than do consumer markets. Consider the case of detergents. When sold into industrial markets, specialized detergents may be required to clean slippery floors in the edible oils industry, for example. Detergents must have special characteristics to cut through the thick grease. These characteristics will differ markedly from detergents needed for other manufacturing applications. The users of edible oils can be readily identified and each will be an important potential customer for purpose-specific detergents. Consumers, on the other hand, will be happy enough if the detergent provided to them is more or less the same as their neighbor receives, if it cleans dishes as it should.

B2B markets can also be more concentrated geographically than consumer markets. Vendors of printed circuit boards are likely to find many major customers for their products within driving distance of cities such as Houston, Boston and Palo Alto, for example, and North American financial services industry customers are concentrated in New York, San Francisco and Toronto, for example. Customers of consumer electronics and financial services suppliers are to be found everywhere, perhaps in greater abundance in some areas than others, but with more fragmented demand than the businesses that supply these products or services.

Concentration of end-user demand offers more opportunity to identify and research B2B customers in depth. Their needs and those of their customers can be explored. The strategies of their competitors can be examined. And a supplier can afford to make the investment to develop the relationship, because the anticipated payoff from such an investment can be very significant.

Technology can help vendors understand their customers in consumer markets but the technology will need more sophistication and modeling than in B2B markets to have the same yield. Companies cannot invest as much time and money to understand each consumer in a fragmented market as they do in more concentrated industrial, commercial, institutional or government marketplaces.

Distribution Channels

B2B marketplaces typically have shorter distribution channels than consumer markets. Often, B2B companies serve major or national accounts directly, smaller ones through distribution channel intermediaries, and medium-sized firms through some combination of one or the other. Companies marketing to consumers often go through multiple layers. In the case of consumer electronics and computers, it is not uncommon for manufacturers to access the consumer markets directly (as Dell does, for example) as well as through high-volume retailers and chain stores and through distributors to smaller retailers.

It has now become more common for suppliers to also bypass their traditional channels and cater to consumers directly. With the advent of the Internet and e-commerce more generally, technology has removed levels in the distribution channel and offered consumers the chance to buy directly from suppliers.

Distribution channel intermediaries will not go away anytime soon but their growth may be more limited if they are not finding ways to use technology to bond with customers and use the vendors' solutions to help them do so. For example, Michelin distributors have long used the tire manufacturer's databases and resources to obtain information about inventory and answer questions about tires, such as what tire is needed for a specific car. This helps the installers provide faster and better service to their customers while Michelin naturally benefits from the efficiency with which orders are handled and the way the company is perceived by its dealers.

Purchase Decision-making

There are four types of buying situations, as follows:

1. Initial buy—the first time a purchase is made
2. Straight rebuy—when the product or service is routinely bought again
3. Modified rebuy—when there is some change to the purchase requirement, and
4. New task situation—when the product or service is being bought for a different application.

For all of these situations, businesses often buy (or say they buy) for reasons that are rational, based on the economics of the offer and for strategic reasons, such as improving the customer's market positioning. When all else is equal or nearly equal, companies typically default to what they consider to be the lowest risk option, buying again from the incumbent, the company with which they already have an existing purchase relationship.

Like businesses, consumers also go through a straight rebuy, modified rebuy or new task situation. When they buy and buy again, they do so for many reasons, including criteria which are not always derived from rational economic arguments. Consumers value both functional and non-functional attributes in their product and service selection decisions, often placing more emphasis on non-functional attributes, such as benefits that are socially visible. Makeup, clothes, cars and consumer electronics must all be acceptable to the peer group for consumers to add the product to the set from which the final selection will be made. If the peer group rejects it, the individual will likely do so too.

Both businesses and consumers want to manage risk, but in the case of businesses, the financial health of the business—near and long term—and the career of the buyer are important considerations. For years, IBM benefited from the phrase that had wide currency in the business community, that "no one ever got fired for buying IBM." Xerox, too, may have benefited from purchase behavior that historically viewed Xerox as a natural selection for photocopying requirements in large businesses.

Even though business managers may talk in terms of rational-economic and strategic considerations, there are emotional and less rational issues at work in some purchase situations. Consider the customer of a vertical market software company that operates as though it could not care less about the individual customer, constantly cutting resources from software support and new product development, for example. Perhaps surprisingly, many customers continue to deal with such companies even though there may be economic arguments to switch. For some, the software is strategic to the business and cannot be easily replaced. Users become familiar with the look and feel and functionality of software, while technical people develop the knowledge they need to support the system and, in both cases, familiarity often argues against replacement.

More generally, B2B purchase criteria may be categorized as described in Table 18. This suggests there can be many categories of criteria that influence purchase decisions and complexity within each category. On the other hand, decision-making criteria for consumers may vary according to many factors, including issues associated with the product category as a whole, the consumer's values and the consumer's perceptions that a given brand may be readily substituted for another.

Table 18: B2B Purchase Criteria

Category	Description
Strategic engagement	Help the company conceive and adopt products, services and processes that will add value for internal and external customers of the company, lowering costs, improving quality and otherwise helping the company to improve its customer performance and competitive position.
Operational alignment	Provide the products to customers when, how and in the volume required, appropriately tagged, stacked, racked and packaged.
Quality	Produce products of consistently high quality and be in a position to demonstrate assurance of that quality, such as statistical process control and adoption of, and conformance with, ISO standards.
End-customer satisfaction	Ensure that products conform with the customer's expectations and specifications.
Cost management	Consistent with the product specifications and ancillary requirements for service and support, for example, ensure that the initial, lifetime and value-in-use prices are the lowest among competing vendors.
Support	Support the products with services, helping to improve the value of the products in use, such as by providing training, vendor installation and maintenance, diagnosis guided by technology and customer support.
Easy, pleasing, professional and caring	Be easy to do business with. Keep internal customers happy. Demonstrate professionalism, caring, responsiveness and attention, helping the company to manage difficult or unexpected situations.

Decision-making Unit, Criteria and Process

Businesses' decision making comprises many different decision makers for most product categories, each playing different roles in a process that can be quite complex and may differ substantially from firm to firm. The decision-making unit often comprises one or more of:

- An initiator, who recommends that a purchase be made
- Influencers, who motivate the purchase decision, guide the process and have input to key decision dimensions, such as the criteria for the decision and the specific selection
- A sponsor, who takes up the view of the initiator and backs the recommendation
- An approver, usually a person in higher authority than the other decision makers, who validates the purchase recommendation, and
- A purchaser, who actually makes the purchase.

Each person in the decision-making unit usually has different criteria for selecting a supplier the first time and continuing to do business with the company. The role each person plays in the purchase decision varies as he or she facilitates the change in vendor or the new vendor selection decision, as well as the nature and timing of that decision.

BUYER–SELLER RELATIONSHIP

In B2B marketplaces, close personal relationships are commonly formed. In B2B markets, customers expect to be recognized for their importance and for their suppliers to take steps to bond with them and their organizations. If this means playing golf with the customer, then the supplier should be able to do this. Interpersonal bonding, comprising a matching of people and process, enabled by the knowledge suppliers have of their customers and the technology to put this knowledge to work, are important components of this bonding.

High-value relationships are often high touch while high-volume relationships are high tech. This is so because the economics and competitive conditions of the highest value relationships typically require human intervention and facilitation, while lower value and higher volume relationships can involve repetitive transactions and value creation for which technology is well suited. As a result, most B2B relationships are typically high touch while many B2C relationships have technology to disintermediate, except where relationships are particularly valuable.

Reciprocity

In B2B markets, it is common for firms to extend their business relationships to become customers of one another. For example, our consultancy uses the products and services of our clients wherever we can, whether they supply computers, computer carrying cases, photocopiers, courier services, Internet access, cars, hotels or airline flights. Our clients have given their trust to us and we return this honor.

By contrast, it is still not common for such a view to prevail in consumer markets and reciprocity is not to be expected here, either.

Mutual Value Creation

Beyond reciprocity is the matter of continuous mutual value creation. In B2B markets, suppliers and customers have the potential to work together to create new products, processes, value chains or even entire businesses and new enterprises, and then to share in the new business value. This may mean opening themselves up in non-traditional ways, such as providing suppliers with access to customers or sharing proprietary knowledge. Those companies that keep themselves closed will invariably achieve less shareholder value than those that unlock their control and look for new value to create and share.

While businesses can collaborate with consumers to create new value and share it, the value creation often employs technology to facilitate personalization and customization in communication and in the product/service bundle. There are many such examples, as is discussed in Chapter 7.

One-Way "Relationships"

A relationship requires the creation of new and mutual value for both company and customer. As in a more personal way, relationships are generally all about mutuality and novelty. So, can a one-sided relationship exist? For some products, most notably those for which the purchase decision is a low-involvement one, the buyer may prefer little in the way of dialog, mutual value creation or other engagement with the vendor beyond the product itself. This situation could apply to consumables and low-involvement capital goods for industrial or other B2B applications.

MANAGING THE B2B RELATIONSHIP

As has been suggested earlier in this chapter, B2B relationships are in many ways more complicated, involve more decision makers and centers of influence, and represent greater opportunity and risk than relationships with single consumers. As such, B2B relationships ought to be carefully planned strategically and operationally so that the relationships can develop and mature. As will be evident from what follows, relationships require a common interest in a positive outcome. Without such commonality, or if interests are substantially unbalanced, the pursuit of a relationship by one party is not likely to result in a relationship. A lack of balance may cause the relationship to break down, depending upon the nature and style by which the relationship is pursued. Among other things, the following should be clear to both parties (i.e., company and customer):

- Definition of mutual objectives and expectations
- The allocation of resources and engineering of processes in support of customer/supplier relationships, including processes and responsibilities for people working on strategic initiatives and those that are focused more on day-to-day operations, technology and operational integration, and service—both for the end-customer and the immediate B2B customer
- Mutual commitments for information sharing, joint planning (including timing and responsibilities of any planning meetings) and operational alignment
- The process for developing a relationship plan to which both parties can commit
- Processes for resolution of any dissatisfaction before any such need should arise, and
- Processes for dissolving the relationship in the event that such should unfortunately occur.

Many companies don't want to develop a relationship plan together with their customers, perceiving that such a plan should be the exclusive responsibility of the supplier. Naturally, while there would be some elements of a relationship plan that a company may not wish to share with its customers, many elements of the plan would benefit from both company and customer being jointly committed to a successful outcome.[1] Should the customer not wish to participate in a joint planning exercise, one would have to ask how strategic the product or service category is to the customer and how important the relationship may be in the first place.

B2B, SOCIAL MEDIA AND PRODUCT LIFECYCLES

Social media has been discussed in Chapter 4 in the context of developing customer relationships and connecting to the people these customers know. Social media can also be used very effectively for B2B customer engagement at every stage of the product lifecycle.

Social Media in the Introductory Phase

In the introductory phase of the product lifecycle, companies often use social media to create product awareness and interest in new offerings, and to identify new prospects for their offerings. For example, technology firm Cisco used a combination of blogs and social networks to encourage potential customers to register for an online launch of their Aggregation Services Router 1000. Cisco's communications mix was anything but traditional. They created a launch environment in the simulated, virtual world of Second Life where the product was "actually" launched.[2] A virtual concert was held in the hours leading up to the executives' speeches. Additionally, targeted network engineers were met on their terms by playing video games (for a prize) in which the engineers were, not incidentally, educated about the product. This approach to social media engagement is called "advergaming" or "gamification."[3] Cisco used YouTube to generate further interest.[4] Cisco also engaged engineers using their mobile devices, Facebook, blogs and widgets.[5] As a result of activities such as these, more than 9,000 people attended the launch, providing Cisco with leads for follow-up.[6]

Social Media in Growth and Maturity Phases

Social media may be used in growth and maturity phases to penetrate existing markets by identifying potential prospects and seeking customer conversion from present behaviors and usage patterns. As an early example of B2B social media being used in the growth and maturity phase of the product lifecycle,

Visa started to use Facebook in 2008 to access small business owners by launching an application designed specifically for Facebook, the first of its type to connect small business owners to one another. Visa formed an online social community because they wanted businesses to support each other and learn from each other's best practices. The application allowed small businesses to search for companies based on demographic information, an idea exchange center that allowed users to chat with one another and a research center with access to popular and Visa-specific content. Within a few months, several hundred thousand owners had personal Facebook pages, an indication of rapid uptake accelerated in part by a $100 advertising incentive provided by Visa.[7]

As suggested by the Visa Business Network example,[8] there are many benefits available to businesses that use social media, most especially including revenue acceleration that can come from identifying, accessing and communicating with existing and potential customers using social media tools such as Facebook, LinkedIn and Twitter—and leveraging communities that use these social media—as well as other approaches that have been in widespread use for some time, such as e-mail newsletters. Many businesses are excited about the potential that social media offers them to develop new leads. Although social media does indeed offer exciting opportunities, potential for engagement goes far beyond this. Social media provides businesses with an opportunity not only to develop initial transactions but also to convert these into relationships and sustain them over an extended period. Social media does this by providing businesses with an opportunity to learn more about their customers and prospects by engaging each in an ongoing dialog similar to that discussed in Chapter 4 for consumers. This knowledge can be put to use by not only learning about customers' unmet needs, competitive disappointments and future requirements, for example, but also positioning the company uniquely to each individual customer. In a previous era, companies would position themselves in markets but now the focus is to position the company uniquely for each customer and do this under an overall market branding umbrella so that customized communication for one customer, if shared with others, will not undermine the firm's overall market position.

B2B Social Media Communications

It is now relatively easy for businesses, even small businesses, to set up a presence in social media. It is a greater challenge to be interesting enough in social media that newcomers are attracted and retained. As suggested previously in this chapter, existing customers are the logical starting point for connecting with new potential customers, as companies try to market one-through-one. More generally, companies ought to consider how best to create value in all their communications and try to make these communications as customer-specific as possible. All communications should be oriented to the perspective of the other, i.e., the customer or potential customer. Communications based on personal ego or a self-imposed commitment to tweet so many times a week will only lead to customers treating the communications as spam. A case in point: a company president keeps tweeting that he is waiting on a runway to go somewhere. If nobody cares, no brand equity, trust or reason to do business has been created or reinforced. The time has been wasted once by the sender and then multiple times by all the followers who may have mistakenly read the tweet. The good intent may in fact have caused a decline in brand value.

In Chapter 3 it was noted that customer sensing is the process by which an enterprise adds to what it knows about each customer. Sensing, it was noted, tells the organization what changes are occurring in its customer's environment—one customer at a time—as well as how customers respond to specific offers, communications and attempts to create value for and with individual customers. B2B companies listen in to individual communications and conversations in a variety of ways, using, for example, Google Alerts to track specific content on the web, Google Reader to monitor websites and blogs, a wide variety of technologies to track and manage communications using Twitter feeds, LinkedIn, Facebook, and so on. A number of these technologies were discussed in Chapter 4.

Many companies monitor Twitter hashtags to keep track of what is being said in specific categories of information in group conversations. Having identified prospective customers, whether from existing customers, LinkedIn or from other Web sources, B2B companies often reach out to engage these connections and are most likely to be successful with their initial connection when their communication solves a problem, recognizes the respondent's interests, serves to identify a point solution, or otherwise creates new value for the information's recipient rather than simply soliciting for business.

As discussed previously in this chapter, there are a wide variety of services that companies use to help them to listen to customers and potential customers as they seek to build customer and market intelligence, develop accelerated responsiveness and find new ways to cater to customers.

Some companies create internal, private social networks. For these purposes, they use tools such as Salesforce's Chatter to provide employees with the information they need to connect with others in the organization who have specific knowledge or connections, obtain real-time updates on people and groups, share documents, and keep track of updates and news, among other benefits.

Companies are also using social search to track and manage conversations. Services such as Samepoint provide companies with a searchable feed that has the potential to access, filter and track conversations taking place across the social web. Trackur is another social media monitoring service that allows companies to monitor their online reputations, news mentions, and the results of PR campaigns, for example. Trackur monitors millions of media mentions across news sites (they claim over 100 million[9]), blogs, forums, Twitter, Google and Facebook.

Companies are using crowdsourcing to develop solutions with their B2B and B2C customers. Crowdsourcing provides the benefit of more widespread input than traditional market research methods, while being less expensive. It can also achieve better results when customers are effectively engaged in developing collaborative solutions because the results can be less stilted and more actionable. Crowdsourcing takes the perspective that online communities can collectively achieve more than individuals can on their own, that these online communities will serve to think more broadly and deeply than would an individual—even an expert—and that the virtual crowd will also serve to filter out bad ideas. There are many examples of crowdsourcing, ranging from the development of new names for companies and products, to organizations that serve as platforms for crowdsourcing and those that function as info-mediaries that distribute crowdsourced content for companies to apply to specific purposes.[10] Platform enablers include companies such as Jovoto, which has facilitated crowdsourcing for companies such as Starbucks to find sustainable solutions to disposable coffee cup waste, Coca-Cola to develop Coke Zero packaging design for a male demographic and Victorinox to find fashionable designs for their Swiss Army knives. Examples of intermediaries that facilitate content sharing include YouTube, SlideShare and iStockphoto.

Entrepreneurs, innovators and small businesses are also using the crowd to help secure financing for their businesses, start-ups and projects. This is so-called crowdfunding and companies such as the following provide solutions in this space:

- Appsfunder for new mobile apps
- Cofolio for small businesses in the local community

- Kickstarter all-or-nothing funding for a wide variety of projects
- NewJelly (Norway) for artists
- Peerbackers for "big ideas"
- RocketHub for independent artists and entrepreneurs
- StartSomeGood for social entrepreneurs, and
- Wefunder crowd investing platform for start-ups.

Social Media and Planning

Different business and communications objectives can be enabled using social media and plans for a social media presence ought to reflect these objectives, leading to the development of internal social media capabilities and competencies, social media strategy and structure, roles and responsibilities, personnel and budget, among other considerations. Plans with content such as this will enable social media to become an important part of the company's communications mix, part of the firm's integrated marketing communications that employs other than social media, and a central element in its overall relationship marketing strategy. Chapter 4 discussed social media planning and many aspects of this consideration can be applied equally here with appropriate adjustments to reflect differences required for B2B companies.

Social Media and the Communications Mix

B2B social media ought to be integrated not only with mass media but also with other online media, most specifically the firm's own website, transaction-based offers that drive traffic and surface potential leads from existing customers and from the market as a whole, and educational outreach that seeks to inculcate knowledge as part of an attitudinal behavioral shift. Additionally, the customers the company is seeking to attract ought to be accessible using social media for, without such accessibility, the company can only seek them out and approach each employee as individuals, and that may not be the best way to open up lines of communication and maintain them.

Processes and Customer Analytics Considerations

As with social marketing more generally, engaging B2B customers through social media requires close attention to marketing processes and analytics. Chapter 8 focuses on customer measurements and analytics. At this stage we note that companies ought to have given thought to the engineering of their marketing processes for customer engagement more generally, and using social media specifically. Firms ought to be clear about customer metrics that matter and follow these very closely. For example, most companies are familiar with the concept of sales funnels for tracking conversion rates of their sales force as they take potential customers through a sales process that starts with customer identification, proceeds to meetings, presentations and proposals, and ends with closing the sale. Companies ought to approach social media in much the same way as they track conversion rates, watching the number and percentage of prospects that visit their websites and become customers in due course. Feedback from data such as these ought to inform the processes and business rules used to engage customers so that processes can be refined and business rules improved. Rapid adaptation is key to competitive advantage. Experimentation and rapid discovery of new learnings from existing customer communications, analytics and observations is a key to driving adaptation and being excellent at the things that matter to customers.

SOCIAL, INTERNAL TO THE ENTERPRISE

As has been discussed in Chapter 4 in the context of social media and consumers, there are a plethora of options companies can consider when developing social media communications strategies. Various forms of social media can also be deployed within enterprises themselves for engaging employees and enabling collaboration among employees. Platforms that enable social communication within the enterprise accelerate information flows between people, making it more likely that the right information is made available in time to make a difference in decision making. By extending collaboration, these platforms can lead to better decision making and greater creativity because every problem benefits by having more than two eyes focused on it. The platforms can also serve to introduce people to one another and lead to the formation of stronger and more focused internal networks.

As with any technology selection decision, strategy ought to precede it. There may be a temptation to deploy these platforms independently of those discussed in Chapter 4 and such a temptation, if it exists, should be resisted. Enterprise social platforms exist interdependently with social media for customer engagement and, like all technologies in a firm's customer-related eco-system, ought to be considered in association with customer engagement and communications strategies.

When considering the deployment of enterprise social platforms, employees as well as other categories of stakeholder should be considered. After all, social media and enterprise social platforms will be used to engage with each category and to develop progressively deeper relationships both within specific categories of stakeholder and between them. That is, the technology environments will enable customers to connect with one another on their terms and not just to advance the enterprise's objectives. The solutions will also enable employees to connect with one another for the employees' own purposes as well as those of the enterprise. Any company thinking more parochially in its narrow interests may find it does not achieve its own objectives or those of its constituents.

The technology environment of the firm ought to enable stakeholders to connect with one another. The example of Best Buy's Twelpforce initiative as a case in point was discussed in Chapter 4. Although apparently self-evident, a number of companies continue to restrict employee access to social media, perhaps believing that unfettered use makes communications uncontrollable and that transparency is a bad thing. On the contrary, subject to reasonable constraints such as limiting communications on issues that are mission-critical, such as new products, for example, the opening up of the enterprise to employee communications can achieve higher levels of customer and employee engagement, knowledge, collaboration and satisfaction.

Because technology solutions come and go, and their relative advantages change from day to day, it is impossible to provide the reader with guidance as to the best platforms to consider, even if the reader's objectives, strategies, resources, communications mix and other relevant factors were known.[11] Table 19 provides a list of selected firms and solutions, which may serve as a starting point for the reader to consider aspects of platforms for social connectivity within the enterprise.

Table 19: Enterprise Social Platforms for Employee Engagement

Enterprise Social Platform	Description of Selected Aspects or Capabilities[12]
Asana	Team-based task management
Blogtronix	Social networking for communities within the enterprise
Bloomfire	Web-based social learning platform for enterprise teams
Blue Twit (IBM)	Enterprise microblogging platform
Brainpark	Internal enterprise collaboration software that connects people with relevant information, data, resources and tools in real time
BrainTrust.io	Internal team-based conversation management

(continued)

Table 19: (*continued*)

Enterprise Social Platform	Description of Selected Aspects or Capabilities
Campfire	Enterprise team collaboration with real-time chat
Cisco Pulse	Search and analytics platform to enable collaboration and discover who knows what
Cisco Quad	Enterprise collaboration platform
Clearvale (by BroadVision)	Cloud-based social enterprise platform that enables businesses to create a network of networks, a social enterprise ecosystem
BizCloud (previously CloudSandwich)	Social business enterprise collaboration platform to facilitate internal and external collaboration
Communote	Professional microblogging service with some similarities to Twitter
Co-op (coopapp.com)	Enterprise connectivity, communications and collaboration platform
Cyn.in (by Cynapse)	Open source group collaboration software for enterprises
Do (previously ManyMoon)	Social productivity platform for managing projects, organizing tasks and conversations for a team
Elgg	Social networking engine for enterprises to create their own social networks
Eureka Streams	Open source enterprise social networking platform for employees to find colleagues in groups, followed streams and communicate— developed by Lockheed Martin
Flowr	Enterprise software for sharing ideas, files, creating tasks and worker collaboration
Glasscubes	Online collaboration, organization project management, information collaboration tool
Hashwork	Connectivity and sharing platform, Twitter-style, to engage the company's community of customers, partners and others on the Internet
HeadMix	Multichannel communications platform to facilitate connectivity within an enterprise and unlock what the company calls "undiscovered knowledge"
HipChat (by Atlassian)	Hosted private chat for a company or team to share ideas and files
IBM Connections	Social software for business that lets employees access a professional network including colleagues, customers and partners
Ididwork	Tracking and feedback engine for employee task and project management
Idonext	Cloud-based service to organize, share and assign tasks, files and activities
Jisko	Open-source microblogging platform for which development stopped in 2010 but still used by small and medium enterprises
Jive	Social business and customer service solutions incorporating social networking, collaboration software, community software and social media monitoring

Joint Contact	Online project collaboration software for small business owners and project managers
Jouzz	Internal enterprise social platform similar in some respects to Facebook, Twitter, LinkedIn and Xing
Kinetic Glue (previously injoos)	Cloud-based enterprise social network and collaboration software exclusive to a company or team
MangoSpring	Social business collaboration software for web, desktop, mobile and tablets
Microsoft Office Talk	Enterprise social networking tool with some similarities to Yammer and Chatter (by Salesforce)—enterprise social network
Moot	Real-time team collaboration, sharing and connectivity enterprise platform
Moxie Software	Enterprise social platform for workforce connectivity, project management, crowd sourcing, and agent productivity management
Novell Vibe	Document collaboration management system/business productivity software for people, projects and processes
Obayoo	Enterprise collaboration tool for microblogging and file sharing
OraTweet (by Oracle)	Microblogging platform that allows employees to broadcast their messages to a wide audience
P2 (by WordPress)	A theme for WordPress that incorporates real-time updates, and posting forms on the homepage
PBworks	Online team collaboration, knowledge sharing and project management, paid professional wiki services
Platform46	Multichannel communications integration and messaging software
Podio	Social work platform for employee and client collaboration
Producteev	Enterprise social sharing software for workspace sharing and collaboration, task assignment and progress tracking
Qontext (by Autodesk)	Enterprise social collaboration platform that facilitates content sharing and contextual conversations across business applications
Regroup	Group messaging and alerts platform to facilitate communication by e-mail lists, SMS, Facebook and Twitter
SAP Jam (previously CubeTree)	Engagement and collaboration platform for customers, partners and employees, optional to tie back into core SAP applications
Sazneo	Enterprise social platform for instant messaging, group chat and online communities into an online group messaging service
Sharetronix	Social networking for communities external to the enterprise
Snipia	Enterprise solution for information and file sharing, and status updates positioned as a corporate Twitter

(continued)

Table 19: (*continued*)

Enterprise Social Platform	Description of Selected Aspects or Capabilities
Socialcast (by VMWare)	Enterprise microblogging platform for employee connectivity and information sharing in real time
Socialspring Streams including Presently	Suite of social enterprise products including microblogging, communications, collaboration and sharing platform from Presently
SocialText	Enterprise social networking and business collaboration software, including wikis
StatusNet	Enterprise social software for collaboration, sharing, problem solving and relationship building
Teambox	Online collaboration project software combining productivity tools and social networking
Tibbr (by Tibco)	Real-time enterprise social networking and problem-solving solution
Trillr (by CoreMedia)	Enterprise microblogging platform for workers, partners and customers to communicate and connect
Wiggio	Free online toolkit for group collaboration including calendars, to-do, sharing, online meetings and polling
WizeHive	Enterprise collaboration, business process and workflow software
Work.com (by Salesforce)	Enterprise social collaboration software for recognition, feedback and coaching of staff
Yackstar	Social software to facilitate interactions and collaboration in a secure internal social network
Yammer	Free private social network for businesses
Yonkly	Open-source microblogging platform
YooLinkPro	Information sharing and retrieval on Facebook, Twitter, and e-mail

In this chapter, we have seen that B2B relationships differ markedly from those with consumers in virtually every aspect of customer needs, decision making, the value each places in a relationship and the value that both company and customer bring to it. B2B relationships demand the planning and execution of an entirely different relationship, using different processes, technologies, people and knowledge/insight, than a firm might have with consumers. This chapter contrasted relationships between consumers and B2B customers and considered aspects associated with the rethinking of B2B relationships in the mutual interests of the company, its business customers and other stakeholders, including employees. The chapter also considered selected social platforms and solutions as technologies that might be deployed to assist and accelerate the development of relationships within an enterprise and between businesses too.

Chapter 6
RELATIONSHIPS WITH MOBILE CUSTOMERS

"A self does not amount to much, but no self is an island;
each exists in a fabric of relations that is now more complex and mobile than
ever before."
                                    —Jean-François Lyotard (1924–1998)

The first fully mobile cellular phone was the Motorola DynaTAC 8000X. It went on sale in March 1983, weighed nearly two pounds and was priced at $3,995. Now mobile devices are small, smart, much more functional and increasingly interconnected. These devices have not only enabled consumers to be mobile and still attend to their computing and communications tasks, they have changed the behaviors of consumers and enterprises alike. This chapter considers the relationship implications of technological innovations that have increased consumer mobility and made communications and intelligence ubiquitous and real time.

Wherever consumers are, they are reachable. Wherever consumers are, they can also reach out, be influenced and influence others, give and receive information, and seek and create entertainment and other content. This always-on, 100 percent–uptime consumer has the same needs as he or she ever had, since needs are innate and never change. But now this consumer has the means to fulfill those needs as never before. The opportunity for the enterprise is not just to reach out to the mobile consumer or to open up the communications environment to new mobile platforms, although it is surely that. The opportunity is also to consider mobility as a basis for increasing both user and workforce productivity and, by so doing, transform the workforce into a mobile one. Although the opportunity for mobile technologies is thus broader than forming mobile relationships with consumers, the focus of this chapter is principally on developing, sustaining and deepening relationships with mobile customers.

DEFINING MOBILE RELATIONSHIPS

First off, it should be noted that there is no such thing as a mobile relationship. There are certainly relationships with mobile customers. These are the same customers with which the enterprise has been seeking to develop relationships as described in the preceding chapters. So why provide a chapter on mobile relationships? Mobility is a key frontier of technology in part because technology enables increased performance and miniaturization at affordable costs, and because the need exists—customers want to connect with one another and with enterprises, even while they move around. Accordingly, companies ought to consider how best to sustain and develop relationships with the mobile customer.

As in the case of social networks, technology ought to be the last thing an enterprise considers when developing relationships with mobile customers. Preceding this consideration, a company should be thinking about which platforms its customers use, what the enterprise's objectives are for connecting, influencing and developing relationships with these mobile customers and what might be appropriate strategies for the organization to adopt in the context of these objectives.

Mobile technologies typically have a number of characteristics in common, including the following:

- Facilitating real-time access to the users of the technologies
- Enabling the users to initiate contact with whomever they want, whenever they want
- Having intelligence resident in the local communications terminal to augment and enrich communications
- Having multiple input options including voice, photography and typing, and
- Facilitating a deeper and more personal interaction with each individual user as a result of having information such as each person's physical location.

Not only can all of these characteristics facilitate better selection of customers and potential customers by the enterprise, it can enable the firm to create strategic capabilities that allow it to also be selected by customers, and, by so doing, invert the historical marketing process. Now the customer chooses the business at least as much as the business selects the customer.

Technologies discussed in this chapter are enabled by virtualization, which enables workload to be spread across more users and infrastructure, and utilization to increase. Organizations are increasingly developing their infrastructure as a cloud-based service in which they use the cloud when they exceed their own capacity, which might be the case when university servers become overloaded by students taking exams, for example. While the cloud and mobile technologies are not linearly interrelated, they do dovetail. For example, some companies use software applications on demand in the cloud to cater to mobile customers, which is known as SaaS—Software as a Service. Some companies do more than this, having application development and a production environment on demand in the cloud, PaaS—Platform as a Service. PaaS may also be beneficial for engaging and sustaining a relationship with mobile customers, depending upon the scalability and design of an enterprise's existing infrastructure. The reader is referred to the case discussion of Dell in Chapter 10, which reviews how this company is using mobility, the cloud and other technologies to help customers engage with medical practitioners and others who are increasingly mobile.

As in the case of Dell just mentioned, relationships with mobile customers would simply not be possible had there not been such widespread adoption of mobile devices such as smartphones, PDAs,[1] netbooks and tablets.[2] Today, most people have either a cell phone or smartphone. There are more than 7 billion people on planet Earth[3] and approximately 6 billion mobile phones.[4] About 40 percent of all mobile phones are in China and India as these countries have used mobile technologies to substitute for, and leapfrog, terrestrial cable for communications. In a number of countries, such as Russia and the United States, there are more mobile phones than there are people. In short, access to the mobile customer is now a fact of life and is no longer a developing trend. As the mobile customer demonstrates increased willingness to upgrade his or her mobile telephony to increasingly sophisticated devices, new and significant opportunities are becoming available to companies who extend their relationship development to cater to the mobile customer in creative ways.

Companies that will succeed in developing deeper relationships with mobile customers will not simply port their existing technologies and approaches into the emerging technologies of the mobile arena. They will rethink their objectives and strategies for mobile customer engagement and develop newly engineered processes and technologies. E-learning companies have themselves learned that they need to develop m-learning (or mobile learning) methodologies to cater to mobile customers and, in much the same way, all companies need to recognize that the Internet access and customer engagement approaches they used yesterday ought to be reconsidered for mobility. This new consideration may include tailoring and possibly providing entirely new solutions for the customer whose cell phone or smartphone is an Internet appliance and is different in terms of form factor (dimensions of the device), processing capability, storage and bandwidth that have been the basis for connecting with and assisting each customer. As is well known, most widely used consumer applications enable mobile access, including social media such as Facebook, LinkedIn and Twitter, e-mail, online retailers such as Amazon and eBay, local applications such as Foursquare and Yelp, and so on.

For some companies, the mobile customer presents not only an opportunity but a requirement to rethink and possibly reinvent their business models. For example, of Google's $38 billion in 2011 revenues, 96 percent came from search advertising, Google AdWords, making search particularly important to the company.[5] This form of advertising has historically required a large computer screen to present options for the consumer to consider and Google has not yet found ways to develop significant revenues from mobile devices where the reduced screen size requires a different approach to advertising. To respond, Google is including telephone numbers in click-to-call advertisements on mobile devices using different ad formats as the firm seeks to achieve increased revenues from mobile devices, at present still a relatively small percentage of total revenues.[6]

MOBILE RELATIONSHIP OBJECTIVES AND STRATEGIES

Strategy in the context of mobility for technology enables new classes of devices that themselves create new opportunities for customer engagement and influence. So which ought to come first, the technology or the strategy? A marketer looks at customer relationships through a strategy lens, seeking first to conceive relationship objectives and strategies before contemplating the technology tools to use. Executives (other than those in marketing or IT) are often more inclined to see the capabilities that new technologies can enable and demand more rapid deployment from marketing and IT, sometimes leaving a patchwork of technologies for strategic knitting, *ex post facto*. Here we take a marketer's perspective and first consider the objectives and strategies that might be considered in the context of the mobile customer relationship while also considering the broader customer relationship objectives of the enterprise. That is, mobile customer relationships ought not to be considered separately from the relationship plans of the enterprise—rather, they should be integral to them.

Relationship objectives are the second component of the CREVITS model of relationship management described in Chapter 3, and are typically set one customer at a time. The enterprise establishes the target behavior for an individual and seeks to advance the customer up a behavioral ladder by encouraging or facilitating behavioral changes that enable this progression. Mobile customer relationship objectives are similar to those for other customers, but provide an additional aspect for the company to consider as it seeks to achieve customer-specific objectives. Examples of the kinds of behavioral objectives a company might seek to achieve are discussed in Table 12 of Chapter 3, Customers' Demonstrated Behaviors on Each Relationship Ladder Rung.

In Chapter 4, social media objectives were discussed in the context of taxonomy for social media. Reputation management, customer management and customer acquisition objectives were explored in the context of informing, educating, communicating, entertaining, collaborating and transacting with social customers. The same methodology applies here where companies are seeking to engage with, and advance their relationships with, the mobile customer.

In short, customer relationship objectives for engaging with customers apply generally because there is no difference between the social customer and the mobile customer—they are naturally one and the same. Accordingly, integrated marketing communications need to reflect customer engagement both socially and using mobile devices. When focusing specifically on the subset of strategies that cater to the mobile customer, Figure 22 suggests that there are a number of interrelated strategies that companies can consider to engage with and add value to the mobile customer. Technology underpins these strategies, serving as both a tool for strategy implementation and, in some cases, providing an entirely new basis to connect, relate and compete. Each element of strategy is discussed after the diagram is presented.

Figure 22: Mobile Customer Relationship Objectives and Strategies

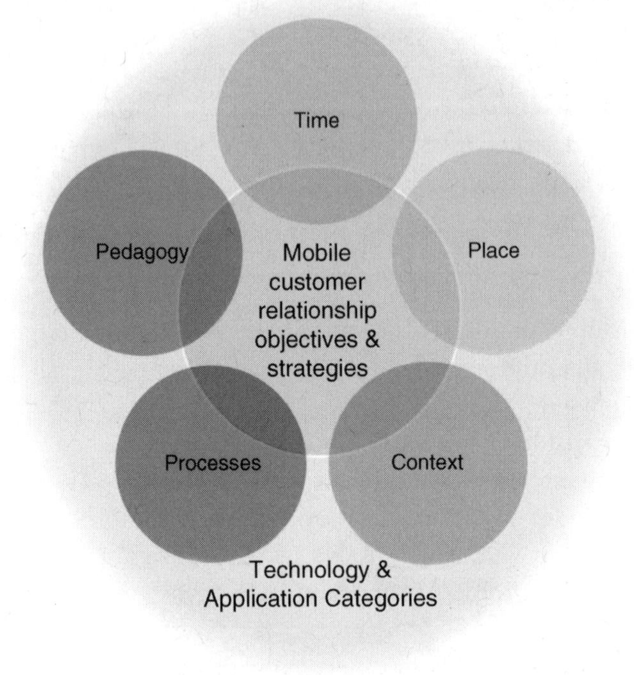

Time

Pedagogy

Mobile
customer
relationship
objectives &
strategies

Place

Processes

Context

Technology &
Application Categories

- Time: Now and Next

    Real-time technologies are important for understanding and engaging the mobile customer, in part because they enable ubiquitous, content-rich access and in part because they provide for a deeper understanding of the context of each individual customer. Linked to place, real time allows companies to know where customers are, where they have been and where they are going. Associated with other customer information, and independently, these data serve to help the company better understand the customer and be relevant because of that understanding. For example, there is potential to predict where the customer will be going next by using or projecting GPS data with known mobile patterns, for example. By associating this understanding with what the customer might want next, say, by interpreting existing data and using predictive modeling, the company can position itself to sell just as the customer is ready to buy and that has the potential to be a significant differentiator and basis for competitive advantage.

- Place: Location and presence sensing

    Most mobile phones enable the company to identify the user's location, commonly by using GPS data, as previously mentioned. By sensing where the customer is, the company can provide location-specific messages or inducements to modify customers' behaviors, such as by providing coupons that can be used in stores that are in proximity to customers. Local marketing environments such as Foursquare invite users to sign in and, in return, users get financial or other benefits, such as discounts, from the retailer. This is another way for companies to know where a customer is at any given time and this sensing, when applied with customer-specific objectives, interaction and transaction history, profile information and predictive modeling, enables strategies to be deployed for the mobile customer. Data derived from customer sensing can also be used for geo-demographic clustering, allowing companies to develop local and micro-marketing initiatives that cater to customers whose behaviors can be assessed in part based on their geo-demographics—i.e., where they are and where they go in relation to their specific profiles and behavioral objectives.

- Context

    Companies can know who their mobile customers are, the interaction and transaction history of these customers and where they are, among other information. They can identify and interact with customers in real time, adding value to the connection when it makes a difference to the customer. The context of the customer—that which surrounds him or her, what he or she could be thinking, what was bought before, what might be wanted next, and so on—is more important than the content the company uses to engage the customer. As important as content is, context is even more so because it provides a perspective on the individual's likes, dislikes, needs, wants and intent. A company using this insight can add much value to the customer relationship. Companies seeking to develop meaningful context integrate information from various customer touch points, sensing and listening—whether the customer has actually communicated something or because behaviors infer a specific requirement or future purchase intent. Listening to—or, more accurately, sensing—the mobile customer requires that companies examine what data they might obtain by engaging with customers' mobile devices and encouraging customers to provide data *in situ*, wherever they are. Feedback from customers can be specific to their immediate requirement, it can be additive to the company's existing understanding—say, key questions that need to be answered in the customers' profiles—or it can be contextual—say, finding out where a customer is at a given point, e.g., when signing into a Foursquare app. Companies need to use these customer data in real time, associating the data with the customer's information file and having an ability to predict an aspect of the customer's emerging requirements, again in real time.

- Processes

    A mobile customer expects to receive different treatment than the stationary one. The difference is a matter of urgency—mobile customers want attention *now*. Someone awaiting customer service while in line at a store, wanting to know why his or her credit card was declined, for example, sees time as even more valuable than a customer calling from a residence or other fixed location because the mobile call is made when time is at a premium and is often associated with other aspects of a customer's life. Companies that understand the importance of the mobile customer's need for immediate attention develop apps that work on the customer's mobile phone or other platforms, such as tablets. These firms have back-office technologies that understand each customer and make customer information files and other customer-specific data available to customer and service personnel wherever they are. The organization also engineers its processes to accommodate the mobile customer. It is in this latter regard that some companies have yet to invest time in the reengineering necessary for meaningful process changes. Paying bills should be possible from mobile phones, as should retrieving account status information, tracking shipment status, seeing catalogues and prices, and obtaining coupons—in short, everything the customer is used to doing in the physical world and from a stationary virtual platform should be possible from a mobile one.

- Pedagogy

    Pedagogy is the art and science of teaching based on an understanding of the theory and practice of how people learn. So what then does pedagogy have to do with the mobile customer relationship? A great deal, it turns out. Mobile customers use their devices and the apps on these devices because they have learned to do so. They buy from companies they have learned to trust. They visit websites they have learned are easy to navigate and have the goods and services they want. In short, if customers are to exhibit new behaviors, they must learn these behaviors and it is incumbent upon the organization to teach them (recall that "T" is for "Teach" in the

CREVITS model in Chapter 3). Innovation, relationships and pedagogy thus go hand in hand as customers become aware of new need-satisfying products and services, engage suppliers and learn what they must to satisfy their needs and potentially repeat the experience. Few companies have fully appreciated the opportunity associated with developing pedagogy to complement their marketing communications. Fewer still have evolved this pedagogy to embrace mobile communications devices and customers. Companies that provide e-learning services can demonstrate some best practices in this regard. These firms seem to have understood from the start that people learn differently online than in classroom environments and developed e-learning capabilities to reflect these differences.[7] When learners began to use mobile devices, e-learning companies were among the first to appreciate the significance of this change and evolve their pedagogy to m-learning, mobile learning, as previously mentioned. Thus a learner using a cell phone while commuting would see a very different screen than would a learner using a larger screen from home, say. Perhaps the mobile device would provide knowledge in association with a handbook and ask questions more succinctly to accommodate the smaller size of the screen.

SELECTED APPLICATION CATEGORIES FOR MOBILE DEVICES[8]

Once companies have considered their relationship objectives and strategies in the context of their integrated marketing communications, one of the next questions to be asked and answered relates to which application categories the company will focus on to engage its mobile customers. There are a number of options that ought to be considered in association with one another. The discussion starts with a review of the mobile Internet and then discusses specific technology categories that relate to or depend on this technology. The order of presentation is not intended to reflect relative importance or priority of each category.

Mobile Internet

Consumers make extensive use of the Internet on their mobile devices and have the potential to make even more use. According to the ITU,[9] of the 5.9 billion mobile phone users, there are 1.2 billion users with mobile broadband subscriptions in 159 countries.[10] The highest levels of mobile broadband penetration are found in Korea, Japan, Sweden and Australia, all of which have over 80 percent penetration. Different areas of China have lower levels of penetration (still more than the United Kingdom or the United States—56 percent and 54 percent, respectively) with over 118 million users of mobile broadband Internet services in this country.[11] Penetration rates such as these provide an indication of the direction for mobile broadband penetration. In short, the mobile Internet may be increasingly referred to as simply the Internet, as consumers access information, entertainment, payments and other benefits via the Internet from their mobile devices. Although the percentage of website hits coming from mobile devices is still relatively small—approximately 8.5 percent, excluding tablets—the clear trend is for mobile devices to be an important and perhaps dominant platform in the future.[12] (By comparison, website hits from mobile devices were just 0.7 percent in 2009.)[13] Many consumers are giving up their desktops and laptops in favor of mobile-only communications. In the United States, 25 percent of mobile users have no desktop and in the United Kingdom, 22 percent.[14] This means that companies thinking of the Internet as a communications channel to the consumer's desktop or notebook at a more or less static location now ought to explore how to engage the mobile consumer through his or her mobile platform wherever he or she is. Increasingly, it will be the growth of mobile Internet connectivity that impacts aspects of customer relationships enabled by mobile technologies. As has been suggested, it's quite likely that many consumers will simply turn off or throw out their desktops and laptops in favor of mobile communications devices. Companies wanting to connect with their customers will need to do that on their mobile devices or they soon may not be able to reach them at all.

Apps

Apps, an abbreviation for the applications companies develop using APIs—Application Programming Interfaces—enable customers to use their mobile devices such as smartphones to engage with the enterprise wherever and whenever they wish. Apps are developed to run on the operating system (OS) of mobile devices and are typically downloadable from the application store of an OS vendor such as Apple's iOS, Google's Android, Nokia's Symbian, Microsoft's Windows Phone or RIM's BlackBerry 10. If you have an iPhone or a BlackBerry, for example, many of the apps you have on your smartphone would fall into this category, whether they be for an electronics retailer such as Amazon or Best Buy, a bank or stock brokerage, the Yellow Pages, and so on, as well as apps that are produced for sale as products in their own right. Many companies will need to deploy new generations of apps if they have not already done so by now to benefit more fully from the trend toward the mobile Internet discussed above.

SMS

SMS or Short Message Service allows the sending of messages with up to 160 characters to and from mobile terminals such as smartphones. Many people refer to SMS as texting which is accurate if texting is text-based communications and not content such as video. Most SMS communications are between people using mobile phones. When used by companies, SMS marketing facilitates highly targeted—if brief—personalized and context-sensitive messages to provide information (e.g., stock market or other financial information, weather and traffic reports) or solicit it, motivate purchase, seek a response—such as a vote or initial contact, or to achieve another change in customer behaviors. Financial and other incentives or rewards such as coupon codes, free music, ringtones, airtime or a draw for a prize can be used to help achieve the desired behaviors. SMS can also be used as a vehicle for financial payments and to generate new revenues by cross-marketing, as in the case of TV programs encouraging viewers to vote and purchase songs from iTunes, as *American Idol* has done, for example. Customers may subscribe to the SMS of an enterprise or opinion leader such as a movie star, for example, and unsubscribe too. Companies pay attention to the communications preferences of their customers and prospects, and manage communications so as not to over-communicate while respecting the preferences of each customer.

Approximately 8 trillion SMS messages were sent in 2011, nearly two-thirds of all messages.[15] This volume makes SMS the most important form of mobile communications. New technologies such as those mentioned below, mobile e-mail, mobile IM[16] and SMS hubbing[17] continue to change the nature of consumer-to-consumer communications and the options available for enterprises to engage with consumers, and vice versa, as application-to-consumer communications. At present, SMS continues to dominate as the principal means of communications but, as was noted in the consideration of the mobile Internet and discussed below for Multimedia Messaging Service (MMS), the growth of mobile broadband Internet connectivity and smartphones suggests that the

249 billion MMS messages sent in 2010[18] will grow significantly as a share of the messaging marketplace, as will the share of communications represented by mobile IM and application-to-consumer messaging.[19]

MMS

MMS, Multimedia Messaging Service, is used to send and receive multimedia content, including photographs and videos from smartphones such as iPhones. Among the capabilities that MMS enable are ticketing (e.g., airline boarding passes), advertising, and e-coupons. For example, companies can send coupons that are accessible and usable from mobile devices.

QR

QR or Quick Response codes are smartphone-readable graphics that are being increasingly used by companies to facilitate rapid access to information. Consumers simply need to use a QR app and their smartphones to be directed to information or other resources that a company wants to make available to consumers. There are many potential uses for QR codes and the list is growing rapidly as companies find new ways to cross-link their content, such as putting a QR code in a television advertisement to encourage consumers to visit the company's website to learn more about their products or a specific event, for example.

GPS

GPS, or Global Positioning System, is a multi-satellite system that provides accurate location (and time) information if mobile phones are GPS enabled, and most have this capability. Location information can be determined even for phones that are not GPS enabled using cell towers but this approach is less accurate. Phones are GPS enabled mostly because of the need for cell phones to be able to hand off the signal between terrestrial cell towers and for the 9-1-1 system to be able to identify an individual's location. The location information, sometimes called geolocation, can be very accurate, to as close as a foot. GPS enables mobile phone users to track their locations using apps such as Google Maps Navigation. GPS is also used for purposes such as geotagging where geographic coordinates are applied to photographs, for example, as well as potentially letting companies know where a phone is at any given time if that capability on an app has been enabled. GPS can be used for geofencing, a capability that allows companies to understand where their vehicles and staff are, for pet owners to retrieve animals or for parents to monitor where their kids are, among other uses.

Advertising

Companies are increasingly employing mobile advertising to reach consumers, as was noted when previous mention was made of Google's AdWords. Other than Google, the major mobile advertising companies include Millennial Media, Apple, Yahoo, Microsoft and Jumptap. Research firm Gartner projects that worldwide mobile advertising revenues will reach $20.6 billion by 2015, with the highest revenue applying to search and maps, and the fastest growth applying to video and audio advertisements.[20] This firm expects companies to significantly increase their mobile advertising budgets such that mobile advertising budgets will comprise about 4 percent of total advertising in 2015. In short, mobile devices bring with them new opportunities for companies to develop relationships with prospects by serving up context-sensitive advertising, such as when specific search terms are employed. As advertising has proved to be a lucrative business model for many advertising, search and map companies, among others it is likely that companies will find new ways to advertise to consumers and engage them on their mobile devices, such as using mobile games, product placement and other novel ideas.

Games

The market for mobile games is estimated to be in the vicinity of $4 billion to $5 billion of the $33 billion games market and is growing by about $500 million a year. Consumers are playing games on their smartphones using either preloaded or downloaded apps that are specific to games, apps for which games are incidental, such as Facebook, or Internet portals directly. Games may be played by just one person or several players simultaneously in Massively Multiplayer Online (MMO) games, including first-person shooter (FPS) and roleplaying (RPG) games.

A number of games have been phenomenally successful and the impetus for entire companies. For example, consumers have downloaded the Angry Birds game hundreds of millions of times for multiple platforms, and over 12 million times just for Apple's smartphones. Produced by Finnish mobile game development company Rovio, the game is a strategy puzzle for consumers to have fun while firing birds at pigs. Angry Birds has also developed a Facebook application for consumers to play on the Facebook site.

Facebook has become an important games environment in general and especially for smartphone users. The world's leading provider of social game services on sites such as Facebook is Zynga, with 240 million monthly active users playing games such as FarmVille and CityVille.[21] Zynga's games are free to play. The firm generates revenue by using virtual currency for consumers to buy virtual goods, and advertising. Facebook Credits is a form of virtual money that can be used to banish ads from screens and to buy pigs for FarmVille, for example. (Yes, really.) Advertising revenues are developed from product placement and sponsorships within game play, advertisements geared to getting information from customers in exchange for virtual currency, ad-supported free versions of mobile games, and display advertising.[22] Companies such as McDonald's, Kia, 7-Eleven, MillerCoors and Visa have advertised in game environments such as Zynga's.[23]

As the examples of Rovio and Zynga suggest—and the proliferation of mobile game developers such as Electronic Arts (U.S.),[24] GREE (Japan), Mobage by DeNA (Japan), Gameloft (France), Glu Mobile (U.S.) and TeamLava by Storm8 (U.S.) confirm—there has been an emergence of new firms and business models that are very different from tradition and which make extensive use of social media and mobile platforms, and free and "freemium" pricing models.[25] As an example of the freemium pricing model, Dropbox, a cloud-based service for file storage and sharing, provides 2 GB of data storage free. Users pay for additional storage if they want more than this.

Geotagging

Geotagging describes the process of taking content and adding geographic information to identify the content by location. For example, a photograph could be tagged with GPS data from a smartphone, enabling the location of the photograph to be identified. Similarly, content such as videos, websites and SMS messages can be tagged with geographic information such as latitude and longitude coordinates. This tagging not only helps to identify locations for specific content but also enables searches to be made by location, which leads to identifying points of interest in proximity to specific coordinates, for example.

Location-Based Services

Location-based services (LBS) makes use of geographic information revealed by GPS-enabled cell phones, smartphones and tablets to pinpoint the location of the user, leading to the provision of services to consumers, such as knowing where family members are (a service offered by cell phone firms), finding the location of a friend, identifying a nearby retailer or tracking a vehicle, parcel or shipment (a B2B application). Other services include providing discounts or advertising to consumers who have entered a specific geographic area and other customer and location-specific information and games. The global LBS market is estimated to be in the vicinity of $12 billion to $13 billion, with advertising comprising an increasing share of LBS-related revenues.[26]

Foursquare is a location-based mobile application that has about 20 million registered users and an average of approximately 3 million check-ins per day. Foursquare provides consumers with social and geographic information, helping consumers to know, for example, where their friends are, what is in proximity to them and also to receive coupons and discounts, among other benefits. Consumers check in to the businesses they visit using smartphones or other devices. They receive points for checking in and these points can be redeemed for various rewards. For example, a restaurant may offer a free dessert to Foursquare customers who buy a main course, obtaining in return increased revenues by attracting local traffic in search of a restaurant, and information about each customer, such as profiles of loyal customers, time of check-in, age, gender and social reach.

Some mobile games also have LBS features. Booyah's My Town 2, for example, is a city-building game for the Apple iOS operating system that uses the user's current location so that the first towns seen are those in closest proximity. Users can check into local businesses and incorporate those into the game. SCVNGR is another LBS-enabled game; this one seeks to have users contribute to the building of a mobile game that incorporates locations into the game. SCVNGR is a gaming platform that uses challenges in local places in what the company calls a game layer on top of the world.

Other popular applications that make use of location-based services and geosocial networking more generally include Yelp and Facebook. Yelp is a local search and review site with LBS, social networking and reputation management functionality, among other capabilities. Facebook uses LBS to enable social users to tag where they have been, where they are now and where they are going. Placecast sends messages and information about deals to customers who enter virtually fenced-off geographic areas. But not all location-based mobile apps have been successful and there have been a number of acquisitions and departures from this space. For example, Gowalla was, like Foursquare, a mobile app that used mobile devices to allow consumers to check in. Subsequent versions of the app allowed consumers to also check in using Foursquare, Twitter and Tumblr. Gowalla ceased operations in 2012. Dodgeball, another location-based mobile app—this one focusing on SMS—was acquired by Google in 2005 and shut down in 2009, replaced by Google Latitude.[27] Loopt was acquired by Green Dot in 2012. This is clearly an evolving arena.

Payments

A number of industry observers perceive that a cashless society is at hand and the mobile phone will be used as the instrument of payment. Phones will be able to buy sodas, coffees, transit tickets—more or less anything—while retaining receipts, displaying tickets, boarding passes and coupons, and providing proof of payment and loyalty information. Google is planning for consumers' wallets to go virtual, with money migrating from something people touch to ones and zeros in the cloud. The Google Wallet mobile app puts users' credit card, loyalty card and PIN information onto smartphones, allowing consumers to pay for merchandise and services by tapping their phones on a reader at the point of sale. PayPal is also planning for a cashless, mobile society where users can view their transaction records and account information from mobile devices, send money and buy merchandise and services. Mobile devices are already used for making payments in a number of countries and it seems likely that some form of mobile payments will be ubiquitous in due course, if not in universal use.

Consumers are naturally concerned about security in a cashless environment that makes use of technologies with which consumers may not be fully familiar, such as near field communications.[28] PayPal maintains that consumers need not be concerned as every payment is confirmed by a PIN or password so unauthorized usage would be highly unlikely. Privacy is also of possible concern as payments organizations become increasingly well informed about consumers' locations, purchases made (and, by inference, rejected), loyalty and trial, spending patterns and profitability, among other considerations. Especially when consumer behavior data is assembled, a comprehensive view of each customer can be developed and predictive models can help companies develop their existing customers and acquire new ones, all the while managing their marketing budgets for greatest impact, lifetime customer management and profitability.

TV

Consumers are increasingly accessing television on their smartphones, creating an opportunity for the operators of cell phone networks, and challenging them strategically and operationally. One of the strategic challenges cell phone operators must address is the potential for substitution of television signals delivered over mobile networks by those that are broadcast. Some cell phone companies are making smartphones that receive broadcast television signals which bypass the cell phone network and, by so doing, create no additional revenues for the network operators. In part to address this threat, some network operators have acquired traditional broadcast media companies. In addition to providing them with content to channel through their local networks, this provides the operators with revenues from converged media, such as advertising revenues from both broadcast and customer-specific media. The operational challenge cell phone network operators face is principally one of capacity as streaming media consumes considerable bandwidth and places new demands on existing infrastructure. The network operators are building out their networks and acquiring new spectrum to be able to handle projected increased demands in capacity.

Coupons

Mobile coupons are virtual coupons delivered to smartphones or mobile devices such as iPads that function in much the same way as paper-based coupons but with greater functionality and customer memory, and with a lower cost of distribution and redemption. For example, LBS can be incorporated into mobile coupons so that offers are confined to a specific geographic area. Generally, mobile coupons require that users download an app that enables coupons to be shown to cashiers in-store. Unique coupon codes are often employed on coupons to reduce fraud and track each customer's use of the coupon. Among the better-known apps for mobile coupons are Coupons .com, MobiQpons, Mobilecoupons.com and Yowza. Walgreens has released its own app for mobile coupons, as have a number of other stores. Grocery iQ is a Coupons.com app that allows users to find and use coupons, among other features. As with many of these arenas, companies come and go, among them Coupious, an e-couponing pioneer that ceased operations in 2012. Companies that engage with any vendor, whether here or in other spaces, ought to assure themselves that their customer and other data can survive even if their partner does not.

Mobile Betting

Betting, lotteries and social gambling are emerging as important application areas for mobile devices. Mobile gambling was in excess of $19.5 billion worldwide in 2011 and is expected to rise to more than $100 billion in 2017.[29] Sports betting accounts for the majority of mobile gambling but casinos and lotteries will become increasingly important areas of transaction for mobile gambling.[30]

About 66 percent of American,[31] 80 percent of Canadian,[32] and 70 percent of British[33] and Australian[34] adults gamble to some extent. Given the large number of gamblers in society, it seems quite likely that the very nature of gambling, including time sensitivity, convenience and social context, will make this an increasingly attractive application area for mobile devices to engage consumers.

Local Deals

A number of firms have capitalized on the power of the Internet to blend mobile, local and social technologies, e-commerce and the physical and virtual worlds to provide discounts to customers in local markets. Groupon and LivingSocial, as well as companies like Keynoir (now part of Time Out) and WagJag, function more or less like local buying groups for consumers. Local goods and service providers benefit by developing new sales, although this frequently comes at a high cost. It is not uncommon for the site to take up to half of the revenues from each deal and the local firms likely benefit over a long time horizon only if they are able to keep new customers that are developed by the initial deals. For some it can be a daunting challenge to sustain high levels of service as large numbers of customers suddenly flock to their stores, restaurants and other businesses, and this obviously does not aid customer retention.

EMERGING TECHNOLOGIES

There are a number of new technologies in mobile phones, applications, communications technologies and cloud-related technologies that provide new tools for marketers and enable alternative strategies. Mobile technologies such as GPS, onboard accelerometers and gyroscopes have provided companies with new ways to add value to consumers with applications as discussed and a new generation that promises to help consumers even more as the trend toward social-local-mobile— "SoLoMo"—continues. Some of the new ideas underpinning mobile technology advancements have emerged from the Center for Mobile Learning and Fluid Interfaces Group at the Massachusetts Institute of Technology's Media Lab, an influential fount of novelty. The Center for Mobile Learning is working on a Google-initiated, Web-based program development tool that can be used by novices to create mobile applications.[35] This suggests that mobile apps will proliferate, be less costly to develop and increasingly be designed by people without software development skills. The Fluid Interfaces Group is working on augmented experiences, responsive objects, collaborative interactions, and programmable materials.

One is left to wonder how the many areas of emerging technologies and opportunities, including context-sensitive computing, databases full of personal information, GPS, QR codes and local, real-time and mobile devices and related technologies will intersect, be commercialized and affect all of us. Some of the technologies are already with us, providing insight into the promise and the short time between conceptualization and commercialization, as in the case of Apple's Siri, for example. Examples such as the preceding suggest that future technologies will likely be yet more mobile, multiplatform and context sensitive. Interfaces will be on a more human scale and more intuitive, with individuals interacting with devices in much the same way as they interact with people in an even more informed, helpful and personal experience. Devices will be omnipresent enablers of people—helping them to remember, find out, understand and connect with others—while not being intrusive. Or so would be the promise.

•   •   •

The focus of this chapter has been on the development and maintenance of relationships with customers who just happen to be mobile. Enabling capabilities of mobile technologies and applications allow management to pay new attention to "place" as a component of their digital marketing mix. Companies not only have an opportunity to leverage smartphones and other mobile devices such as tablets but to integrate their one-to-one communications with a wide variety of digital communications in an integrated communications mix. For example, a consumer might be prompted by LBS to take advantage of a nearby deal and, when entering the store, might be thanked by a store employee for coming back and to recommend a specific next purchase. The employee, in turn, may have been prompted by his or her mobile device to engage in this communication.

The technologies are here that could make some of the scenes in the movie *Minority Report* a current reality. In the movie, the protagonist, Chief John Anderton, receives custom messages on in-store digital billboards as he enters the Gap. Although such messaging may be a little too public for what should probably be private communications, the potential does exist to integrate digital, intelligent communications with place to be even more relevant to each individual, on their mobile devices, socially and locally. A number of interrelated strategies that companies can consider to engage with and add value to the mobile customer were discussed in this chapter. These included setting objectives and catering to the needs and expectations of mobile customers in respect of time, place, context, processes and pedagogy.

Chapter 7
MASS CUSTOMIZATION

"I swear nothing is good to me now that ignores individuals."
Walt Whitman (1819–1892)

To the extent that individuals have expectations, interests, wants and experiences that differ from one another, they need to receive individualized treatment. This is the very essence and starting point for management of customer relationships. Individualized treatment, in turn, requires that organizations think about how best to modify their own products, services and processes to engage with each individual customer uniquely. For many organizations, one outgrowth of this consideration is mass customization. This chapter explores mass customization and considers selected alternative strategies and implementation considerations.

MASS CUSTOMIZATION DEFINED

Mass customization can be defined as the process of providing and supporting individually tailored goods and services, according to each customer's preferences with regard to form, time, place and price, and doing so profitably. Mass customization considers customization of each aspect of the 4Ps: products and services, pricing, promotion and communications, and place/distribution channels.

Mass marketers historically viewed mass customization as interesting in theory but too expensive to implement practically, particularly if mass customization would result in considerable additional expense, such as could be the case for new equipment or a plant overhaul. Today, mass customization is considered more practical because technology costs have declined, business processes have become more flexible, and enterprises are increasingly willing to develop and apply customer-specific strategies for engagement and many aspects of value creation.

AN EXPENSIVE OPTION?

Still, some companies may see mass customization as an expensive option they cannot afford. These firms may sometimes say that they are committed to customer-specific relationships, even though they are not pursuing mass customization. Unfortunately, customers will be able to tell that the enterprises are not fully invested in deepening and expanding customer relationships. Customer strategy really *is* that transparent. So, if the company is to commit itself completely to a strategy of customer relationships, mass customization is not just a concept or an option. It is a necessity. Although the practical reality is that few firms can afford to provide infinite customer choice by allowing and implementing every possible combination and permutation for mass customization, most companies can make major strides toward giving customers genuine choice in terms of what matters most to each customer, and connecting with each customer on his or her terms.

Those companies that say that mass customization is too expensive may wish to consider the barriers that impede their adoption of mass customization. Some might find mass customization provides a new start, an opportunity to shed anchors to the past such as outmoded business processes. For example, car companies still offer a fairly narrow range of colors for their vehicles. Why not offer customers near infinite choice when selecting a color for the car? Car companies say it is too expensive or hard to do. They might remember that Henry Ford famously said that customers could have any car as long as it was black. General Motors surpassed Ford in part because it offered customers more color choice. It's curious that both companies still have a limited palette at a time when technology could enable many more colors without materially increasing vehicle assembly or even collision repair costs. It is in situations such as this that mass customization offers not only an opportunity to build deeper relationships but also provide competitive advantage.

TECHNOLOGY FOR MASS CUSTOMIZATION

Technology offers many more opportunities than even the previously mentioned example would suggest. Consumers have become used to assembling the value they want on their screens. Many companies have built their businesses with this variability as part of their strategy, designing their production, distribution, service and organizational flexibility to provide an increased array of offerings suited to individual preference. To illustrate a pioneering effort, about 20 years ago, Morrison International of Sarasota, Florida, reinvented the way eyeglasses are made. Traditionally, eyewear involved custom-grinding lenses for differently shaped frames. Morrison fitted pre-molded lenses into snap-together frames that adjusted to fit any face. By rotating the lenses to any of 180 positions in the frame, 26,000 prescriptions could be filled using a stock of just 152 lenses. And now many companies, like Goggles4U, have taken eyeglass customization yet further and in the process cut substantially into the highly profitable business of optical retailing.

Some approaches to mass customization are more appropriate than others for a given industry and firm. Buick's long ago slogan, "Can we build one for you?," required that Buick secure individual customer preferences and develop processes to build some uniqueness into its vehicles. But Buick has made no attempt to build fully customized cars. If you want a five-cylinder engine, manual transmission, red upholstery, side airbags and fins, forget it. When capital-intensive goods are produced, there is a requirement for core functionality to be established and a range of customization options and degrees of variability to be pre-specified so that the goods can be manufactured. Goods producers typically identify modules that can be mixed and matched, to allow the customer some choice. In so doing, manufacturers make trade-offs in the degree of uniqueness they are prepared to offer, preferring to provide individualized products rather than truly unique ones to balance the costs of uniqueness with production and other constraints.

Although it can be costly to provide an expanded array of alternatives when customizing goods, the same cannot be said for the customization of services. Here, opportunities likely remain for companies to further extend their thinking with regard to mass customization. That is, while it may not be economical to provide full customization for the design and manufacture of an automobile engine, for example, there is no reason a leasing package cannot be custom designed for an individual customer. If you want to buy a car by making a down payment of the cash in your wallet, not pay for three months, make a balloon payment of whatever bonus you expect to receive this year, then pay a minimum of $50 a month until next year's bonus and so on, why would the car company not enable this? Systems and processes should allow this to occur, and frontline people should be appropriately trained to help the customer achieve whatever each wants.

Just as consumers can choose to customize products for their requirements, so can business customers. When American Cyanamid invented glow-in-the-dark green chemicals, they invited businesses to identify applications for the product, and soon firms were packaging and marketing Cyanamid chemicals for photolabs (it will not expose most photographic film), fishing lures (fish race to the lure like lawyers to accidents), runway lights to outline rural landing areas, safety lights for kids to wear at Halloween, and lights to be held up by the audiences at rock concerts. In developing the unique chemical technology and supporting it with custom engineering processes, Cyanamid created a mass-customized approach to allow their customers to market a value-added chemical to a number of micro-markets.

ENABLING RELATIONSHIPS THROUGH MASS CUSTOMIZATION

In addition to the ability of an organization to sense and understand individual customers, there are a number of important considerations that enable companies to use mass customization to interpret customer-specific needs into point solutions, services and communications. These are described as follows:

- Assembling unique offerings
- Customer appreciation
- Adaptable technology and processes, and
- Support of intermediaries and suppliers.

Each of these issues is discussed below.

Assembling Unique Offerings

Unique offerings can be assembled by customers or by the company on their behalf, or a combination of both. If unique offerings cannot be made, as in the case of the five-cylinder automobile engine referred to earlier, an opportunity for mass customization is limited to customizing only service and other intangible dimensions of the product.

A furniture manufacturer may establish mass customized processes to produce sofas to individual preference, allowing customers to choose among such things as fabrics, styles and quality levels and charging a premium for this choice. Alternatively, a manufacturer may provide standard knock-down kits of unfinished furniture for customers to assemble and finish to individual taste. Another possibility is that the manufacturer provides the retailer with the ability to customize certain aspects for the customer, such as custom cut shelving for wall units, assembly of manufactured furniture modules, providing relevant brochures, literature, expert advice or videos and running training sessions on furniture finishing. The furniture manufacturer can then produce a standard product, while the customer receives a customized one, with the retailer playing the mass customization role.

The manufacturer has a responsibility in owning the processes for mass customization and for individually tailored communication. To illustrate, Andersen Windows put multimedia kiosks into retail operations for customers and salespeople to collaborate on the design of a window and see how it would look.[1] Taking this information, the system developed manufacturing specifications, communicated with the plant and provided pricing information, among other benefits. Today, Andersen Windows allows customers to design their own casement windows online, selecting colors for the interior and exterior, hardware, glass and size, among other options.[2]

Customer Appreciation

Customers will value and respond to a unique product/service bundle tailored to their requirements, and will reward the company for having mass customized.

If the manufacturer decides to provide a mass-customized solution to customers, it should target those needs that are key purchase criteria, not "nice-to-have" components of the product or service selection decision. For example, the customer with a bad back might want a vehicle manufacturer to provide seats contoured to the individual's shape. A company offering this will find new customers, additional revenues and potentially increased margin. Back sufferers will pay almost anything for more comfort. But if the car company chose to offer custom colors for trunk interiors (to pick one rather absurd area), few customers would derive sufficient new value from this to warrant the associated investment in technology and process.

In the previously mentioned furniture example, there are a number of customizers of sofas that have survived and grown over the years while some segments of the more standard sofa industry have been in decline. Apparently, there are enough particular and fashion-conscious customers who will pay the premium to make the customization of a sofa economical for the builder. The incremental revenue from mass customization should not be only profitable but more profitable than existing business to warrant the effort. If this is impossible, at least it should provide the company with revenues that can be sustained in the face of competitive threats.

Mass customization can also reduce costs. Dell showed the computer industry how this could be done when they pioneered build-to-order processes that engaged the customer, leading to reduced parts and finished goods inventory carrying costs and write-downs associated with end-of-life products as well as other benefits such as faster introduction of current technologies.

Adaptable Technology and Processes

Technology and processes are sufficiently flexible and adaptable to accommodate mass customization. First, the company should have made investments in the necessary data and other technology underpinning a mass customization initiative. This means that the company should see the architecture of technology as being a key component of the infrastructure needed to mass customize processes. That is, the choice of the architecture determines what is feasible in mass customization.

In particular, the data warehouse should be central to the architecture, and all other processes for mass customization of production, communication, customer care, pricing and channels should be linked to this warehouse. Without a data warehouse, a company will never know what it does not know and will continue trying to reach its destination by running faster without knowing if it is on the right road. And if it has the knowledge but not the processes to make the warehouse the engine of mass customization, each customer will be denied his or her personal solution.

Support of Intermediaries and Suppliers

Channel intermediaries and suppliers must be amenable to customizing their processes. Typically, mass customization processes will need to involve others beyond the walls of the company. If distribution channel intermediaries and suppliers need to be involved, they too will have to appreciate the value to be derived from modifying their technologies and processes. For example, if Chrysler is to provide customers with choice in the interior trim of minivans, it will need to change not only the processes by which customers order in Chrysler's stores and assembly processes in the plants but also the processes and technologies that link Chrysler to Magna, the company that supplies the interior trim for the minivans. If Magna is unprepared to allow customized selection of interior trim, Chrysler will have to abandon the project or get another supplier. And if Magna agrees to the changes, it, in turn, will need to secure the agreement of its suppliers of fabrics and other materials to any required changes in processes and technology. All these changes will need to be underpinned by sufficient new value being created for each customer so that new revenues and margin can be derived and shared along the entire chain of relationships.

APPROACHES TO MASS CUSTOMIZATION

Mass customization can take many forms and it is not always easy to decide which approach should be adopted. The following discusses specific alternatives for mass customization that suggests selected choices companies have as they decide which combination of customization to employ. The main dimensions in which customization may be applied to a standard offering are as follows:

- Product customization
- Services and auxiliary or augmented product dimensions such as installation, delivery and financial terms, and
- Communications for individual customer engagement and dialog, as well as the communications channels to be employed.

Price and value are also dimensions of customization and are associated with customization of other elements of the marketing mix, usually product and service. Chapter 9 considers selected aspects of pricing pertaining to the assembly of customized value for individual customers so this issue is not explored in additional detail in this chapter.

While companies within specific industries may position for mass customization in terms of any or all of these dimensions, in practice some industries lend themselves to mass customization in specific areas more than others.

Firms within the accounting industry, for example, compete to provide services at costs considered fair by the customer. As seen by the customer, the "product" may have limited customization. Even though the accounting firm may see it otherwise, many clients consider accounting services to be a more or less commoditized service they require for regulatory compliance and other reasons. However, accounting firms can find new and permissible ways to customize their services to create new value for both the firm and each client.

CUSTOMIZATION VERSUS STANDARDIZATION

Some of the main choices available to companies when mass customizing include customization of product, service or other auxiliary or augmented product dimensions, and communications. The principal combinations companies adopt may start with personalizing and customizing communication with the customer, then providing either customized service or product, before potentially customizing all dimensions. Three customization options are as follows:

1. Standard Product, Standard Service, Customized Communication
2. Standard Product, Customized Service, Customized Communication
3. Customized Product, Customized Service, Customized Communication

Obviously, as levels of customization increase, so too, does the cost of providing such benefits. To be profitable, these costs must be offset by increased customer value or reduced costs in other areas of the business.

Each of these options has different implications for customer bonding. The firm's best customers will be able to provide additional perspective on the implications for bonding and customer value, and should be consulted—most will appreciate the engagement. Additionally, each option will have cross-organizational impact, which the relationship marketer will need to manage in the context of each specific business. For example, while customized communications may be limited to the functions historically found in the marketing department, customization of service and product are far reaching, and would likely involve people from design, development, engineering, operations, customer service, installation, and so on. Where the implementation challenge is complex, multidimensional and cross-functional, the relationship marketer should adopt a team-based approach to implementation and would likely include senior staff from the affected functions. At a later date this may be less necessary if the organization is shaped according to the customers with which it collaborates and the processes it employs, rather than the functions it performs. Most organizations are not yet designed this way.

Companies customizing all three dimensions of product, service and communications will be expected to have the closest customer relationships and be most open to the customer, at every stage at which value is created for the customer. The other approaches to mass customization previously mentioned had more standard components to the business processes and technologies. There were fewer choices and combinations. Complete customization requires that virtually all investments link to customization and that the best customization engine of all—the human mind—be active at the customer interface, knowing what is possible, what can be made possible and how to help give the customer what each wants. Complete customization increases the complexity of the business and raises its scope of operations. It will require that suppliers and channel intermediaries themselves be integrated into the initiative and committed to the direction.

Complete customization is the most difficult to fully conceive and implement, and it is the most costly. But, precisely because it is difficult, opportunity remains in most industries to achieve advantage by adopting this approach. By expanding the array of options at the outset, rather than by providing an infinite customer choice, the company can manage its costs and progress without collapsing under the weight of change.

A MASS CUSTOMIZATION PLAN

A mass customization plan is a subset of a broader plan to manage customer relationships. The focus here is on what the organization intends to change about itself rather than how it plans to guide and manage the behaviors of individual customers.

When considering what to change about the company, an organization may ask itself a number of important questions, the answers to which may help to guide its strategies for mass customization. The following are among the key questions that might be asked in this regard.

How Much Mass Customization?

The costs of mass customization can be high. In order to manage these costs, an organization might establish an overarching vision for mass customization and then identify the specific steps to be taken to achieve the vision. That is, develop a plan for full mass customization, and then select specific modules for fast tracking. The best ones to choose will obviously be those most desired by customers and those which make the most significant competitive difference. Although customers may not see the full benefits of mass customization at once, over time the benefits will become apparent while making the costs manageable.

To illustrate this stepwise approach to mass customization implementation, suppose you made off-the-rack suits. Recognizing the retiring of baby boomers, declining interest in suits in general and witnessing how some are cramming themselves into too-tight trousers, would you not consider how best to produce suits in lot sizes of one instead of longer runs? Perhaps you would focus first on the processes for training and providing incentives to sales staff, ensuring that customers are sold on the benefits of made-to-measure, then getting customers measured, transmitting measurements to the plant, implementing technology to produce in unique runs and processes to ship suits back to customers quickly. Later, you might focus on opportunities to expand the range of fabrics, develop customer data warehouses, expand the range of clothing for which you will mass customize, develop a distribution outlet further afield, serving more remote stores, and so on. Such costs as these can wait.

In-Source or Outsource Each Component of Mass Customization?

Another consideration for managing costs is whether your firm should undertake the mass customization itself or if third parties, such as channel intermediaries and end-customers, have a role to play too. For example, in the computer industry, resellers provide customers with the computers they need as well as extended utility by assembling a total benefit bundle for the customer, integrating hardware, software, networking, delivery and installation and offering financing, service contracts, evergreen programs, repurchase of existing computers and training, among other non-product-related benefits.

Before deciding who will perform specific components of mass customization, a company could ask questions regarding four areas:

1. Customer Involved Directly
2. Customer Involved Indirectly
3. Custom or Standard
4. Supply Chain

Customer Involved Directly

Should the customer perceive that the product or service has been mass customized for him or her, or should he or she simply be delighted with the benefits he or she receives? If they are to perceive that customization has taken place, they will likely need to be involved in the customization process, requiring changes to technology and processes.

Customer Involved Indirectly

Customers need not be directly involved in customization. For example, a customer who checks into an hotel and is offered a non-smoking room on a low floor that doesn't overlook the parking lot may have received a customized service but may be oblivious to this customization. Companies need to decide whether to engage customers directly in customization for their benefit. If they decide to involve customers only indirectly, as in the previous example, companies need to engineer their processes to facilitate this indirect engagement.

Custom or Standard

Another decision a company needs to make is the extent to which customers will be allowed to customize. At one end of the spectrum, companies do not allow for any customization—they market a standard product, with standard services using pre-defined communications, whether one-way or bi-directional. The firm thus has three main arenas within which mass customization decisions need to be made, as follows:

- Product
- Service, and
- Communications.

The firm needs to decide if customers are to be allowed to make decisions about the components, modules (comprising components that have been aggregated into modules), sub-assemblies (of modules, possibly including components with modules), and assembled products. The company also needs to decide where to allow customers to customize each of these aspects. Customers could be engaged at any stage of the value chain, whether for conceiving products or services, or designing, developing and/or producing them. Companies need to decide whether to allow all or some of this customization to take place.

There are many different approaches to mass customization of products, well described in the literature. As suggested above, the basic concept often involves definition of modules that can be shared in different ways within mass-customized products. Modules may involve the sharing or swapping of components and they may be assembled to order from sub-modules and components.

The second arena within which companies make mass customization decisions relates to service. Service, by its very nature, offers many more options and alternatives for variability than do products and this is both a positive for the customer and a potential negative for the enterprise if not managed effectively, for costs can and usually do migrate toward solutions that are most variable and please most customers—but not necessarily shareholders. Companies can decide whether to offer standard services and to package them as such, or to allow for variable service elements such as the following:

- Auxiliary aspects of service, where supplemental help is needed by customers and for which they might decide to pay. For example, a customer might decide to buy a new car or home stereo and have the retailer install it—for an additional price.
- Augmented services that would have the effect of magnifying, increasing or extending existing services. Examples would be an extended warranty on a new home appliance, longer financing terms on the purchase of a computer, or out-of-hours support for maintenance and repair of an industrial installation such as air-conditioning, a boiler or plant controllers.
- Disaggregated services that allow customers to choose service providers, including, but not limited to, the company selling the goods. When buying a car, a customer might be steered to a recommended set of banks that provide vehicle financing, for example. A purchaser of an industrial installation could decide which firm is to provide after-market service, again subject to some input and management from the OEM (original equipment manufacturer).
- Non-conforming services that allow customers to depart materially from the services originally envisaged by the manufacturer without voiding manufacturer warranties. For example, some customers may want to "tune" their new cars with a variety of after-market products to enhance appearance and performance. A vehicle manufacturer might develop a list of approved suppliers who are trusted to provide non-conforming services that would still allow the non-replaced items to be warranted by the manufacturer. In another example, a customer might want a retailer to deliver furniture outside business-hours to a new residential condominium as this is the only time the elevators are available for moving, and the retailer would need to decide if it will cater to requests such as this and how such services might be provided.

Communications is a third arena within which mass customization should be considered and decisions taken in respect of the amount of variability that the enterprise will find acceptable and where and how this is to be managed. A number of chapters of this book have explored aspects of customer communications and engaging customers in a dialog that will lead to progressively and mutually deeper and more valuable relationships.

Supply Chain

The fourth area in which a company could make decisions that affect mass customization pertains to the supply chain and the potential for it to be disaggregated. Would customers and the company benefit from an approach to mass customization that involves disaggregating the supply chain so that, for example, different companies produce mass-customized components? Or should the primary creator of customer value remain in control of the total customized solution?

The historical view of production and supplying customers was called a "supply chain"—whereby suppliers operated according to a process described by Figure 23 once the standardized design and development processes had been completed.

A supply chain could be viewed as "inside out" thinking that sees the customer as the end-point of consumption of a more-or-less standardized

Figure 23: The Supply Chain

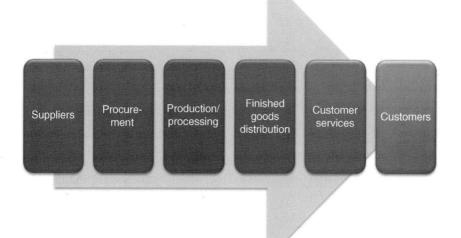

product. Mass customization calls for a rethinking of this process of creating value for customers because the process really starts with the customer, not with suppliers and manufacturers. It may be more accurate to think of the supply chain as a demand cycle that starts with the customer and then proceeds among some of the members of the chain of relationships, leading to goods being made to customer order rather than being built on spec or to fulfill production plans or targets.

Companies such as Nike, Apple and Dell have approached mass customization with a view to managing brand value as well as product and other value-creating processes such as those that enable quality. Even some vehicle assemblers have explored mass customization in a virtual environment, such as Volkswagen's truck and bus plant in Resende, Brazil (150 km from Rio de Janeiro), a 3.3 million square foot facility. There was initially just one Volkswagen employee in the entire place; other personnel are employed by suppliers that bought space in the plant to be in proximity to the other vendors' operations. Workers from companies such as Iochpe-Maxion, Meritor, Remon, Aethra Karmann-Ghia, Carese and Continental undertake production of parts for the chassis, suspension, axle, tires, wheels, seats and instrument panels and so on, and assemble the vehicles and paint them. Volkswagen owns the processes for vehicle manufacture and quality, and customer, dealer and supplier relationship management. And VW obviously owns the brand equity of VW. Beyond this, they may not need to own much more.

Mass Customization and Relationship Objectives

Without mass customization, or with too little, relationship objectives become challenging to achieve. On the other hand, with too much mass customization, the company may experience costs that are untenable, especially if they give the customer more value than the relationship warrants. The job of planning for more mass customization in a company should go to the head of a company's relationship marketing function, working in a multidisciplinary team to assess issues such as the following:

- Do our best customers want a mass-customized solution? Will they pay more for it? Will they pay more for it from us (how are we positioned with them)? How much more will they buy from us and our partners if we offer customized solutions for them?

- What are the key dimensions of the solution that must be mass customized, from the perspective of the customer?
- Will our existing capabilities—people, technology, knowledge/insight and processes—allow us to deliver the mass customization customers want? Do they have the right context, content, skills, flexibility, willingness, focus, structure? In particular, do we need a major makeover of the processes and technology in the company, from design/development, to production and onwards through the demand cycle? Do we expect any changes in customers' behaviors to make mass customization work effectively?
- How much will mass customization cost us, if anything? (Can we save money through mass customization?) Can we do mass customization in steps, according to what we can afford and what is necessary, rather than implementing a full-scale initiative at once? Will this initiative be economic, considering earlier questions regarding pricing, needs and incremental value?
- What do we have to change about ourselves to deliver the mass customization benefit? Will our existing organizational structure accommodate the change? Will our capital base? Will our culture? Do we have the leadership commitment? Importantly, is there a business case for the initiative?
- If we implement a mass customization initiative, what will be the competitors' response? How will we, in turn, respond?
- What are the barriers to exit if we implement a mass-customization initiative? What have we burned and what have we built by going down this road?

• • •

This chapter has discussed mass customization as an opportunity for providing value tailored to the individual customer. An approach to planning mass customization was reviewed and core elements discussed, including the four elements for customizing communications with each customer:

1. The environment within which communications are to occur
2. The degree of communications control that customers want and which the enterprise is prepared to provide
3. The sequence of communications that the company enables
4. The degree of collaboration that the company will allow

Mass customization, and customer management more generally, requires the support of both customers and stakeholders other than customers, as well. Stakeholder contribution to customer value is critical for relationship management to create new value for every stakeholder, including the chain of relationships with stakeholders such as investors/owners, boards of directors, management, employees, labor unions, bankers, knowledge capital suppliers (such as ad agencies and consultants), equipment suppliers, raw material and consumables suppliers, IT vendors, channel intermediaries, customers, media and political stakeholders.

Chapter 8
CUSTOMER ANALYTICS

"If you cannot measure it, you cannot improve it."
William Thomson, a.k.a. Lord Kelvin (1824–1907)

"In North Wales, from where I come, we measure a man from the chin up."
British Prime Minister David Lloyd George (1863–1945)

Chapter 3 discussed a process for customer engagement that included organizational sensing, understanding customers individually, interpreting this understanding and responding to each customer. This chapter focuses principally on the two cornerstones for engaging with customers and developing enduring relationships: understanding each customer and interpreting this understanding into solutions that customers value. Collectively, these cornerstones are called customer analytics and may be defined more generally as the processes by which companies use data and analysis to optimize customer engagement. To achieve this end, organizations do the following with a view to informing the development of customer-specific strategies, tactics and other factors that affect and advance relationships with customers:

- Sense customers' behaviors
- Learn from this sensing
- Frame questions, objectives or hypotheses
- Inform questions, hypotheses or potential strategies and tactics to the extent data permit the required analysis, predictions and optimizations

- Interpret their considerations into experiments or solutions using customer-specific knowledge
- Implement solutions or experiments, and
- Measure implementation outcomes and understand transaction and profitability results.

These elements are described in Figure 24. Customer analytics used to be thought of more narrowly as data mining but today customer analytics is generally considered to be a more widely applicable term that incorporates data mining as well as the surrounding processes that use information to add value to the customer. Customer analytics places the customer at the center of the analysis, while data mining suggests that data itself is more material than are customers. Customer analytics uses data to better understand each customer as an individual and predict what he or she may want next so that the enterprise can prepare to be of benefit and be seen to be of benefit in a meaningful way, leading to a progressively deeper relationship.

Figure 24: Customer Analytics

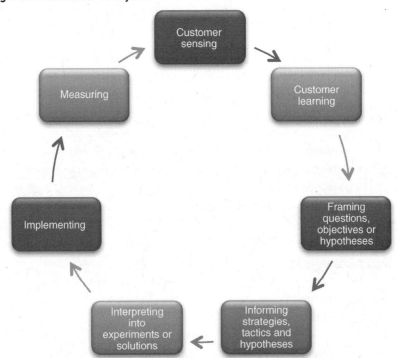

Organizations often find that the associations and other insight they develop from their data could not have been previously predicted. For example, one department store found from their data that it would be a good idea to place their cosmetics counters in proximity to their candy counters, in part because the shopper was the same person in both cases. By doing so, sales in both areas went up, leading the company to realize that the indulgent female shopper buying cosmetics might treat herself to candies if the opportunity was right at hand, but might not do so as a considered decision if the candy had to be sought out.

Increasingly, customer analytics is achieved in real time as organizations receive data describing customer interaction and transactions with the enterprise and use these data, combined with data already on file for both this customer and similarly profiled other customers, to predict what the focus customer will want and engage the customer on his or her terms as a result. In this way, customer analytics is increasingly becoming transparent to the customer and part of the very fabric of the organization's processes so that intelligent engagement is no longer surprising to the customer, but expected. Just as the customer benefits from this intelligence, so too does the enterprise, of course. For example, by being able to predict how customers are likely to behave under different scenarios, some cell phone companies cluster customers and seek to understand not only individual customers but the groups to which they belong so that the enterprise can take the actions it needs to reduce attrition.

Market researchers have long employed standardized processes to understand markets and market segments to guide their marketing strategies. Companies are now using customer researchers and new technologies to listen and develop data to inform and understand each individual customer so that engagement strategies can be tailored to each person. The following are some of the tools companies use to listen to customers:

- Call center conversations
- Customer complaints
- Customer councils
- Customer feedback to employees
- Customer focus groups
- Customer surveys
- Feedback or comments on website
- Online communities

- Real-time customer responses to online surveys or questions
- Snail mail
- Social media, and
- Suggestion cards.

Companies now know that customer-specific knowledge has a finite shelf life because the company has only so long to influence customers' behaviors before customers act, so the longer it takes the firm to put customer-specific knowledge to use, the less effective, relevant and influential the company is likely to become. If companies are to use customer analytics to create shareholder value, the data they derive for each individual customer must be relevant and sufficiently comprehensive that data interpretation is meaningful in the customer's context and sufficiently timely so that the data is fresh enough to be used. The closer the company comes to making all of this happen in real time, the more likely it is that solutions will be relevant to customers.

Amazon understands individual customers and uses a recommendation engine to provide real-time and relevant options for online customers to consider. Pandora's algorithms interpret individual customers' music preferences into a portfolio of music that each is likely to enjoy and usually does. By putting customer analytics to work in real time, companies such as these cater to customers, often before customers know that they would benefit from the proposed offer and, in the process, create less opportunity for competitors to enter into purchase decision-making. This chapter discusses key aspects for the application of customer analytics to advance customer relationships.

THE META IS THE MESSAGE

Customer analytics seeks to optimize organizational performance by developing data about people and putting these data to work in ways that benefit both customers and shareholders. Even while customers talk of the importance of privacy, they seem increasingly willing to share data about themselves, perhaps because some types of personal information seem less "private" than others. Additionally, companies that warehouse customer data in massive data mines have the power to gain deep insight into individual and collective behaviors. By putting these data to use with insight into individuals' interactions and transactions, companies can develop a picture of each person that is so comprehensive it has the potential to almost mirror the customer him or herself.

Some decades ago, Marshall McLuhan famously said, "the medium is the message"—and by that he meant that the channel of communication was more important than the content itself. In today's marketplace, it may be said that context trumps content and that this context needs to be developed into progressively higher levels of data abstraction to make sense of it. As a result, it might be said that the medium is no longer the message. Rather, metadata, which is data about data, now mirrors people, providing the ability to understand each among us and inform one another in areas such as history, perception, behavior and attitude. The potential exists to use metadata to predict what people will do next, often before they themselves know, and this is frequently done, as is discussed in this chapter. Seen this way, the *meta* might be said to be the message. Now, people become productized objects that the data describes and on which the data acts. As metadata mirrors people, each almost becomes an avatar in virtual reality, making hyper-reality—where meta-data augments physical presence in real time—not only plausible but quite likely. There are already indications that this augmentation is in our near future. Google's Project Glass makes conventional glasses into an interface device that observes, processes and augments environmental information such as temperature, a call or text. Data and images are projected onto the glasses just above the individual's sightline. Just as a device such as this can be applied for individual consumers, so too could it be applied in a retail context, for example. Here a cashier could use glasses such as these to engage more effectively with each individual customer, with customer intelligence enhancing the communication in real time and data being communicated to the cashier just above his or her sightline in the glasses.

Figure 25 observes that four elements are central to the message being meta. Relationships depend on organizations adding value to people in much the same way that they added value to products in previous eras. That is not to say that companies do not focus any longer on their products—of course they do. But now they focus equally on the data that helps them understand and interpret each customer. Seen this way, people become products about whom organizations seek to inform themselves so that they might engineer a stronger connection and a product that has more value. As organizations gather data about people, so too do they gather data about communications, including how people respond to offers, the media channels they prefer, what turns them on and what turns them off. These data are used to make each communication progressively more valuable and helpful and, in a genuine listening relationship, the communicator assumes the role of the recipient,

Figure 25: Meta Is the Message

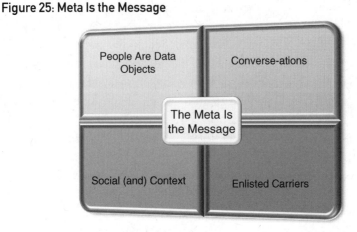

knowing in advance how the communications will be received. This type of conversation might be termed a "converse-ation" because of the converse roles that customer and enterprise perform as a result of conversation, becoming more connected and developing awareness and understanding of the other party. For example, understanding customers leads companies to predict customers' requirements, and the products and offers to which they will be most receptive, and suggests how to speak with each person. Customers used to undertake these roles but now companies do this as a matter of course. Customers decide price, location of product purchase and the specific components of value they choose to assemble in a product. These are roles that the company used to perform before converse-ations took place to determine the why, when, where, what and how of each transaction.

As noted previously, content is important but the context within which the customer finds him or herself is even more so, especially the social context. The enterprise uses customer data to shine a light on customers' social connections and context so that the firm knows the customers' group setting, both physical and virtual. As a result, the organization is better prepared to treat each customer not only according to the value that each represents, or even the future value that the customer might account for, but also the value of each customer's connections and the influence of customers over potential customers.

As the company understands each customer as an individual and as a member of the group, the enterprise is better able to use data to guide and inform customer communication and the communications that may serve to influence each person. Companies reach out to people who will carry their message, brand values and specific offers, and who will serve as decision-making influencers for other individuals. These are the carriers companies enlist to benefit the firm, customers and their constituencies. For example, a company might enlist a well-known blogger to review its new game or hardware product, knowing that this review will be seen by a number of identified customers in the company's prospect and current customer databases.

THE UPSIDE OF CUSTOMER ANALYTICS

Customer analytics has the power to deepen and extend relationships. Customers may rarely appreciate how companies put their data to use, offering them products they knew they wanted or perhaps products they didn't even know they wanted. Facebook, for instance, knows an enormous amount about its users. Beyond basic demographics such as age and gender, Facebook knows relationship status and contact information by e-mail and cell phone. From Timelines and geotagging of pictures, they know where people have been physically, and from Like buttons on other websites, also where people go virtually. From some mobile apps, Facebook can identify users' friends, birthdates, locations and Likes.[1] Perhaps surprisingly, information may also be collected from users even if their Like buttons are not pressed, which still provides Facebook with information about people's preferences in music, products and much else. From information such as this, Facebook is able to identify the songs most popular with people who enter a relationship or leave one. They are able to make informed guesses about the advertisements most likely to appeal to people in circumstances such as these and serve these ads up.[2] Users may not fully appreciate that the product or service that now seems so right for them was identified using social analytics methodologies and tools focused on creating relevance rather than "simply" responding to customers' needs.

One of the early pioneers in customer analytics was Harrah's, a gaming company with investments in hotels, resorts and casinos. In the mid-1990s, Harrah's recognized that they were probably not going to be successful competing with major casinos on the basis of property distinctiveness and features. Competitors such as Bellagio and others were spending over $1 billion to build single casinos; Harrah's properties at the time were much less expensive and somewhat depreciated. Harrah's perceived that an opportunity existed to compete on customer relationships and the guest experience, and chose to invest in customer data as a key capability to achieve this strategy. Harrah's was among the first companies in any industry to recognize that data can be a fundamental basis for competitive advantage. The most visible customer manifestation of the customer analytics process was the Harrah's Total Rewards loyalty card that was provided to guests. There were three levels to this card: gold, platinum and diamond. Guests' spending behavior led to credits being earned, tracked for each card and differential rewards being provided back to guests based on spending behavior and selected other behavioral considerations. Harrah's guests were offered benefits so that the right guests would receive the right incentives at the right times, sufficient to modify their behaviors accordingly. Harrah's also made sure the firm did not spend money on the wrong guests or even overspend on the right ones. Not only did Harrah's use these data to develop customer-specific initiatives that individuals would value, they used these data as an input into a plan to manage customer relationships more generally. This led to a number of actions, such as improving wait times in the lines that mattered most to customers, structuring reporting relationships so that properties were run by marketers rather than property managers, modifying how call centers and employees engaged with each customer, and so on. Although this initiative did not generate a significant number of new customers, it did dramatically increase per-customer revenue and profit. One of the main reasons for this success was the ability of Harrah's to select and serve spectacularly well a customer cluster that had previously not received much attention from the major casinos: the low-roller, i.e., the customer who spends relatively little. Harrah's was not only able to encourage and bring about repeated visits of low-rollers but also increased the number of visits customers made to other properties in the Harrah's chain.

This initiative worked so well because it wasn't an initiative at all. It wasn't a program, or a flavor of the month. It was a fundamental strategy of the enterprise, one to which the firm thoroughly committed itself and which it considered central to its business. Harrah's perceived the competitive opportunity inherent in relationships, understood that a relationship gap existed for a specific audience and put in place an affordable, cost-effective, customer-specific marketing initiative. The link between competitive advantage and customer analytics was evident as the firm began to use and rely on customer analytics as an important enabler of strategic change.[3] In an example such as this, it is clear that significant opportunities can exist for companies to change the competitive dynamics of an industry and improve their own performance using customer analytics as a linchpin for their strategic relationship plans.

There is a significant upside to be had from customer analytics but the upside should not benefit just the company. For customer analytics to achieve meaningful results, it must enable and add value to customers, too. Most customers want the enterprise to do something useful with the data they know the company has been collecting, perhaps because they signed up for a loyalty card or opted into permission marketing on the firm's website, say. Customers naturally appreciate it when they see a benefit from the provision of these data, like a complimentary upgrade to first class travel, a nicer suite or larger rental car, for example. And equally, customers wonder why some among the companies who serve them do so little with their data. Why would car retailers not use service data that shows who is spending a significant amount to repair old cars to help new car sales staff make productive sales calls, for example? Why would airlines not review travel patterns and make offers aligned with the patterns but with some expectation of behavioral change, such as going to the same destination a little more often? Data is gathered about so much in the lives of every person. It seems surprising that so many companies put their customer data to such limited use.

On the other hand, some companies do use customer data extensively and some among them do so in an intrusive way, not only by using these data for their own purposes but reselling it for others to use. Customers then get offers from companies with which they have little or no connection and can be surprised by the specificity of the offers or communication. For example, an insurance company might choose to purchase data profiles from a social media firm that the company then correlates with healthy people. Perhaps the insurance company has found that people who repetitively mentioned some form of exercise in their communications are less likely to experience certain kinds of maladies, such as depression, or are likely to live longer and this insight might lead them to tailor insurance to specific customer clusters. Customers who receive approaches for this insurance might find it to be extremely helpful but the potential also exists that some among them might find the approach to be perhaps a little too perfect and feel that they have been observed too closely. Activities of this type may sound a little far-fetched; they are not.

Customer analytics can not only make marketing more effective, it can also make it more efficient. For example, customer analytics can reduce some marketing costs, such as market research and pilot testing. Customer analytics helps replace market research with customer research. Customer analytics also enables organizations to formulate thoughtful experiments and hypotheses that they test in real time to help determine, for example, the validity of an hypothesis, which among options they are considering is best, and what would achieve highest financial return. Customer analytics can thus make expensive tests less costly but, even more importantly, it can also accelerate the outcome. One of the great benefits of customer analytics is that it helps organizations succeed faster. It also helps companies frame and test hypotheses that can help them to fail faster and take speedy corrective action. Customer analytics enables firms to know much quicker which customers, clusters and options are unlikely to be productive paths to a more profitable future.

PUTTING CUSTOMER ANALYTICS TO WORK

Every connection a company has with its customers provides a data point that can have a number of actions performed upon it after data capture, both after storage and in real time. The following are selected categories of analyses that companies may perform with customer data. More than one category may apply in specific circumstances. For example, a company may use both correlation and longitudinal analysis to develop the understanding they need. A brief discussion of each of these elements follows.

- Classification

    Customer data can be classified according to a variety of discriminating variables and factors such as group membership. For example, customers may be classified according to their demographics, transactions, interactions with the enterprise or lifetime profitability, a combination of these or other factors. One of the approaches companies use to develop this understanding is CHAID—short for CHi-squared Automatic Interaction Detection. CHAID enables companies to consider alternative approaches for grouping customers. It does so by exploring the interaction between variables over which the company typically has control (say, price and quantity) in relation to a variable the company does not directly control except through the other variables (say, profitable market segments).

- Aggregation

    The data may be aggregated with other data for a specific customer (data describing customers in a specific group or who match a given profile, for example), in order to inform specific questions or to derive estimates or interpretations that may not have been considered at the outset.

For example, the company might be seeking to understand whether certain behaviors are general in nature or are specific to given individuals. If they are general in nature, the company might want to understand the underlying drivers so that they can act upon these.

- Correlation

    The data may be used as a basis for interpreting consumer behavior as suggested by the preceding either for a specific individual or for a group. Interpretation may include data correlation, comparing data about which the company already has a deep understanding with data the company does not. From this action, inferences can be made regarding the unknown data set but correlation does not imply causation so care should be taken when making inferences based on correlations. For example, a company may be able to compare the dates on which a consumer buys with the products they buy and the known weather patterns should they wish to plan short-term advertising or one-to-one advertising based on the predicted weather, such as offers for snowblowers or trips to sunny destinations.

- Association

    The data may be used to determine if an association exists between the purchase of specific products and services. Imagine a situation where a retailer is considering asking suppliers to bundle some of its products, or if it is wondering whether to offer a service in addition to the product, such as installation services for the air-conditioners that it already sells. A supplier might use association data to cross-market its products with others that might be manufactured by complementary vendors. To illustrate, perhaps a manufacturer of hand tools uses data to understand that buyers of these tools also typically purchase a certain breakfast cereal, magazine or vitamin. Some of these associations might have been reasonably hypothesized previously but in many cases they would not have been. Some associations reveal certain consumers' conscious or unconscious thought processes.

- Prediction

    The data may be used to predict consumers' future behavior and likely needs, a most important use of customer analytics or perhaps even the main reason for using it. After all, if a company can position itself to sell when a customer is most likely to be ready to buy, it has an opportunity to create a monopoly position in the mind of the customer and further advance, extend and deepen the customer relationship. Prediction goes beyond this to include data modeling to understand customers who are most likely to buy, to leave the organization (e.g., "churn" in the cell phone industry), to attract more customers who are like the existing customer in some way, and so on. Companies use curve-fitting techniques (discussed next) and other approaches, including algorithms that employ Bayes' Theorem, which uses conditional probabilities, and Naïve Bayes, which multiplies probabilities of events or outcomes that are assumed to be independent for the purposes of modeling.[4] Other techniques include the Kaplan-Meier estimator for predicting customer survival and churn, and the CRISP-DM methodology for using databases to assess specific issues and options, and predict outcomes.[5]

- Curve fitting

    The data may be used for curve fitting to predict future results and behaviors, as suggested previously, but it may also be used to establish whether certain characteristics or rules might be inferred from the data. For example, data may be backcasted, the case when companies try to prove whether a predictive model works using historical data as the model output rather than using the data as input. Regression analysis seeks to understand the relationship between an independent variable such as purchase frequency, say, and a dependent variable such as customer profitability. Regression analysis may seek to fit a line to the data points as it looks for a so-called linear relationship between the data. Regression analysis may also apply non-linear curve fits in order to find a function that most closely approximates observed data.

- Clustering

    Organizations often use customer data to cluster their customers into behavioral groups within which customers are similar to one another to the extent that their behaviors are alike. For example, customers might be clustered according to the specific transactions in which they engaged, their responsiveness to offers, the frequency of visits to the store, frequency of missed payments on the store's credit card or the value they represent to the enterprise. Cluster analysis seeks to answer the questions: Which customers are similar and in what respect? Are they similar because of who they are, where they live, how they think, what they buy, how much they purchase, the value they represent to the enterprise, the reasons they have for buying what they do and not buying other things, and so on? Clustering is very different than segmentation although some of the same techniques, tools and approaches may be used. But behavioral analysis is more important for managing customer relationships, for reasons that have been discussed elsewhere in this book and below, and so clustering is more important than segmentation if customer behaviors are to be managed.

If customers within a group that has been clustered according to the similarity of their behaviors are then compared according to their demographics (or other non-behavioral bases for segmentation), they may be seen to be very different from one another demographically. It can sometimes come as quite a surprise when companies conduct focus groups with valuable behavioral clusters to better understand them and discover that these customers may be very different in terms of attributes such as age, gender, income and education. In much the same way that companies used to pay considerable attention to market segments in the era of mass and segment-based marketing, today companies are paying much more attention to behavioral clusters within which customers are grouped according to demonstrated behaviors such as their interactions and transactions with the enterprise. Segment-based marketing posits that the market segment ought to be understood *a priori* (i.e., in advance of purchase decision making) if the marketer is to achieve his or her marketing objectives. Cluster-based marketing posits instead that the outcomes of marketing ought to be the starting point for assessing inputs and that marketers should understand the factors that motivated people to behave similarly rather using traditional approaches to understand consumer behavior. In this way, companies are better able to understand what consumers do, why they do it, what they are likely to do next, why this might be the case and the nature of external inputs that consciously and unconsciously motivate consumers.

- Conjoint analysis

    Companies often want to understand customers' key purchase criteria and the relative importance of these criteria. Using conjoint analysis, customers may be provided with hypothetical or real options in an experimental design geared to understanding how customers rank specific attributes and rate currently available or proposed alternatives in respect of these attributes. Using this approach, companies assess the trade-offs customers make when considering a value bundle and this understanding can provide guidance for alternative strategic options. In the case of an auto manufacturer considering the costs and benefits of positioning its vehicles in terms of safety or fuel efficiency, this approach could help them decide how customers value safety and fuel efficiency and the inter-relationship between the two variables, if any. Conjoint analysis can also be used to model expected market performance of new products or services, among other benefits. Conjoint analysis is part of a series of systematic approaches used to assess customers' behaviors and to explain the trade-offs they make among competing preferences.

- Longitudinal analysis

   Longitudinal analysis means understanding how things change over time. Companies often want to understand individual and collective customer behaviors over an extended period. They may do this by designing experiments to track specific segments or behavioral clusters, or simply monitor individual customers' interactions and transactions to understand the nature and direction of behavioral change over time. Longitudinal analysis is often associated with correlations as previously discussed, such as the impact of specific levels of discounts on customer retention, development and lifetime value.

- A/B tests

   Many types of organizations and even politicians make extensive use of A/B tests to understand which between two of the options they are considering is the best way forward. This approach is done frequently when designing improvements in the online customer experience. Companies develop two or more solutions to the same problem and funnel online customers to the alternative solutions in order to measure the difference between outcomes, such as greater click-throughs, stickiness (i.e., keeping customers longer on the website) and increased expenditures. For example, President Obama's 2007/2008 fundraising initiatives made extensive use of A/B tests to decide how best to portray the candidate and raise money online. From this, the campaign learned that more online visitors clicked on the "Learn More" button than on "Sign Up," which led to increased donations. Similarly, a black-and-white photo of the Obama family was received better by visitors than a previously used image.[6] Companies such as Google, Amazon, Netflix and eBay are reportedly adherents of the A/B test method.[7] A/B tests have a number of advantages over previously used processes for deciding how to proceed. The most important among them is that test results are based on actual outcomes rather than what people perceive will likely drive results. Companies that used to make decisions based on the opinion of the most senior person in the room now use data to make decisions. They find that this results in alternatives being informed by reality, unclouded by opinion, independent of hierarchical points of view, with a reduced implementation risk. Data so used also makes the firm more welcoming of revolutionary changes as it takes calculated risks that lead to discontinuous, stepwise actions that are material departures from current practice rather than the more modest, evolutionary changes that used to characterize organizational decision making.

- Speech analytics

    In addition to understanding how customers behave and interact with an enterprise in a physical setting and online, companies are increasingly paying attention to what customers disclose verbally. Firms use speech analytics to help them make sense of customers' interactions with the call centers, especially. By analyzing what customers actually say rather than how the call center representative interprets this communication, companies are able to use speech analytics to identify root causes for specific problem areas, focus on process and personnel issues, and find ways to provide feedback and restitution that keep customers and deepen the relationship. CallMiner (callminer.com) and Nexidia (nexidia.com) are two somewhat different applications used for speech analytics. Among other activities, CallMiner analyzes speech that has been converted to text, tags a wide variety of types of content as well as evident emotion, and categorizes these data to facilitate analysis. Nexidia makes unstructured audio and video content searchable using a phonetic algorithm as the basis for identifying opportunities.

- Pricing analytics[8]

    Pricing, like other elements of the marketing mix, is variable and may be made specific to each customer or circumstance to the extent that technology allows and marketers permit. Many companies employ dynamic pricing to optimize their pricing to better manage issues that impact business and profit objectives. These issues include assessment and management of the following categories, for example:
    - Product or service characteristics such as the categorization of the item, and current and changing inventory levels
    - Purchase decision-making characteristics such as elasticity of demand and other demand characteristics which may include evaluation of issues such as the time of day or week, inventory levels, velocity of inventory turns, and response to offers

- Communications channels, including examining issues developed from, for example, Google AdWords, Facebook, Twitter and LinkedIn recommendations
- The competitive pricing environment
- Financial considerations such as unit profitability, product carrying cost and the cost of lost sales or out of stocks, and
- Factors that impact customer-specific purchase contexts, including customer profiling and clustering, purchase history, product or service interest and willingness to pay.

Companies use considerable customer analytics to facilitate pricing optimization but not all companies want to make their pricing variable. They are concerned about the cognitive dissonance customers might have if customers receive different prices at different times. Accordingly, some companies use aggregators or other methods of disposition to rid themselves of surplus inventory, whether airline seats, unsold car rentals or last year's fashion items that still remain in inventory. Examples of disposition channels can include firms such as Expedia, Priceline.com and eBay retailers. Pricing analytics is important because it not only helps companies to dispose of slow-moving or otherwise obsolete inventory but, more importantly and when effectively managed, helps the firm match supply and demand by helping to ensure that customers who are willing to buy, typically do make a purchase.

In addition, companies use a wide variety of other approaches, tools and techniques to extract information and insight from their databases, and to optimize the use of the data. These approaches include neural networks and rule induction that looks for rules that are implicit in data and which underpin logic or conditions, decision trees that describe alternative logic paths, and personalization and interaction management engines that manage behavior and serve content to individual customers.

Table 20 and Appendix A discuss software for customer analytics in areas such as those just discussed, as well as selected additional categories of solution such as anomaly detection, data visualization, discovery visualization, outliers, sequence analysis, social network analysis, text mining and Web analytics.

As companies deepen their customer understanding, they not only want to know why customers behave as they do but also why some customers do not behave as predicted. It used to be that any particularly revealing insight would depend largely on asking insightful questions—and this remains the

Table 20: Selected Social Analytics Companies, Solutions or Service Providers

Company (and Web addresses)	Description
BrandTweet Statistics (stats.brandtweet.com)	Helps companies understand issues such as the network of Twitter contacts that are most relevant to them, see who among their Twitter contacts are online at present, and review those who are posting the most Twitter links.
Brandwatch (brandwatch.com)	Identifies and organizes social media conversations so that clients can act upon the data. The firm crawls for relevant Web mentions which are analyzed for factors such as content, query matching, sentiment and topic extraction. Mentions are stored and indexed to facilitate client analysis.
Empire Avenue (empireavenue.com)	Offers approaches to help organizations expand their social media audiences and engage with new potential customers. They offer metrics to help companies better understand how they are succeeding with their social media initiatives.
HubSpot (hubspot.com)	Provides page-level analytics and other services to help companies improve customer conversion and other aspects of inbound marketing.
HootSuite (hootsuite.com)	Social media management to manage and measure social networks. As noted previously, the firm manages multiple social profiles, schedules messages and tweets, tracks brand mentions and analyzes social media traffic.
HowSociable (howsociable.com)	Measures the social presence of brands and the level of activity occurring around a brand.
Klout (klout.com)	An influential organization that provides a score to help companies assess the influence of their customers, an important area of consideration as discussed in Chapter 3.
PageLever (pagelever.com)	Social media monitoring to understand audiences, measure success, and optimize content. Includes page alerts and post tagging.
PeerIndex (peerindex.com)	Provides metrics on individuals' authority and influence in social media. The firm uses an algorithm to consider an individual's content recommendations to assess issues such as the knowledge a person has in a particular topic area and a person's authority when others comment on specific posts.
Trendrr (trendrr.tv)	Provides a solution to enable assessment of factors such as sentiment, demographics and influencers that affect sales and the changes in media and link attention so that companies can understand brand equity and other impacts.
TweetReach (tweetreach.com)	Gathers data to inform users of Twitter regarding the impact of their tweets (including hashtag, brand name or URL), such as the number of people who received each tweet and specifically who those people were.
Twitter Counter (twittercounter.com)	Statistics of Twitter usage. Provides widgets and buttons to add to blogs, websites or social network profiles.
Twitter Grader (tweet.grader.com)	Allows people to compare Twitter profiles with other users, also a measure of influence.

case but, as paradoxical as it sounds, customer analytics also offers an opportunity to develop revealing insight without formulating deeply thoughtful questions in advance of obtaining useful answers. How else would some supermarkets know that it's a good idea to locate the diapers in their stores close to the beer?

ONLINE CUSTOMER ANALYTICS

Increasingly, customers engage with enterprises online. Customer analytics makes extensive use of online data to benefit both the company and the customer. Companies make use of data, analysis and related services from organizations such as Google Analytics, Omniture, Webtrends, IBM Coremetrics, Yahoo, Quantcast, comScore, Facebook, Chartbeat, DoubleClick (by Google), StatCounter, ClickTracks, Nielsen and Crazy Egg to help them better understand their online customers and customer-related issues. These considerations can include the following:

- Blog mentions
- Bounce rates (the number of visitors to a site who saw only one page before leaving)
- Competitive intelligence (e.g., visitors' online behaviors gathered from their toolbars)
- Customer conversion rates (orders—or other desired behavioral outcomes— as a percentage of total unique visitors)
- Facebook Likes and Google+ interactions
- New visitors
- Online visits
- Page views
- Pay per click (PPC)
- Posts
- Search terms
- Sources of referral (i.e., from where the traffic comes)
- Stickiness (time spent on a page or site)
- Popularity of specific components of their Web content
- Profiles
- Repeat visitors
- Twitter mentions and retweets
- Unique visitors

- Web page and website abandonment and exit (from which page did they leave)
- Where on a web page customers click, and
- Other important custom variables specific to a given company.

Individually tailored advertising programs are also offered by some among the companies mentioned previously. Data about customers can be segmented or clustered almost instantaneously so that companies are better able to understand Web traffic, customer demographics, online behaviors, lifestyles and much more.

Some vendors refer to some of the online data and analysis provided by firms such as those mentioned as "clickstream" analysis. In general, the reader should interpret this term to mean online customer analytics. In addition to data of the type discussed here, companies use online surveys to engage their visitors in real time. Among the survey companies that provide such service are iPerceptions' 4Q Survey, which is a free online survey solution that asks questions such as the experience the customer had in visiting the site, the customer's main reasons for the visit, whether he or she accomplished the intended purpose in visiting the site and a number of other questions.[9] Companies such as Kampyle (kampyle.com) use online survey instruments and customer analytics to develop sales leads from customers who identify themselves as sales prospects.

There are literally hundreds of ways for companies to measure aspects of social media.[10] A number of books have been written on this subject. In *Social Media Metrics*,[11] Jim Sterne argues that all metrics should be aligned with objectives: either increasing revenue, lowering costs or improving customer satisfaction. Like advertising, reach and frequency are important considerations but with social media, reach doesn't necessarily translate into access, so influence is more important than the theoretical number of people who might have been exposed to the communications. Influence can be gauged in part by examining message multipliers such as the number of times a message has been retweeted.[12]

A number of organizations help companies to apply social media metrics to better understand their social media impact. Customer analytics in this arena is sometimes called social analytics and many companies provide services here, including those listed in Table 20. As the intent of this discussion or the chapter as a whole is not to inform a vendor or point-solution selection decision, the reader is referred for additional detail to the respective websites of companies such as these, should this be of interest. Any discussion of specific technology firms is necessarily never complete as companies come and go; the tables provided in this section are not intended to be comprehensive but rather indicative of the kinds of firms that occupy this space.

Companies such as the following offer broadly based social mention monitoring and other social media solutions:

- Alterian SM2 (alterian.com)
- Attensity (attensity.com)
- Collective Intellect by Oracle (oracle.com)
- Converseon Conversation Miner (converseon.com)
- Conversition (conversition.com)
- Cymfony by Visible Technologies (visibletechnologies.com)
- Cogito by Expert System (expertsystem.net)
- General Sentiment (generalsentiment.com)
- Heartbeat by Sysomos (sysomos.com)
- InsideView Sales Intelligence (insideview.com)
- Lithium (lithium.com)
- Radian6 Social Marketing Cloud by Salesforce (salesforce.com/socialmarketing)
- Scup by Direct Group (Brazil) (scup.com.br)
- Sprout Social (sproutsocial.com), and
- Telligent Systems (telligent.com)

In addition to the firms noted above, a number of other firms provide focused solutions in specific areas, such as Social Mention (socialmention.com), which provides social monitoring services and analysis, among other benefits and services.

CUSTOMER ANALYTICS SOFTWARE

Organizations use customer analytics software to discover meaning and for other purposes from their customer data, including the following applications:

- Anomaly detection
- Associations
- Classifications

- Clusters
- Data visualization
- Discovery visualization
- Outliers
- Regression
- Sequence analysis
- Social network analysis
- Text mining, and
- Web analytics.

Customer analytics software may be either open source (i.e., free) or commercial (i.e., available at a price). The most widely used open source software is R, used by nearly half of data miners.[13] R is a programming language and software environment that enables data miners to undertake statistical analysis as well as classification discovery, cluster discovery, regression discovery, association discovery, text mining, outlier discovery, data visualization, discovery visualization, sequence analysis, Web analytics and social network analysis.[14]

There are many providers of customer analytics software. Appendix A provides a selected list of companies that offer data mining software solutions. Solutions such as those mentioned have the potential to extract meaning from data and provide the firm with the insight it needs to engage each customer in a progressively deeper and more meaningful relationship. The potential also exists for companies to use the data ineffectively, possibly even leading to customer antipathy. As an example that shows the potential intrusiveness of data mining and predictive modeling and the downside of sensitive execution, the American mass merchandiser Target developed a "pregnancy prediction" score based on their analysis of a basket of goods purchased from the chain. The score included an estimate of a customer's due date and the retailer sent out coupons linked to pregnancy.[15] Some customers reportedly became irate. The father of a high school girl felt the retailer should not be sending out these coupons—until he discovered to his chagrin that his daughter was indeed pregnant. Now the retailer masks the communications by including non-targeted products with coupons for goods they suspect the customer will soon need. Some companies call this approach "dumbing down" communications so that it is less intrusive and less likely to impact negatively upon relationships.

CUSTOMER ANALYTICS AND THE CLOUD

"The cloud" refers to processing, application and storage capacity being available online. For the most part, users of the word "cloud" assume that data, applications, platforms and infrastructure in the cloud are external to their own computing environment and, as such, an individual would not need to manage or maintain anything that is resident there. Rather, users expect that this external cloud computing will provide them with what they need from computing on demand, more or less as expected from software as a service (or SaaS), or platform as a service (PaaS), other widely used terms that in some ways are partially descriptive of the all-encompassing term "cloud." Much of the data that companies need are already external to their enterprise, such as social media data that they want to better understand. As such, the cloud lends itself to customer analytics that are also in the cloud and which can be engaged in real time to understand social network sentiment, for example. Some enterprise solutions also integrate internal social networks and calendaring, among other functions, to facilitate collaboration and rapidly forming social networks as a requirement linked to listening and responding to customer sentiment in real time, among other benefits.[16] When companies already have their CRM databases external to the physical enterprise, as would be the case in using Salesforce, for instance, other tasks such as social listening, earned media analysis and CRM analytics and business process integration may best be accomplished by also using the CRM database vendor's tools in the cloud. Many companies that use the cloud for customer analytics and CRM report a cost advantage from so doing.

Increasingly, companies also consider that CRM in the cloud is potentially a new paradigm for customer engagement and social connectivity, with customers being part of the fabric of the technology and process infrastructure that firms implement as their CRM 3.0 initiative—a cloud-based environment in which the customer has control over many or all processes with which he or she can engage the enterprise.

Perhaps the issue is not as much where the analytics takes place—whether in the cloud or not—but *that* it takes place so that companies optimize the customer's experience with the enterprise at all available touch points. When asked, many customers say they don't perceive a competitive difference and this suggests opportunity remains for companies to use customer analytics to delight customers and create competitively superior customer value to advance profitability as in the case of Harrah's (as previously discussed).

NET PROMOTER SCORE

In a seminal article[17] and book,[18] Frederick Reichheld argued that the most important customer loyalty metric derives from a single question, now frequently called the "likelihood to recommend" question: "How likely is it that you would recommend Product X to a friend or colleague?" That is, rather than using a Customer Satisfaction Index that is derived from the weighting of responses to multiple questions, Reichheld proposes the use of this one question. Respondents answer from 0 to 10, where 0 is "not at all likely to recommend" and 10 is scored as "extremely likely to recommend." Customers considered promoters of the organization would score 9 and 10, while those who are viewed as detractors score up to 6. Those who score 7 and 8 are thought of as passively satisfied. The Net Promoter Score takes the percentage of customers who are promoters and subtracts from this the percentage of customers who are detractors. Customers who are passively satisfied are not included in the calculation. This calculation yields the Net Promoter Score, the one number a company needs to grow in order to increase its customer loyalty, according to Reichheld.

It may be observed that the Net Promoter Score is a *descriptive* calculation, not a *prescriptive* one. As such, it provides a view—an important one, but still a single snapshot—of customer loyalty at a particular point in time. It remains for each organization to establish how best to achieve an increase in the Net Promoter Score and for this companies may choose to turn to other tools, including those that help the organization understand why promoters are supportive of the organization and why detractors are not. Obviously, this can be established by asking customers open-ended questions. Companies can also be more rigorous by identifying each customer's or each segment's key purchase criteria and weighting these for their relative importance. This can be done based on customers' answers in response to questions or by inferring their responses based on customers' behaviors, although this is a less well-developed discipline. Company performance can be rated in a similar way, say, in response to questions. By combining these two assessments, an organization can arrive at an overall understanding of importance and

Figure 26: Assessing Criterion Importance and Company Performance

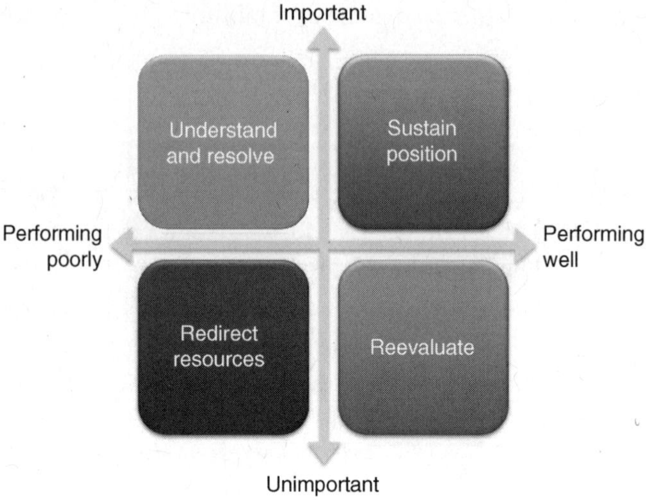

performance, leading to remedial action to sustain and improve customer and market position, as described in Figure 26.

• • •

This chapter has considered selected issues pertaining to the analysis of data that can serve to inform customer relationships and help the organization to better understand its customers. Most organizations can no longer rely on rules of thumb or ad hoc techniques to develop and sustain durable bonds with customers. Rather, companies will need to see data as a basis for creating new customer value, develop an approach to gather data across all customer touch points, derive insight from these data, and develop an ability to interpret data, ideally in real time. This chapter has reflected upon alternative ways of making effective use of customer data to engage customers on their terms, according to their drivers, in the context of their thought trains, behavior patterns and social networks. Specific point solutions were introduced in this chapter and also appear in Appendix A to help interested readers begin the process of considering aspects of software for customer analytics as needed.

Chapter 9
TEACHING CUSTOMERS NEW BEHAVIORS

"The learners themselves do not know what is learned to advantage until the knowledge which is the result of learning has found a place in the soul of each."

Plato, *Laws* (424–348 B.C.)

Change is accelerating. This occurs not only because technology makes change possible but because customers are rapid adopters, actively engaged with innovation rather than being bystanders or passive users. Customers see innovation, learn about it and play with it as they explore why it is in their interests to embrace the new and abandon the old. If consumers were not to change their usage behaviors, no amount of marketing would make an innovation succeed. Marketers could yell louder but it would be into the already deaf ears of consumers. Adoption of innovation and the very success of new products depend on the ability of marketers to change customers' behavior. This, in turn, depends on customers learning, and learning quickly, because if customers don't learn fast enough, innovation languishes, adoption is retarded and companies can perish if they haven't planned for a long adoption cycle. It happens all the time.

Customer learning isn't just about innovation. If customers are to adopt *any* product or service to substitute for what they now use, they will need to learn powerful reasons why. Learning requires teaching. Marketers must now act as customers' teachers if customers are to behave differently and as though customers are interdependent with innovators in one another's mutual interests, as indeed they are or could be.

Successful companies depend upon innovation in one or more dimensions to improve shareholder value. Some companies innovate with new products and services, some with process innovation or in their value chains, others with their business models, and so on—but most firms now realize that not innovating is equivalent to stagnation and stagnation leads to demise. By its very nature, innovation requires two things: an innovator, and what might be termed an "innovatee"—one or more people who embrace the output of the innovator at least once and, in all likelihood, repetitively, and may advocate for others to also welcome the change. The innovator, in this context, is the company that brings change to its customers and potential new customers. And the innovatee is the customer or prospect who is willing to consider and accept the change. If customers are to accept change, they must understand the nature of the change and, for this, they must be willing to learn.

The implications of the very concept of teaching customers new behaviors are many and include the following:

- Existing customer behaviors are somehow deficient and need to be changed
- The organization can identify new behaviors that would be mutually beneficial to both the company and the customer
- The organization can describe pedagogy that can, as an end result, migrate customer behaviors to those which the company has identified as being desirable
- Customers are willing to learn and be taught, and
- Customers see it to be in their interest and are willing to embrace new behaviors.

The following engages these topics by first reflecting on existing customer behaviors, innovation in the context of customers' learning, then pedagogy and customer learning.[1] The chapter concludes with a consideration of teaching customers by entertaining them. Who said learning couldn't be fun?

WHAT'S WRONG WITH EXISTING CUSTOMER BEHAVIORS?

A discussion centered on the changing of customers' behaviors may have the premise that there is something wrong with the existing customer behaviors. There may not be. Customers may be very content to continue their existing purchase behaviors and the enterprise might be very happy with this continuance. Some companies have found the path to making frequent changes and having customers embrace these changes as often as they occur. Companies such as Apple and Harley-Davidson are among the companies that have been particularly successful with new products and other innovations. Firms such as these have benefited from customers who find it easy to learn the benefits and applications of those new products quickly, to find out how the products work, and to share what they have learned with friends. The fact that such a small percentage of new products succeed (more than 95 percent do not) underlines the importance of teaching customers and finding ways to advance customer learning. A product introduced according to the traditional marketing model called AIDA—which stands for Awareness, Interest, Desire, Action—may not succeed if the Interest phase is not accompanied by teaching. Interest is not self-evident or self-generated, except for the most obvious of need-satisfying solutions. Who would be interested in a new smartphone if customers did not learn why the old phone paled in comparison to the new one? Any product that is somewhat different than current offerings or that requires engaging a customer in consumption or usage which is technological to some extent will require teaching that leads to interest.

There simply are not that many companies that have focused on teaching customers new behaviors as part of a plan for innovation, the very essence of growing a business in these fast-moving times. There are few markets that are so mature, with industry structures so entrenched and static, where innovation is so unnecessary that existing customer behaviors can proceed indefinitely without changing. Just as novelty enhances customer relationships if there is value sharing, so static conditions depreciate relationships. Companies that are not changing at the speed of possibility and customer willingness to learn and embrace change are conceding opportunities to their competitors. It is only change that makes relationships durable for, as discussed earlier in this book, relationships are all about novelty and mutuality—that is, innovating and value sharing—and without these two central elements, relationships erode over time. Change requires, among much else, customer engagement. Engaged customers are willing to learn and be taught and, importantly, are willing to be taught by the company, which they may see directly or implicitly as a trustworthy teacher.

In successful innovation after successful innovation, consumers have learned what the provider wanted them to know. They were willing to leave their investments in old products behind as well as the knowledge inherent in the previous solutions as they embraced new alternatives. Think about any Apple product you have ever owned. Consider what you had to change about yourself and your own behaviors in order to leave the old behind and embrace the new. Apple's pedagogy—the art and science of teaching—is resident in its very products. Their products are typically very different from anything else available or in use. The products are also beneficial to the user, simple, intuitive and easy to use, and look good and provide a stimulating initial experience. Apple is excellent when it comes to creating product awareness, a necessary first step to changing customers' behaviors. Although I have consulted with Apple, I have no firsthand knowledge as to whether or not they have pedagogy on their innovation agenda, but the layout of Apple's stores and the simplicity of the customer interface and user experience suggests they do. Companies such as Apple often have someone on staff who focuses on the user experience, human factors and ergonomics, for example, but not something as important as teaching. Most companies do not teach customers—they let customers learn of their own accord, at their own pace and with uncertain learning outcomes. It is no wonder that so much innovation does not succeed.

So what is wrong with customer behaviors? Maybe nothing today—and maybe everything in the course of time. Every market is materially affected by change eventually and every company innovates at some point to lead the change or respond to it. As already mentioned, change requires the collaboration of two parties, both company and customer. While companies can choose to learn at whatever pace they like, delayed response by customers opens windows for competitors and may render innovation completely valueless. There is a window of opportunity for innovation and profit can only be made for that time. Slow adoption by customers—adoption that is impeded by a lack of knowledge—narrows the window and lowers the potential profitability that can be realized from innovation. That customers can and must be taught should therefore be evident to any innovator. The question is "what method of teaching would be thorough, fast and effective?" Now that customers target companies more than companies target them, how should companies go about teaching their customers and potential customers?

PEDAGOGY AND TEACHING CUSTOMERS

Marketers need teaching strategies that help customers learn but few companies have the processes, structures and roles to develop and guide the correct use of teaching strategies. Pedagogy applied to customer learning can correct this shortcoming as part of innovation planning. This pedagogy would involve creating and reinforcing new customer behaviors and extinguishing old patterns of behaviors that are no longer required or even dysfunctional from the company's perspective. For example, Research in Motion (RIM), the creator of the BlackBerry, may not have been thinking in terms of pedagogy when it innovated its BlackBerry mobile communications device but it certainly achieved most of the desired outcomes of consumer learning. The interface was intuitive, the multiple benefits self-evident, especially for e-mail, the package enticingly small compared to the alternatives then available and the firm's dealers well trained to teach potential customers. So complete was the intrinsic reinforcement and social approval that consumers called their BlackBerrys "crackberries" for some years, likening their benign addiction to the device to a far more destructive one. Even the marketing muscles of previously entrenched and deep-pocketed competitors were, for a time, unable to shake RIM's hold on this market, again summoning up the analogy of marketers yelling to deaf consumers. In time, Apple's iPhones demonstrated how consumer convergence appliances could reimagine the nature of communications, outstripping the prevailing strategic thinking of RIM and other competitors in this regard, and teaching customers another set of new behaviors.

Traditional approaches to educating customers rely primarily upon cognitive marketing principles according to which buyers' behaviors derive from their attitudes, which are in turn formed by perceptions. Accordingly, most companies focus on managing customers' perceptions as the gateway to influencing their behaviors. That is, according to cognitive marketing principles, the pathway to purchase is accelerated when marketers create desired perceptions by initiating one of the following in the context of customers' values, motivations and beliefs:

- Communicating product or service benefits effectively, such as by advertising the selling propositions of a laundry detergent
- Creating a context within which the product or service is to be used (examples include lifestyle and celebrity advertising), and
- Positioning the brand, product or service to emphasize how it differs from competitors' with respect of one or more key purchase criteria.

Many marketers have found that traditional marketing principles no longer work as well as they once did. As noted previously, there are a number of reasons for this decline, including the increasingly rapid pace of change associated with product introductions and discontinuations, the individualization of markets that have made them customer-specific, and the social connections that have transformed the nature of marketing communications. Marketers used to think in terms of three key objectives in their marketing: informing, reminding and persuading, and their communications plans typically employed the AIDA model as mentioned previously, as they used mass media or segment-based media to reach out to achieve their communications objectives. It can take a long time to influence customers in the traditional way just described and time is no longer on the side of innovators. Innovation is simply occurring too quickly; every product seems to have a short life cycle and a shortened window of opportunity, as mentioned before.

Consider for example the FLY Pentop Computer from LeapFrog, a California-based developer of multimedia learning platforms and related content and learning toys. This computerized pen, when used with special paper and software, assisted students with subjects such as math, spelling and geography. LeapFrog achieved a complex solution by innovating in both the product and ancillary requirements such as the paper, and complementary products such as software, while also launching the total pen/software/paper solution to consumers and the distribution channels. There was not much evidence that children learned why they should quickly put away their calculators, dictionaries and maps and embrace the LeapFrog solution set. Apparently the device took time to learn, wasn't intuitive and had some bugs. This became a gee-whiz technology in a world not short on devices to compete for consumers' time, attention and wallet share. Adoption of the FLY wasn't quick enough to ensure ongoing success and manufacturing of the product ceased in 2009, about five years after being introduced. It would seem that LeapFrog needed to teach kids new behaviors, and parents too. LeapFrog may also have experienced a challenge motivating retailers. After FLY was launched, it took about a year for the product to appear in stores.[2]

Pedagogy varies according to whether marketers consider that an emotional, cognitive, behavioral or individual/social model—or some combination of these, such as social behavioral models—best describes customers' learning behaviors. Mention was made previously of the AIDA model (for Awareness, Interest, Desire and Action) that advertisers use. Although cognitive models such as this have merit for advertising and may serve to inform and thus teach customers to some extent, they are insufficient for fully describing options for teaching customers. Figure 27 provides taxonomy for alternative pedagogies, with a hierarchy implied.

Figure 27: Emotional/Affective,[3] Cognitive,[4] Behavioral[5] and Individual/Social[6] Pedagogy

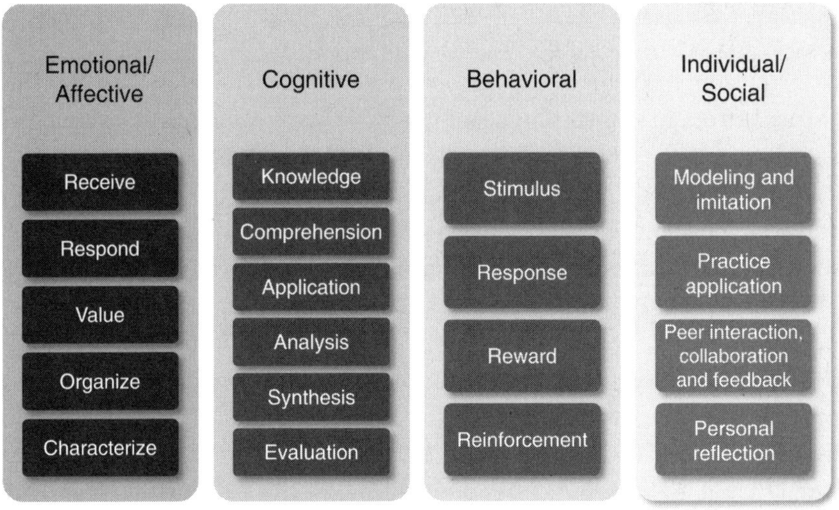

Emotional/ Affective	Cognitive	Behavioral	Individual/ Social
Receive	Knowledge	Stimulus	Modeling and imitation
Respond	Comprehension	Response	Practice application
Value	Application		
	Analysis	Reward	Peer interaction, collaboration and feedback
Organize	Synthesis		
Characterize	Evaluation	Reinforcement	Personal reflection

The first-mentioned competencies or outcomes should generally be achieved before those mentioned next within the construct of a specific model noted in Figure 27.

All models have a place when it comes to teaching customers new behaviors, as discussed next.

EMOTIONAL/AFFECTIVE PEDAGOGY

Emotional (also known as the affective domain) pedagogy requires, as a precondition, that customers have empathy and receptivity to new ideas and solutions. A well-satisfied or emotionally unavailable customer will not be as open to behavior modification as a dissatisfied but emotionally available customer. An early challenge for a marketer employing this model is to connect emotionally with the customer, posit a problem and offer a solution, thereby simultaneously creating dissatisfaction and dissonance to extinguish inappropriate behaviors while creating new and desirable ones. While it is necessary that customers have empathy for the teacher and willingness to engage the content to be taught, it's at least equally necessary that the company have empathy and respect for its pupils, its customers.

The following is a hypothetical example: Toyota could conceivably identify owners of older models of gas-guzzling eight-cylinder cars as potential targets for their hybrid, fuel-efficient Prius vehicles. The challenge for Toyota would then be to determine the emotional availability and information receptivity of this customer cluster. Research could be conducted to understand how this cluster learns emotionally and cognitively, perhaps exploring issues such as valuable content, authority figures and the development of learning communities. If developing a learning community, Toyota might message this cluster and seek a response to the emotional and behavioral signals the company sends, generally one small step at a time. That is, there should be evidence of an emotional connection, not just behavioral compliance. Consumers need to value the information they receive and put it in the context of their beliefs, motivations and values. Continuing with the hypothetical example of a learning community, could Toyota create an online Green Club of and for current Prius owners that potential owners could approach directly to listen to and learn from? Depending upon how this cluster learns, such an approach might help consumers embrace the Toyota vision of "green," and accommodate Toyota's approach as personal characteristics within their very being, helping to further improve Toyota's brand equity. In this case, Toyota may have little to do with the actual teaching other than setting up the initial community and driving traffic to it, if you'll excuse the pun.

COGNITIVE PEDAGOGY

If we look at customer learning through a cognitive pedagogy lens, consumers would need to know that an innovation had been created before they could understand it fully. This corresponds in part with the A in the AIDA model—Awareness. More than this, if the customer is to have knowledge about a possible solution, he or she should have sufficient mastery and recall of the subject matter to be able to comprehend and appreciate the potential benefits to be had from the innovation. To illustrate: just a few years ago customers did not understand the importance of carbon dioxide emissions, so innovations that reduced such emissions did not achieve much success at that time. Once the customer has knowledge of and can comprehend the importance of the innovation, the customer must be able to appreciate how to put the innovation to use. This is where the marketer has an important role to play in communicating, demonstrating and otherwise teaching how the innovation can solve customers' problems. Then customers can analyze their observations and perceptions of meaning, and synthesize the recently acquired understanding with existing knowledge to create a new, integrated whole. Finally, customers are in a position to make a reasoned choice.

Companies that adopt this approach to teaching customers new behaviors often seek to maximize the sensation by which customers engage with their products and services, and the company as a whole, while minimizing the intellectual load expected of each individual customer, giving customers one fact at a time, presenting customers with one thought per sentence or paragraph, and organizing thought trains very carefully so that the customers are nodding in agreement as they proceed through the process of being trained.

BEHAVIORAL PEDAGOGY

Behavioral pedagogy considers how to reinforce desired behaviors using the so-called stimulus response model. In this regard, the name Pavlov rings a bell for many marketers. Ivan Pavlov (1849–1936) was a Russian psychologist, physician and physiologist who taught dogs to salivate on command. The work of the American psychologist B.F. Skinner (1904–1990) is also of interest to behavioral marketers. Skinner developed the operant conditioning model whereby he demonstrated that people learn to modify their initial behaviors depending on the success of behavioral outcomes. Many marketers subscribe to these theories of learning to reinforce existing behaviors. For example, a soft drink company might show a hot desert scene in in-theatre advertising, stimulating an exodus of patrons to the concessions to satisfy their thirst. In another example, loyalty programs that give customers points for their purchases are essentially mechanisms that reinforce and stimulate similar behavior, much as medals motivate athletes and soldiers, and reinforce their performance. Marketers generally use price to change undesirable behaviors, as some banks do when they charge customers more for service within the branch in order to steer customers to the ATMs. As in this example, unlearning is important if Luddite behaviors are to be extinguished. Unlearning remains among the hardest of tasks for marketers to conceive and master with sensitivity and effectiveness.

Companies focused on this approach to pedagogy pay particular attention to presentation of facts, and the design, observation and measurement of outcomes. Feedback is provided frequently to help ensure that customers are appropriately reinforced.

INDIVIDUAL/SOCIAL PEDAGOGY

Modeling and Imitation

This book has already noted the importance of the individual in the context of his or her social environment and using this understanding to influence the individual and his or her connections. We have seen that customers want to simultaneously fit in and stand out from their peers, an apparent paradox that marketers ought to bear in mind to tailor simultaneous appeals to both interests. That is the general context, but it applies also to customer learning in that customers learn both individually and from their peers, and often their motives are the same—to fit in and stand out at the same time. Customers teach one another and, in the process of doing this, learn themselves. In both cases, customers and potential customers can be taught by the enterprise to teach one another and to personally benefit from the experience. Consider the case of a preferred customer provided with a market-ready version of a product soon to be released. Perhaps the customer is taught in a hands-on way, in a simulation or virtually, such as through a YouTube video, how to use the product. Or perhaps the customer has demonstrated through prior behaviors, such as purchases, statements to peers or interaction with the company, that he or she can learn how to use this particular product or service easily. If the customer now puts the product to use in a setting where peers can observe this firsthand, the potential exists for these peers to model the same behavior, leading to imitation by their friends and, by ongoing repetition, marketplace penetration.

The potential also exists for each individual to perceive innovation, application, brand and environment uniquely and situationally such that it is specific to the individual. Each person forms his or her own constructs of the world based on the experience and prior learning of a lifetime. These constructs are most often very different person to person, yet every opportunity to learn has to be situated within an individual's own constructs and models, either bypassing or integrating with his or her filters of the world, and so that each can make sense of what is being witnessed before putting this understanding to use. In the process, individuals convert apparent randomness into orderly design in such a way that it makes sense to them, and, in doing so, it's quite likely that this order would not be as comprehensible to another. That is why individual constructs are so important. This is also the reason why companies ought to engage with these constructs as they conceive what it means to teach customers new behaviors by helping them to personalize information and the usage experience, and convert both the information and experience into a personal, comprehensible activity. This activity needs to align and fit with who each person thinks he or she is, the projection of the individual into his or her environment, and what each person feels excited to embrace going forward.

There has been much discussion of Apple in this book. Not to dwell on this firm, but part of Apple's genius has been to make standard solutions fully comprehensible to each individual, easily learned and taught, fitting within multiple reference frames, with highly personal usage and social acceptance experiences.

Practice and Application

Some customers might be inclined to discontinue their use of a product after a brief initial trial, in part perhaps because it is difficult to use or some other reason. A customer helped through this process may be more inclined to continue its use and, by practicing, derive ongoing benefits. Many people believe that adults learn best through doing. By putting products to use, by finding practical application, perhaps as envisaged initially by the company but more importantly as each person thinks is best, products and services find their way into the fabric of life of an individual. Then, through each person, the individual introduces his or her network of friends and colleagues to the benefits as he or she perceives them. Each person who receives a communication is more likely to embrace the message because of the trust placed in the communicator, the customer's understanding of each recipient and the usage context. It is for reasons such as these that the company needs to develop a following that will carry the message and become ambassadors for the brand.

Companies can foster practice. When a kitchenware company sets up a demonstration at a retailer, they might put their products on display. A good sign that I once saw in such a setting said, "Please touch." When car companies invite potential customers to go on a test drive, they are also providing a hands-on experience. But don't send the salesperson with the customer. Let him or her learn on individual terms. Let each feel trusted. Unless, of course, the company perceives that customers are not to be trusted—then there would be more work to do before customers can ever be taught anything. When a company does not trust its customers, customers can sense this and are more likely not to trust the company and not to listen, and are therefore unlikely to learn.

Peer Interaction, Collaboration and Feedback

Customers, like anybody, need interaction and reinforcement from peers. They need to collaborate with them to see whether and how best to use any innovation, especially those that are fraught with social and other risks. Should I really buy this new skateboard? What will my friends think of the style, design, ergonomics, technology and how it handles? Before some early adopters could face down stares of friends, they might need to know answers to questions such as these. Answers will come from peer group interaction and collaboration. It will also come from their feedback.

Customers, like any pupils, need ongoing feedback in order to adopt and continue engagement. Companies can engineer their products to invite not only individual engagement but peer group sharing so that feedback leads to reinforcement. Opportunities for feedback can of course be engineered directly into a product or service, such as via an error message that might be prompted if a customer tries to do something that a software product, say, wasn't designed for. The feedback can also be performed in non–real time—such as by collecting data from the device and providing occasional feedback to the user, online or offline. As an example of the latter, Roche Pharmaceuticals markets Xenical, a branded gastrointestinal lipase inhibitor that prevents the dietary absorption of some fat. When the firm used nurses as call center agents to engage with Xenical users online and to develop healthful habits with customers, providing feedback on their activities, customers continued to use the product longer than customers who were not so engaged, leading to healthful benefits for customers and financial benefits for the company.

Personal Reflection

Customers who think about their purchase and usage experiences are more likely to think positively about the company, especially if the company can guide customers' thinking. This is why individual surveys can be vastly more important than simply obtaining information from individual customers. Surveys can perform the more subtle role of helping each customer to reflect on his or her constructs and expectations, models and filters, by asking thoughtful questions that will help someone engage much more deeply than simply asking about the "likelihood to recommend" or another standard question. Thoughtful questions might be considered longitudinally and in an open-ended manner, such as, "why did you buy this product in the first place?", "why did you not buy it sooner?", and so on. Each individual can be encouraged to think about him or herself first by encouraging self-assessment using high-level archetypes from appropriate modeling or classification systems, such as the Myers-Briggs Type Indicator (MBTI) psychometric assessment, which helps to classify a person's personality type, strengths and preferences. Obviously an entire questionnaire cannot be used but the intent might be to understand if each type of person—INTJ,[7] for example—thinks, feels, buys and interacts with the product differently. More importantly, each person can be asked a revealing question to help him or her reflect more deeply and imaginatively on his or her own so that each reaches a more informed conclusion of a personal nature. For example, is someone more likely to see him or herself as guided by conscious perceptions or unconscious ones, or focused more on the logic that enables objectives or the logic that is inherent in a situation? If a company wanted to engage customers' unconscious perceptions, symbolism in the product and communications may be as or more important than the overt communication of features and benefits. A customer who needs to see how the logic of the solution will help him or her reach personal objectives will need to interact differently with the communications, product or service than a person who needs to see the "big picture" context. In short, companies focused on this pedagogy model would pay attention to the possible engineering of individual connections and direct and indirect engagement (such as customers using products or services hands-on) differently and in a planned manner according to the typology of each individual.

In the previous example that discussed Roche Pharmaceuticals' marketing of Xenical, the firm might help individuals achieve positive results from behavioral change by understanding the nature of personalized communication, especially how information is received, processed and integrated into personal models. Should the company focus on logic and objective-setting for health goals, such as weight loss, or social aspects, such as the intrinsic and peer acceptance benefits of losing weight? Perhaps a company such as this could consider creating opportunities for reflection such as surveys that individuals can self-administer, forums and blogs for customers to share results and reinforce one another, and reinforcement by the company itself. The latter could include recognition of an individual's learning, progression and assistance, providing tangible and/or intangible rewards, and, by asking the customer for additional help, engaging him or her on an important next challenge. In short, there are many opportunities for companies to consider their goods and services in the context of customer learning; as with the management of almost all change, it starts with a plan.

DEVELOPING PEDAGOGY FOR TEACHING CUSTOMERS

Corporate pedagogy for teaching customers needs explicit treatment in a formal plan that ought to recognize the interaction between the company's own innovation process and objective-setting in two dimensions, as follows:

1. Customer learning capabilities
2. The engagement of social networks for one-through-one marketing and prospect development more generally

Figure 28 suggests that the company's innovation process ought to engage customer learning and customers' social networks.

Market success that depends on the behavioral change of customers requires that the behavioral innovation of customers occur simultaneously with, or lag only slightly behind, the product and service innovation of the enterprise. By linking customers' learning capabilities with the innovation process, each aspect of innovation could potentially interact with an element of customer learning. For example, the design phase of innovation might be used to assure the company that customers have sufficient knowledge to use

Figure 28: Innovation Process, Customers' Learning and Social Network Engagement

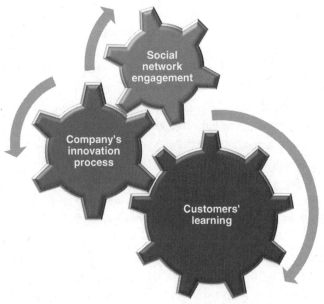

the product's interface. The development phase of the innovation process might be used to create, among early adopters, customer knowledge and comprehension through sampling or test-marketing. Apple has long been particularly astute not only in developing eye-popping, simple designs but in understanding how to make it easy for customers to use technologies that were previously regarded as too complex for the average consumer to use. The very earliest Macs, as well as the iPod, iPhone, iPad and Mac OS, are cases in point. Press a button—hear music. Press another button—surf the Internet. And so on. Apple makes its products very simple to use so that customers need little or no training to use each device.

Having identified objectives for the customers' learning capabilities, companies can consider and optimize the various touch points by which customers connect to the company, as they go through their purchasing and consumption lifetime. That is, companies can determine how learning objectives are to be achieved through the various channels of connection such as advertising, the Internet, call centers, direct mail, installation, personal sales and invoicing. Table 21 provides a framework for companies to consider the development of pedagogy for each potential interaction between the enterprise's innovation process and the customers' learning process, or those specific intersections that make sense in the context of a specific business. This table suggests that customer learning comprises six main phases: knowledge, comprehension, application, analysis, synthesis and evaluation. This is one model for customer learning, the cognitive model, as discussed previously. The company might develop pedagogy to ensure interaction with each of these phases of customer learning, causing each aspect of its innovation process to reflect upon the

Table 21: Pedagogy for Each Intersection of Innovation and Customer Learning

Innovation Process	Customer Learning					
	Knowledge	Comprehension	Application	Analysis	Synthesis	Evaluation
Conceive						
Design						
Develop						
Produce						
Distribute						
Market						
Sell						
Service						

potential for customer engagement and collaboration. For example, what is the enterprise doing right now to engage customers in the conception of a new product or service? What knowledge do customers need to have and what do they need to understand about the company's product development process and how to have input into it?

LEARNING RELATIONSHIPS

Companies that have adopted CRM strategies and technologies usually seek to create and maintain a learning relationship with individual customers. If they achieve their goals, these companies typically understand individual customers well enough to predict their future needs and know when the customer is likely to be ready to buy so that they can position themselves to sell. When customers give a company an opportunity to learn, companies ought to seize that opportunity, retain the information, add value to it and be ready to use it in future. For example, the customer using an automated teller machine to withdraw money is giving the bank information about his or her withdrawal patterns, information the bank can use to predict future use for both the individual, that specific machine, the bank branch, various services and the IT infrastructure more generally. Not only does this provide an opportunity to accelerate customer service and be more relevant to each individual customer, the bank can save money by cutting wait times, possibly reducing the number of machines it needs, and so on. Why wouldn't all banks simply tailor their options to the customer's last withdrawal, say, asking if the customer wants the same amount he or she took out last time?

The previous chapter considered customer analytics and aspects of predictive modeling as a basis for learning about customers and developing a relationship that grows progressively more meaningful as companies put customer-specific data to work. It should be noted, however, that customer analytics and predictive modeling can be employed without developing a learning relationship, or at least a relationship where both company and customer learn about one another and progressively teach one another in ways that are both overt and transparent. A relationship absent this progression ultimately depreciates past achievements, perhaps a major transaction or a good feeling about the enterprise. For any relationship to thrive, something new has to be learned and put into play in a way that will be appreciated and in a way that value can be derived and shared.

There is a major difference between education and indoctrination, just as there is between listening and advertising.[8] In this one-to-one world of customer engagement, where listening, interaction and dialog have replaced the "buy me, buy me" entreaties of advertising, the teacher—whether the enterprise or the customer—ought to seek out one-to-one connections, exchange new ideas and find ways to both talk and hear, listen and apply, anticipate and predict, and expect progressively more from one another. Certainly, the company sending out coupons for customers to use on their birthdays is showing early evidence of an interest in developing a learning relationship. But the company that does only this has necessarily limited itself to first-order opportunities and cannot reasonably expect to drive significant shareholder value from such basic outreach.

BEST PEDAGOGY PRACTICES

Whichever model of pedagogy is adopted—whether emotional/affective, cognitive, behavioral, individual/social or a combination of these or others— a company must achieve behavioral change for the investment in customer learning to pay out. There are many perspectives on motivating customers to learn and engaging each on individual, personal terms. Based on consulting experience when conducting assignments to help firms in respect of customer learning, the following are selected observations that might be termed best practices. It may be better to call these "thoughts for consideration" as "best practices" suggests that all practices are known and the best have been selected from among them. That would not be the case for most best-practices engagements and it is not the case here, either.

In addition, as with any best-practice consideration, whether or not a given practice ought to be adopted by a specific company would depend very much on individual circumstances, objectives, budget and experience, among other considerations. With that as a qualifier, the following could be considered by companies exploring how to teach customers new behaviors:

1. Plans

    Plans determine customer learning and behavioral outcomes, so have a teaching plan at the outset of innovation planning.

    - Keep customers, customer learning and the process for teaching customers and having them learn in continual focus.

- Have a perspective of pedagogy that serves as a touchstone and is employed throughout the plan.
- Be clear about what you want customers to know and how you want them to behave. That is, what metric will you use to assess a successful outcome at the end of a planning horizon, say, one year?
- Apply pedagogy to each element of the innovation process so that the customer is engaged throughout.
- Ensure that the plan has appropriate levels of funding to support its intent, whether enhancing innovation, incorporating the customer into changed innovation processes, content development and enhancement, and upgrades for ongoing and refreshment costs of technology and content.
- Integrate customer learning objectives with metrics and assessments to ensure that customer behaviors do change as intended.
- Employ feedback into the planning process to incorporate learnings from the above-mentioned assessment.

2. Implementation considerations
    - Limit barriers to customer learning. Make capabilities available for free wherever possible and help customers train one another in forums, blogs and testimonials, for example. Do not charge for individual courses in Web-based training.
    - Pilot test everything possible. If using an online user interface, employ A/B tests, or pilot test options if not. The options need not be limited to product options—they could include service options and process alternatives, including considerations that deal with points of contact with the enterprise.
    - Provide adequate support such as via telephone and e-mail, and ensure that standards for customer engagement are in place and are delivered.
    - Use a development team comprising personnel with multidisciplinary knowledge of, for example, customer behavior, content, technology and human resources.
    - Ensure that there are opportunities for customers to engage with human beings as well as with technology from the enterprise so that they obtain a more complete experience and can engage on multiple levels.
    - Do not repurpose content used for other purposes in order to teach customers new behaviors. Start with a clean sheet of paper and design

everything to reflect the desired objectives in the context of pedagogy and plan elements noted above and earlier in this chapter.

- In general, and except for companies that operate exclusively online, the Internet does not determine all aspects of customer learning outcomes. More generally, technology is a tool and should not drive customer teaching decisions. Customer knowledge transfer and opportunities to engage with and between customers should make use of the enabling characteristics of specific technologies.
- Use simulations and interactive questions to provide opportunities for the customer to engage new concepts, teach the enterprise about him or herself and reflect on aspects of the purchase, use and adoption experience, for example.
- Use subject matter experts to assist with each aspect of plan design and plan implementation.

FROM TEACHING TO ADDICTING

As has been discussed, companies can and do teach customers new behaviors. In the extreme, some companies also want to make "addicts" out of their consumers by providing them with products or services so compelling that consumers will want to repeat the experience again and again and again ...

THE CONSUMER AS A FUNCTIONAL ADDICT

"Addict" is defined as follows: "v. Devote or apply habitually or compulsively ... n. A person addicted to a habit ..."[9] In other words, addiction need not be limited to potentially destructive arenas such as drugs or alcohol, for example, but applies equally to any behavior that becomes habitual and, for reasons known or unknown, is repeated. In other words, addiction may apply equally to arenas that are constructive or value-neutral. Constructive arenas could include an habitual focus on self-improvement and the needs of others, such as habitually volunteering to help the less fortunate, for example. Those that might be deemed from a societal point of view to be neither excessively constructive nor destructive might include habitual timeliness, cleanliness, tidiness and respect for authority.

Considered this way, customer loyalty may be said to be a form of addiction, if a very mild one in most cases, and one which, because of its mildness and limited consequence, is not demanding of change—at least not because society ought to demand this change. (Competitors may want to change this behavior but only to replace one manifestation of addiction with another—their products!) Extremely loyal customers may be said to be addicted to a brand. To see what this form of addiction means, just try to take away someone's iPhone, Wii or Harley-Davidson. The reaction may be not dissimilar from trying to wean someone from drugs or alcohol. Addictive behavior considers how companies create, reinforce and sustain behavior in customers sufficient that these customers want to repeat their behaviors and it is this repetition that comprises addiction.

Addicting Rewards

Addiction starts with rewards to which consumers just cannot say, "no." The rewards may be intrinsic or extrinsic. Intrinsic rewards are those that integrate or resonate with innate or natural elements of a person's psyche and cognition. Extrinsic rewards are those that focus principally on an individual's behavior, and factors external to the person. An example of intrinsic rewards may occur when a game player becomes hyper-stimulated as a result of a game speeding up and providing more threats and rewards as the person progresses through different levels. The game player continues the game because he or she derives direct enjoyment from it and sees the game as an end in itself. An example of extrinsic rewards includes providing consumers with points as they accomplish tasks or spend more. The points may be convertible for goods or services, or may simply allow individuals to display their accomplishment for others to see, as will be discussed shortly. When people modify their behaviors to achieve more points, and do this repetitively while rationalizing their behaviors, they may be converting extrinsic rewards into intrinsic ones. Thus, by repetitively working on behavioral change so that behaviors are changed, companies can, over time, also modify cognition. People eventually comprehend and integrate what it is they do, even if this requires some rationalization, as mentioned. In short, companies do not need to go through perceptions and attitudes to modify consumers' behaviors—they can work on behaviors directly.

Behaviors have the potential to become habitual when consumers are rewarded and derive pleasure from their behaviors. The superego (the "policeman" in Freud's perspectives on what governs consciousness), helps channel behaviors into socially approved outlets. Historically, rewards consumers derived were from the consumption of goods and services to satisfy a consumer need. For example, if the consumer's plates were not clean, Brand X dishwashing detergent might promise to get them so. By using Brand X dishwashing detergent, the dishes would be cleaned, the problem would go away, the consumer would be rewarded, and the pattern of behavior would likely repeat. Loyalty programs established a parallel value system whereby consumers would be given points or other rewards redeemable for similar or different goods and services. By creating an abstract value system operating in parallel with the core benefits delivered by the focus product or service, the consumer has the potential to be rewarded in more than one dimension. Loyalty points are one example of a parallel value system. Loyalty points are more or less like sugar in coffee—they provide more than one reason to consume a product, creating reinforcements that Skinnerian psychologists would call operant conditioning.

There are many forms of operant conditioning that form parallel value systems to the benefits inherent in a good or service. Beyond the perceived intangibles that companies have long been seeking to build, parallel value systems may offer rewards such as those described in Table 22.

Table 22: Rewards and Operant Conditioning

Maslow's Need Hierarchy	Category of Reward	Examples
Self-actualization	Spontaneous experience	Points to travel, unexpected pathway to proceed to a higher level in a game, prize awards for being the nth customer
Esteem	Status and respect of peers— e.g., restricted access or items in short supply	Backstage passes to rock concerts provided to frequent or high-volume consumers
Friendship and love	Friendship	Quantifying friends (such as counting Facebook friends), even though the quality of the friendships may be variable
Safety and security	Protecting health, person or assets	Points to convert into need-satisfying goods or services that make a consumer feel safer, e.g., Nike+, a sports community that enables individuals to set, track and share sports goals, potentially a healthful outcome
Physiological	Few rewards programs operate at this level	

New Media and Addictive Behavior

New media in general and games in particular have created additional opportunities for reinforcement to reward behavior and seek its repetition. Many of the hours previously spent watching television are now used for new media and games playing. To recognize this, marketers are thinking out of the (TV) box to engage games players and provide them with short-term stimuli and longer-term recognition and rewards.

Loyalty programs have long provided consumers with opportunities to collect points that let them fly somewhere or buy additional products. Now it is common for virtual environments to provide consumers with opportunities to collect points that are redeemable for virtual rewards—rewards that are more or less without value. Companies such as 7-Eleven, JetBlue, H&M and Tesla Motors and brands such as Olay, Travel Channel, Green Giant and Microsoft Windows have employed virtual games to help achieve their marketing communications objectives.[10] Game players may obtain points by visiting properties in a virtual space and the points are used within a game such as MyTown or FarmVille. Sometimes the motivation for collecting the points is simply to improve one's score or elevate one's status within a game for all to see. Adherents to Maslow's needs hierarchy could perceive a social need being met here as people collect points so that others see and appreciate their considerable efforts. It is also possible that motivating behaviors go beyond this. Some people may feel that they derive intrinsic rewards from these point-collecting behaviors, such as feeling better about themselves from accomplishment in a virtual arena, a possible compensation and an offset for not being able to achieve as much in the physical world. By providing leader boards so that game players can see their status, games reinforce point-collecting habituation.

Points programs have long used a version of leader boards to differentiate their customers. The highest mileage travelers on airlines receive higher rewards for their accumulated points to recognize their importance to the airline and travelers are provided with physical manifestations of their points standing, such as luggage tags that serve to communicate their status to other travelers. While there is potential for virtual points to be perceived as valueless, they do have the near-term benefit of modifying behavior—after all, consumers do play these games and collect points from so doing, and the results can be rewarding for enterprises as brand equity improves and as behaviors are internalized from virtual worlds, creating the potential for new or modified behaviors in the physical one. Virtual games can also be used for education, leading to the teaching of new behaviors. For example, Tesla Motors offers potential customers an opportunity to answer quiz questions in exchange for points, potentially leading to more product-informed consumers purchasing Tesla cars.[11]

In their book, *Game-Based Marketing*, Gabe Zichermann and Joselin Linder note that games played with consumers tend to have a number of key components that provide consumers with status and levels, points, rules and demonstrability.[12] Status and levels refers to an ability to display achievement outwardly. Points provide a scorekeeping system and basis for comparison. Rules provide a mechanism for proceeding through the game or system. Demonstrability allows people to demonstrate their accomplishment and status. Zichermann has further noted that the main categories of reward offered to consumers may be described by the acronym SAPS, which stands for Status, Access, Power and Stuff. He considers that cash rewards can be overrated in part because they can turn users off if the rewards are not rapidly seen as good ones, and that they do not motivate consumers better than chance would.[13] Perhaps so, but price still remains a key weapon in the marketer's arsenal, especially when it comes to changing behaviors, as discussed next.

Using Price to Teach Consumers

If consumers are to learn, they need to be provided with an opportunity to act, to use, to apply, to taste, to test, to make mistakes and to see for themselves. It can be that simple—and that difficult—for marketers to teach consumers. If you want adults to embrace your product, service or solution, give them an opportunity to try it out. Put it in their hands and encourage use in a safe, risk-free way. Marketers have long used samples to encourage free trial to start the change of consumers' behaviors, typically for consumer non-durables such as soap, razors and breakfast cereals. Trial, these marketers reason, leads to evaluation and evaluation leads to adoption of a new offer. This interrupts existing behaviors and creates new ones. Coupons can perform much the same function as samples, although coupons most typically provide a discount and thus an incentive for the consumer to switch or try a new or competitive product. However, the consumer usually still needs to pay something with the coupon and this makes the purchase decision still not without some risk to the consumer.

This raises the subject of "free." If consumers need material incentives to change behaviors, if they need an opportunity to try something out, if they are to entrench new behaviors, why not give them an opportunity to use the product for nothing? In this, the absence of any price functions as a positive reinforcer, a reward for spending time to assess the product or service. The only problem with giving things away for free is that, rather than the goods or services themselves, an absence of price has the potential to become the reinforcer of behaviors. People then seek things out for nothing. That is, reinforcement occurs in an inverse sequence because the reinforcer needs to follow the desired behavior. Even though there is potential that the pursuit of free becomes the reinforced behavior, behaviors will have been modified with repetitive use of the free goods or services. This leads to adoption nonetheless.

In addition to giving away goods for free, marketers have long given away information and ancillary products, such as T-shirts. In his book *Free* (which isn't), author Chris Anderson recounts how Jell-O was selling poorly at the start of the 20th century but all that changed after free recipe books were given to consumers showing them how to use Jell-O together with custard and other toppings to make it a tasty dessert.[14] In the company's first 25 years, it printed and distributed about 250 million cookbooks door-to-door, making it one of the largest consumer education initiatives in the pre-TV era; it was an important reason for Jell-O's marketplace success.

The so-called freemium business model is now widely used by many companies seeking to change consumer behavior. A product or service is given away at little or no price for the consumer to try. If the consumer wants an enhanced version or additional features, this is sold. This model is widely used for the sale of apps such as from the Apple App Store. It is also used in various forms for the sale of cable TV, cellular services and so on, with low initial prices used to change behaviors and then prices escalate as behaviors become entrenched.

Giving things away for nothing obviously doesn't mean that the company doesn't expect to earn a profit at some point. Customer acquisition carries with it a cost and companies plan this acquisition cost as part of their marketing plans. These plans are enabled by a fundamental truth that applies in many businesses today: fixed and indirect costs are much more material than direct costs. Often this means that the cost of producing an incremental item—the $n+1$ unit—is almost nothing anyway so the company's profitability will not be materially harmed by giving away some incremental units. Software, telephone services, airlines, hotels, car rentals, banking services, movies, music and many others have cost structures that are skewed toward high fixed costs with proportionally lower variable costs. It costs a lot to develop a software application but, once developed, the cost of producing one is proportionally quite small.

In some cases, where high initial or one-time costs can be regarded as sunk and written off when incurred, there can be even more incentive to give away goods or services to penetrate markets and gain customer share, especially if there is an expectation that customers' behavioral changes will drive improvements in business profitability in the medium term. Most companies think that three to six months is a reasonable horizon for behavioral changes that are initiated by giveaways or steep discounts to become entrenched. Some firms use contracts to enforce this perspective, such as cell phone contracts that escalate after three months with egregious escape clauses. Such approaches may be profitable and may sustain businesses in the near term but run counter to the concept of relationship development. Over time, approaches such as these lead to consumer disengagement. Rather than having customers love the company for what it is and what it does, customers become disenchanted and are more likely to switch at the end of a contract period. This leads to accelerating churn of customers and companies continually giving away their goods or services to attract new customers rather than keeping the ones they already have by using business practices focused on sustaining relationships.

In the previous example, companies offset the free or low price of a good or service with the expectation that future sales to the same consumer will subsidize the initial acquisition cost. There are other forms of offsets that companies use to make free possible. The following describes some of the main forms of offsets, arranged alphabetically (not in order of importance):

- Attention

   Just as marketers used to use the interruption model of advertising—where consumers would have their free viewing of a television program interrupted in exchange for watching an advertisement—marketers today provide free online viewing or product or service discounts in exchange for watching an online ad, for example.

- Bundling

    Bundling of goods and services into a discounted group or even a promotion such as BOGO (buy one, get one) is a form of offset, but different in the sense that a number of products and services are grouped together to provide a discount for all of them. Bundling has the additional benefit to companies—and disadvantage to consumers—of creating barriers to switching because consumers would experience an increase in costs of their remaining goods or services if they switched away from one.

- Customers

    Companies will frequently give away or discount their products or services if consumers attract new customers to the company or even if they help in the possible attraction of these customers. This is the basis of the "Friends and Family" promotions used by a number of retailers, cell phone companies and others. In some cases, per-customer incentives are provided and this can lead consumers to obtain a good or service for less than nothing—they are paid for the privilege.

- Financing terms

    Financing terms often offset the purchase price, for example, monthly payments that are waived for a few months at the front end of a long-term vehicle lease. A variant of this is the mail-in-rebate (MIR), where companies obtain the consumer's money now in exchange for information and a rebate later.

- Information

    Companies may seek something other than money in exchange for providing a product or service without charge. Information is most commonly sought, e.g., information about the customer, the product or the purchase experience. Starbucks might say, "Tell us how we did today and we'll give you a coupon for a free coffee."

- Money

    Some companies create their own money as part of their business model and to offset the cost of entry or customer attraction. Real cash is paid in exchange for virtual cash in some games. On YoVille, a customer would use Yocash to buy a kitty, say; on FarmVille, Farm Cash or Facebook Credits are used to buy things as players cultivate their farms, buy animals and harvest crops and trees.

- Points

  This chapter has discussed parallel value systems such as points and how these are used to stimulate primary demand one consumer at a time. Points are obtained by consumers in exchange for their purchase behaviors and these points are exchanged for goods and services, sometimes when these would otherwise have gone unsold or unused, such as hotel rooms in non-peak periods.

- Product upgrades and virtual "things"

  Companies often use revenues from premium versions of a product to enable the less well featured products to be given away. This frequently occurs in the software application sector. Rovio Entertainment's well-known Angry Birds game is provided for free, for example, but customers pay if they want a Mighty Eagle or an ad-free version. Apps that take people into virtual worlds often provide the game or experience at low or modest cost but charge for digital enhancements, such as a special digital weapon in an online war game or an animal in Zynga's well-known FarmVille game.

- Recycling

  Consumers may be encouraged to repurchase by taking back their end-of-life products, partially used or recyclable products in trade for discounted new ones. Taking back end-of-life products to provide a discount or to secure the next sale requires that the company establish a reverse distribution channel, one that takes goods out of markets rather than supplies them to markets.

- Systems, collectibles, samples and comps

  Companies subsidize the sale of one product in order to achieve sales of other ones, especially when the product that is given away is part of a system that would benefit from the use of other products. An example is giving away razors to make money on the blades, something Gillette has done in the past. Some manufacturers of computer printers have a variant of this model, with the printers being sold below cost in order to make money on the toner.

Another variant of the system is the collectible, where consumer behavior is triggered by beginning a collection sequence, with early goods given away, discounted or bundled to secure ongoing sales of later ones by the collector. Supermarket encyclopedias used to use this approach and current examples are to be found for companies such as Pandora when collecting charms, e.g., purchasing three charms might give the buyer a color cord for free.

Samples are of course also a well-known approach to stimulate trial and adoption, and examples are to be found in many consumer goods industries.

Complimentary products are also often given away to stimulate trial and change behaviors when the desired relationship is a valuable one and the cost of the product is modest in relation to the value of the relationship. This can occur when the incremental cost of the item is low or the asset is a wasted one without use, e.g., seats on airlines or at concerts, long-distance telephone time, out-of-season or low-period car rentals and hotel rooms, etc.

- Time

  In the previously mentioned example, where a company gives away or steeply discounts its product or service in order to secure future business, current sales are being offset by future ones. Time is being used as an offset. Any form of sampling would serve as an example here.

- Work

  Companies exchange work a consumer does for something the consumer is likely to value, or as a requirement such as to log-in to a website, for example. In the latter regard, consumers often complete two codes (called "captcha" codes) prior to logging into a secure area of a website. One code is required for security and authentication. The other serves to provide the company with an accurate conversion of an image into text. This is free work that the consumer does, helping the company make text readable where machines have already tried unsuccessfully.

It has long been said that there is no such thing as a free lunch. There is a cost to everything a person chooses to use. The only question is what each person is prepared to give in order to get. In the case of free, what a person is

Figure 29: Pricing and Offsets

prepared to give—at least for now—isn't money, but it may be other things, as suggested by the above discussion, summarized in Figure 29.

The Perils of Price Reductions

In the preceding section, some of the benefits associated with teaching customers new behaviors through price reductions and even by giving products away for free were discussed. Price reductions have, as an implicit assumption, a requirement that volumes will increase to offset the price reduction or that the lifetime value of customers will increase. Ideally the price reduction would be offset in its entirety through volume lifts or customer value increases, or at least any price reduction would be affordable. It is helpful to consider just how much of a volume increase is required when prices are reduced. It is often much more than companies perceive. Figure 30 provides iso-profit curves for specific percentages of variable

Figure 30: Iso-Profit Curves[15]

**Percentage volume must increase for profit to remain unchanged
when reducing prices**
Curves based on variable cost (VC) as percentage of original selling price (SP)

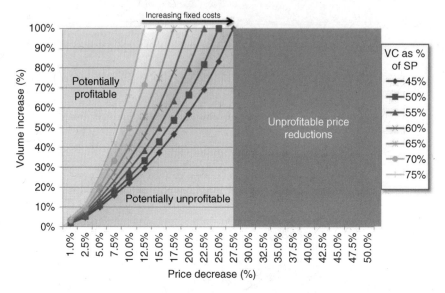

costs. Each curve shows the volume increase that a company would need to sell for a given price decrease if profits are to remain the same. The company needs to arrive at a judgment as to whether they could likely sell more than the curve suggests is a minimum requirement for their specific business. For example, assume a company has a business model with variable costs that comprise 55 percent of selling prices today. In this case, if the company were to reduce its prices tomorrow by 15 percent it would need to achieve a 50 percent volume increase over a comparable period for its profits to remain unchanged. Given market and competitive conditions, most firms would find such an increase very difficult to accomplish. The area under each curve is a zone where profits will likely go down for a given price decrease while the region above each curve indicates a zone of increased profit potential.

Figure 30 also suggests that price increases above about 28 percent will generally result in a profitability decrease unless a firm is able to more than double its sales, depending on the firm's cost structure. This would usually be very difficult to accomplish. Because the potential exists for price reductions to also reduce profitability, any organization attempting to change customer's behaviors through price alone should consider doing so only if one or more of the following conditions can be met:

1. Price reductions can be applied to only to a small percentage of the company's total potential customer base
2. Prices can be reduced for a brief period of time after which prices go up again
3. Costs are cut before prices are reduced
4. Changes are made to the company's business model as part of the price reduction

Figure 30 also suggests that companies with high fixed costs as a percentage of their total cost structure (comprising fixed and variable costs) would generally benefit more from price reductions because a given price reduction requires a lower level of sales increase to cover the profitability decline from the price reduction. For example, a company with 55 percent fixed costs (45 percent variable costs) would need to increase revenues by about 22 percent if it reduced its prices by 10 percent. A company with 25 percent fixed costs (75 percent variable costs) would need to increase revenues by about 67 percent for the same price reduction of 10 percent. That is, companies that have higher variable costs as a percentage of their total cost structure would generally need to sell more for a given price reduction than those firms having variable costs that are a lower percentage of total costs.

Just cutting prices without any limitations or changing any other aspect of the business has the potential to put profitability at risk. Figure 30, as well as related considerations for the volume decreases a company can sustain when increasing price, has implications that go beyond teaching customers new behaviors; this subject matter engages the issue of competitive advantage and other aspects of business strategy.

● ● ●

This chapter has reflected upon the importance of teaching customers new behaviors, particularly when it comes to new products or services. Innovation demands that customers embrace the new products and to do this, they must learn. Customers can either learn themselves or they can be taught and, for this, companies need to plan pedagogy. The plan might be based on one or more of four main pedagogical approaches: emotional/affective, cognitive, behavioral and individual/social pedagogy. This chapter discussed each of these and selected implications for helping customers to learn.

Best practice companies understand that customer learning can be considered a vital element and perhaps the key aspect of customer loyalty because the customer who learns with the company is more likely to bond with that firm, trust that firm, be early to try and forgiving of mistakes. These firms see that customer knowledge should be regarded as learning capital—necessary to earn out the lifetime value of customers.

The chapter discussed addictive behaviors in consumers and considered a number of rewards for modifying consumer behaviors,[16] using new media and even games as learning environments and no or low prices to introduce customers to new products and services, and begin the process of behavioral change. Companies ought to reduce their prices with care because of the potential profit impact. A price/volume sensitivity analysis should precede setting of price.

This chapter did not explore the ethics of addicting consumers. Certainly, there are many examples all around us of companies that offer ancillary benefits. As manifested in law, there is no quarrel with most parallel value systems but you will obviously make your own judgment on this matter.

Chapter 10
CASE STUDIES: MAKING IT HAPPEN

"The secret of education lies in respecting the pupil."
Ralph Waldo Emerson (1803–1882)

This chapter discusses a number of cases from the private and public sectors in the United States, Canada and the United Kingdom that serve to illustrate selected principles that have been reviewed in preceding chapters. The cases are presented as they stand, complete in the sense that they reflect actual practice within these organizations and serve to illustrate key principles in the book, including social media outreach—one-through-one—and teaching new behaviors to existing customers. These cases have been selected because they reflect leading-edge practice in one or more dimensions, in some cases of a pioneering nature as organizations identified and addressed new customers and new customer relationships. Conversely, the cases were not selected to illustrate the completeness of every aspect associated with the management of stakeholder behaviors in each organization. Cases for organizations are reviewed, in alphabetical order, as follows:

- Dell
- Leicester City—National Health Service, United Kingdom
- New York City—Health and Human Services
- TransGaming, and
- TransLink.

DELL[1]

Background

Dell is obviously a well-known computer and computer systems company. This case focuses on one of Dell's lines of business—the firm's provision of cloud-based medical archives that enable healthcare organizations to improve and accelerate processes for diagnosing and treating disease. Dell works with multiple categories of stakeholders, including medical practitioners, radiologists and other healthcare professionals, healthcare organizations, governments, and providers of software and imaging solutions. In order to manage the end-customer relationship, Dell needs to manage relationships with multiple relationship categories. This case provides an overview of how Dell accomplishes this objective.

A quick introduction to Dell's medical archives business: Dell provides on-premise storage and cloud-based medical archives—a unified clinical archive—that seeks to improve the retention, management, communication, sharing and collaboration of healthcare images required by medical professionals in the diagnosis and treatment of disease. Now medical professionals can access and share images wherever they might be, whatever handheld or other image access devices they might be using and whatever imaging modalities might be transmitted, such as x-rays, CT and MRI, patient files, images and reports.

Partners

Dell collaborates with technology partners to bring a comprehensive solution to customers and acts as the voice of the customer to its partner community, while simultaneously being a consultant to end-customers, framing for them what it is that technology makes possible. In so doing, Dell performs three main supplier roles: of knowledge, technology solutions and integration services. Dell's sales organization has responsibility for relationship management with end-users such as radiologists and the healthcare IT community. Subject matter experts support relationship managers by providing information to facilitate consultative engagement with end-users. Dell situates itself between different categories of stakeholders to manage information flows to ensure that the end-customers' needs are met and the solution delivered using a combination of Dell hardware and solutions, and those from external partners. Dell sees itself functioning at the fulcrum of stakeholder relationships and technology, acting to inform an environment in which end-customers generally know that change is required.

Innovative Solutions

It is becoming increasingly clear to customers that the traditional ways of accessing medical imaging and results are time consuming and cumbersome and that technology can readily accelerate processes to save time for both medical practitioners and patients, while likely improving patient outcomes. Historically, medical images have been stored in traditional storage devices that were directly attached to the image-producing modality or image-producing application, such as PACS.[2] In addition to implementing new technology solutions to facilitate anytime-anywhere access to digital medical images, collaborative support for the new technologies is needed across all stakeholders because the technologies bring with them process changes. The ability to share information has become particularly important and Dell engages with partners and end-users to explain to them how to achieve what they want to do by deploying available technologies and protocols.

Teaching Customers—and Partners

By providing customers with knowledge leadership that derives from lengthy experience and partner engagement, and training to ask the right questions, Dell is able to listen to customers and help them learn what they need to know. Dell then becomes a critical player in the team to bring the solution forward. It is clear that Dell does not see itself in the business of providing hardware or even hardware solutions, but rather in the business of helping end-customers learn what might be done and then what should be done before doing anything at all. To do this, Dell deploys the knowledge of subject matter experts who have clinical and technical experience in healthcare, medical imaging, PACS or medical archives. Dell provides these experts and relationship management personnel with the training they need. This includes a process to create customer value by helping customers talk about and recognize the problems they have, and then solve the "I don't know what I don't know" issue.

Dell has developed business cases that inform common customer situations such as the process of migrating from a legacy PACS solution to a more fully featured one, or the case of a customer implementing an electronic medical record that wants to enable physicians to access medical records and images from a wide variety of different imaging applications and displays.

Dell knows that customers typically have unresolved questions such as the nature of resource demands, costs, interaction and collaboration requirements, how workflow will affect radiologists and referring physicians, for example, and how to plan implementation to successfully achieve the desired end result.

While working with end-customers in this way, Dell similarly deploys strategic marketing and procurement people to engage its partner community, both to keep abreast of technology and other developments there and also to collaborate effectively and seamlessly in the common interests of joint customers of partners and Dell. While helping customers to learn, Dell also helps its partners to learn. For example, Dell develops partner understanding in areas where there are customer, technology or other knowledge gaps in the partner community that Dell perceives it might close.

Customization without Custom-Development Costs

Dell has partnerships with five companies that provide DICOM software to ensure that the best possible option is made available to the end-customer in the context of the customer's need.[3] It is uncommon to sustain so many relationships in one category of solution. Dell has elected to have multiple partners in order to facilitate what it calls "pseudo-customization"— essentially allowing it to accommodate the varying needs of its customers without writing custom software to achieve different articulations of the same strategy. Similarly, Dell also has multiple relationships with vendors of data management tools and viewers of medical images, for example, so that Dell is able to readily offer and deploy solutions that vary in complexity. As a result, Dell provides a customized feel to its solutions so that customers have an appropriate combination of storage, data management, viewing and data distribution, for example.

Partners trust Dell to put together a team of integration resources with the necessary depth to collaborate and integrate a wide variety of partners to deliver an appropriate solution. Because Dell assembles modular components, it is able to implement quickly and less expensively than fully custom solutions, and support its customers' mixed environments using a pre-existing support team.

Engagement

In summary, Dell engages with various partners to align them behind a customer objective that Dell frames with customers. Customer engagement leverages the trust that comes in part from success already achieved by acquired entities and the knowledge of experienced subject matter experts, sales personnel and Dell's partners. Dell's approach to customer engagement includes listening before speaking, teaching before selling, finding system solutions rather than emphasizing point solutions, and delivering customization benefits through a mix-and-match approach to the right partners in the right situations. Additionally, Dell leverages an initial point of entry already established in accounts for hardware solutions to identify opportunities to broaden scope of service in the account. This approach has been helpful for Dell to penetrate accounts and migrate its customer base toward progressively larger institutions and more complex opportunities for cloud-based clinical archives.

LEICESTER CITY[4]

Introduction

Social media has been widely used by many types of organizations to connect with and engage their customers, audiences and constituencies. Still, it is relatively rare for public sector organizations to have deep commitment to social media and to have actively sought to engage their stakeholders in non-traditional ways. An example of one organization that has used social marketing to access demographics that would not have been as readily engaged using other marketing approaches is the City of Leicester's National Health Service. The following discusses NHS Leicester City and its Teenage Kicks social media campaign.

NHS Leicester City

NHS Leicester City buys health services for delivery by healthcare organizations and other professionals to the people of Leicester City, which is located in the East Midlands of the United Kingdom, not far from Birmingham. The range of services procured by the city includes emergency and acute care, GPs, rehabilitation and therapies, mental-health care, ophthalmic care, pharmacy and dentistry. In addition to supporting treatment, NHS Leicester City seeks to prevent ill health by, for example, providing people with information with respect to smoking, sexual health and lifestyles.

Background

In 2007, the teenage pregnancy rate for Leicester City was 51 percent higher than the UK national average. In Leicester City, the conception rate was 50.1 out of 1,000 females aged 15 to 17, while the national average rate was 40 per 1,000 females in this group. NHS Leicester City worked with a number of stakeholders, including the Leicester City Council, teenage parents, health practitioners, youth workers, and local schools, and conducted focus groups, interviews and surveys with the target audience prior to designing its social media campaign.

The Campaign

The "Teenage Kicks" campaign started with a video purportedly showing a teenage girl giving birth on a school field in Leicester. The video appeared to have been filmed on a teenager's mobile phone and was placed on YouTube in the knowledge that it would most likely be removed for breaching the website's graphic content policy if it appeared to be real. YouTube removed the video within 24 hours of its posting and this apparent banning led to a significant increase in traditional media coverage. Local media reporting of this incident led to additional media coverage locally and internationally. A media campaign followed immediately with a new, sourced version on YouTube, which led to additional coverage and awareness of the issue.

A website and Web community were established, allowing teenagers to obtain information, interact and leave comments anonymously on the website, and several hundred did so.

A drama series was created to message the target audience in a colloquial style. Teenagers from Leicester City acted in the videos to both perform and shape content based on their own experiences, providing a reality feel to the production while leaving content control with the video's originators at NHS Leicester City. Facebook web pages encouraged young people to engage with the "story."

The videos were produced into a DVD for schools and other groups working with young people, launched with lesson plans and discussion guides to help teachers engage with the intended audiences.

Results

The budget for this campaign was £100,000. The campaign resulted in 2.7 million views of the videos, with approximately 15,000 people—many local—watching each episode of the drama. There were 75,000 hits to the campaign website and research with young people locally determined that 66 percent had seen or heard about the campaign, with more than 80 percent saying they would now consider acting differently. In addition to local market media attention, out-of-market coverage included Sky News, CNN, *USA Today*, Germany's RTL, *Taiwan News* and *AdelaideNow*.

Because of the multi-factorial nature of the issue, it is impossible to state definitively that this campaign led to a reduction in teenage conceptions but the subsequent rate of growth of teenage pregnancies in Leicester City was approximately half that of the UK national average.

Learnings

NHS Leicester City suggests that there are two main categories of learnings that they derived from this experience. The first is that they needed to understand the attitudes and behaviors of small groups within their target audience. The second was that the board which approved the plan and expenditures needed to be willing to engage citizens on their terms. To do so, members of the board needed to be prepared to set their own personal values aside and consider the values of the target audience. They also needed to be willing to accept criticisms from constituents outside the target audience or who were uninvolved in the process and for this they needed to be willing to face the challenge of those who said their approach should not be adopted, always a challenge but particularly so in public sector organizations.

NEW YORK CITY, HEALTH AND HUMAN SERVICES[5]

Background

New York City Health and Human Services (HHS) has adopted innovative approaches for managing individual cases that serve the city's 8.3 million residents, workers, and business owners. By using lessons learned from private-sector experience in areas such as CRM and fraud detection, HHS has accelerated technology deployment times and cut its IT budget significantly while seeking to improve case outcomes. The city's HHS Connect initiative integrates information technology among nine city Health and Human Services agencies to provide coordinated benefits and services to residents, share data among agencies and reduce duplication of effort. HHS Connect improves how clients, caseworkers, human services agencies, and providers interact with each other, obtain and share information, and access city programs and services.

Technologies

HHS Connect technologies comprise the following five components:

1. Common Client Index (CCI)

    Master registry of client links across five different HHS case management systems to standardize and match client records from different agency or source systems based on demographic data, such as name address, Social Security number and date of birth. This expanded view of client information enables caseworkers to identify which clients are being served by more than one agency.

2. Worker Connect

    Integrates with CCI to enable caseworkers from seven city agencies to access client demographic and case/program-specific data across agency system boundaries to improve how they serve their common clients.

3. Document Management

    Enables the City's HHS agencies to share documents and images stored in agency repositories by creating a federated document index.

4. Client Portal

    Provides users with more advanced features and functions, reduces the number of in-person visits to agencies for assistance, reduces the number of phone calls or letters to agencies and enables information already provided by clients to be used by other agencies.

5. Enterprise Architecture

    Identifies the architectural standards and designs the common components to be implemented by the HHS Connect initiatives, including master data management, document management, data exchange, security components and infrastructure. The Enterprise Architecture team is also responsible for the governance processes to ensure that these components are consistently utilized by the program.

Cross-Agency Platform

HHS is focused on achieving better outcomes for its citizens and making more effective use of its own budget. It does this in part by using solutions that are proven and require limited customization, having a 360-degree view on each client derived from a cross-agency platform, and engaging citizens on their terms. For example, HHS obtains data from those who engage with the city agencies throughout their lifetimes, starting with Child Protective Services and ending with services to the aged, as well as obtaining data associated with food stamps, Medicare, Medicaid, cash assistance, homelessness, corrections and probations, for example. In the latter regard and to illustrate, data used to serve people coming out of New York City's Rikers Island, the world's largest jail, is used to help focus discharge planning services, such as cash planning, and finding a place to sleep and medications.

HHS has a policy of "no wrong door," so that any client who accesses city services in one way should also receive attention in the context of other agencies. To illustrate, patients who enter a hospital without Medicaid are enrolled, and people entering homeless shelters are asked at point of entry a number of questions that go beyond the immediate need for shelter and seek to understand other aspects of the individual's life so that the right services can be provided. It is the cross-agency focus of HHS that enables the potential for just-in-time questioning of clients and real-time outcome management.

Outcome Management

Because HHS has access to many skilled employees, third-party studies and data of measured outcomes can be reviewed and these have led to rules being established to help ensure that the desired outcomes become more widely achieved. High-level outcomes are broken down into micro-outcomes and causal factors and rules sought to help achieve each individual outcome that is the root cause of, or contributor to, the larger outcome. For example, it has been found that children who do well in fourth grade math classes tend to also succeed in eighth grade math classes, and these children are then more likely to find their way into higher learning and other productive pursuits. So, by starting at the end and then working backward, the city may ask how to ensure that success is achieved on those aspects that are key contributors to success, such as helping children to achieve good results in fourth grade math classes, for example, as part of a rules-based and holistic approach to assessment and improvement.

Performance Improvement

HHS tracks case visits and uses contextual analysis and expert systems to help inform caseworkers, reduce paperwork and even to identify fraud—say, when a call has reportedly been made but it did not actually occur. Now caseworkers can be better informed when they visit clients because their tablets are equipped with heat-map and GIS[6] information that show, for example, increases in domestic violence in certain areas. Caseworkers have case notes delivered in real time to the tablets, with a rules recommendation engine running on the tablet in real time that allows the caseworkers to ask specific questions and make better-informed, objective judgments that are then captured on the tablet and used to generate automatic reports. This saves time for the caseworker and manager, provides more opportunity for the child to be served and potentially leads to better outcomes.

Privacy and Confidentiality

HHS pays close attention to management of information to respect the privacy and confidentiality of its clients. It operates within guidelines for privacy and public accountability such as the Health Insurance Portability and Accountability Act (HIPAA) for medical data and the Family Educational Rights and Privacy Act (FERPA) for educational data. HHS does not maintain a database but federates existing databases and manages permissible access to these data.

Analytics and Metrics

Analytics used to help inform outcome management make use of some of the same approaches that are commonly used by private sector CRM practitioners. These approaches to analytics include root cause analysis, clustering, machine learning, induction, expert systems, social network analysis and predictive analytics, all repurposed in the context of public sector data assessment. These analytics are dependent upon detailed data gathering and HHS is focused on gathering the required data to enable the analytics, tracking, for example, who the heavy users of services are, how many patients in hospitals do not have Medicaid, and so on.

In addition, client surveys are conducted to assess users' perceptions. Client drops are examined on specific web pages to understand why users didn't proceed to achieve their original purpose. Other metrics that are tracked include the time to serve constituents using the HHS solution versus the time that it would have taken without these approaches.

Learnings

HHS has shown that technology-enabled client management approaches can be applied in the public sector in much the same way as in the private sector, data-based outcomes can be analyzed and managed, and significant implementation and operational savings can result while performance also improves. That is, performance improvement and costs are not opposing considerations. The initiative has benefitted from a mayor who is committed to the thoughtful use of technologies to find new efficiencies in non-traditional ways and a governance model that seeks results, confidence and transparency. Leadership of the HHS Connect initiative includes governance by a board functioning much as a private sector board of directors would, with representation by the commissioners from the HHS agencies, the Office of Management and Budget, the CIO/executive director, HHS Connect and the deputy mayor.

TRANSGAMING[7]

Background

TransGaming is a multinational computer games company that specializes in enabling, creating and distributing interactive entertainment. TransGaming enables PC video games to run on Apple Macintosh computers. Among the games they have enabled for the Mac platform are The Sims 3, Spore, FIFA, Assassin's Creed, Dragon Age, LEGO Universe, Tom Clancy's Splinter Cell, Grand Theft Auto, and City of Heroes. They also distribute video games digitally via television set-top boxes used by cable television companies.

TransGaming maintains relationships with three categories of organizations: content companies (the makers of PC video games), technology partners (such as Intel and manufacturers of set-top boxes) and cable companies. Their content company relationships include companies such as Electronic Arts (EA), Ubisoft, Sony Online Entertainment (SOE), The LEGO Group, NCsoft, Activision, Rockstar Games and Disney. TransGaming's technology partners include Intel, Apple, AMD, Nvidia, SoftKinetic, and Amino Communications. The firm's principal cable company relationship is with the second largest cable company in France, Free—a subsidiary of Iliad. TransGaming provides Free with a software-based on-demand gaming solution for Free's next generation of set-top boxes.

TransGaming also pays attention to relationships with end-consumers, particularly in respect of set-top boxes as these stream video games to consumers in a manner whereby TransGaming's is branding its GameTree TV service in a fashion similar to NetFlix (i.e., a consumer-oriented brand).

Building Relationships

TransGaming categorizes its individual customers according to whether they are in B2B, B2C or B2B2C—the last mentioned would apply to software in the set-top boxes distributed by cable companies to end-consumers. Trans-Gaming focuses on building trust with customers, demonstrating results and delivering compelling value propositions to acquire B2B customers. Having done so, the firm focuses next on customer retention. For example, TransGaming forged a close relationship with EA over five years and now works on a continuing stream of games coming from many EA studios and on a variety of EA's strategic endeavors. Once the games are released into the marketplace and perform well, this becomes further reason for EA to continue to work with TransGaming.

Relationships with Games Companies

TransGaming has essentially all of the business that their customers have for games that require PC to Mac conversion. As a result, TransGaming doesn't compete for share of customer within accounts but does seek to work closely with customers to ensure as many of their games as possible are converted to Mac platforms. They also focus on collaborating with the strategic initiatives of their customers, such as games for smartphones, for example. TransGaming's intent is to continue to meet the key relationship criteria of its customers and to cultivate relationships with games companies so that its customers have no reason to consider competitors.

Relationships with Cable Companies

Many cable companies are experiencing revenue loss to customers sourcing content that bypasses cable operators, such as by using an Internet-connected TV, PC or smartphone. TransGaming's value proposition allows cable companies to compete against these alternatives by providing games content to consumers through set-top boxes. Once TransGaming has integrated its technology, services and platform with the cable companies, the relationship becomes long term in nature as long as customer retention and financial results continue to be achieved.

TransGaming collects a great deal of consumer data when subscribers interact with the TransGaming software (GameTree TV) on the set-top box, including information on the games consumers play, the prices they pay (and hence the business model that works best), the times that games are played and for how long consumers play games. This information is shared with the cable companies in aggregate to help cable companies be better informed about their consumers and the marketplace more generally.

Relationships with Technology Companies

TransGaming has invested heavily with technology partners such as Intel to develop more senior relationships and then broaden their visibility into other divisions and platforms while the partners recognize the importance of gaming as a chip opportunity. TransGaming values the opportunity to leverage the reputations of technology company partners to build its own marketplace reputation and respect. For example, Intel showcases partners such as TransGaming to Intel's own customers, which has led to an even closer relationship between TransGaming and Intel.

Underpinnings for Relationship Development

TransGaming's plans for relationship development start by recognizing key touchstones as the basis for all the relationships it develops, including the firm's integrity and reputation, and manifesting the right company values. TransGaming seeks to achieve two key relationship objectives: being easy to do business with and delivering high-quality performance. TransGaming perceives that customers generally do business with people they like, but only if they receive quality service and results from their relationship with

TransGaming. To help ensure consistent attainment of these two relationship objectives, TransGaming has framed five values as touchstones for their employees: respect (for one another internally, and for partners and customers), taking personal ownership, innovating, collaborating and achieving results. These values have become part of the fabric of the culture of the company. Each employee at the company is considered the CEO of his or her individual job, empowered to do his or her best and to conduct him or herself according to the values of the enterprise. As a result, TransGaming pays less attention to policy manuals as they expect employees to be guided by values.

TransGaming recognizes that its own success depends on the success of the companies with which it has relationships. TransGaming focuses on the alignment of outcomes and the sharing of rewards. This also helps ensure that both TransGaming and its customers support and encourage one another and to make the most compelling and complete value proposition for the end-customer.

Customer Selection

TransGaming has a marquee list of accounts that it wants to support, but finite resources to allocate, and must necessarily make resource allocation decisions. TransGaming values partnerships and stratifies relationships based on the length of the relationship, the strength of the brand, the content customers have and the annual flow of business. TransGaming considers the balance between customers and the company's immediate and long-term revenue opportunities on the one hand, and the cost and complexity of applying technology to a particular title on the other.

Internal Marketing

TransGaming seeks to develop relationships with multiple touch points in each account and manages each connection carefully. As a result, the fluid nature of employment and structures in accounts does not put TransGaming's overall relationship into jeopardy when change inevitably occurs. In addition, if one particular contact point experiences some degree of stress, this also doesn't put the overall relationship at risk as other connections will seek to bring the relationship back into good standing. TransGaming believes that e-mail and telephone are no substitute for personal contact and that business is done between people.

Creating Value

TransGaming has established a technology and product foundation; it develops customer-specific value by focusing on the problem each customer has and then developing a solution for that problem. Once TransGaming understands the problem, it develops and articulate solutions to create a memorable, differentiated impression that leads to subsequent discussion of business opportunity. In some cases, TransGaming innovates for accounts—as in the case of Free, where they recognized the strategic opportunities the company likely needed, such as an opportunity for revenue lift, and then brought set-top box solutions to the account. In other cases, TransGaming innovates with accounts in a collaborative process that engages customers in a questioning process that leads to TransGaming's problem-solving capabilities. When changes are required from a standard solution, TransGaming is generally willing to make those changes, and values customers who help the company adapt rather than viewing the anticipated changes as an impediment, cost and barrier.

Teaching Customers New Behaviors

Customers are constantly adopting new devices, lifestyles and behaviors, making these facets part of the business landscape to which every company must adjust. TransGaming seeks to be at the forefront of behavioral change by helping customers learn new opportunities to satisfy their needs because Transgaming understands that it is more likely to succeed if it modifies customers' behaviors than if it responds to new customer behaviors, such as those that competitors might have changed. TransGaming recognizes end-customers are most likely to change behaviors when change is part of what customers already know and do—that which customers consider reasonable and appropriate, and for which behaviors are already ingrained. Then Trans-Gaming modifies customer behaviors at the margin of what customers do now rather than expecting them to do something very different all at once. When TransGaming priced games for set-top box and cable distribution, the firm used the concept of cable "channels," which customers know from their television viewing, to bundle games into tiers. TransGaming now offers an "Adventure Games" channel, a "Puzzle Games" channel and so on, which allows customers to click on a tab to get the games within that tier. As customers get used to the channels, TransGaming modifies the user interface a little further, and customers are able to accept and adapt to each small change one step at a time without viewing any as being particularly unusual.

Social Media

Social media is part of TransGaming's marketing mix both to touch customers individually and to communicate with the marketplace more broadly. Trans-Gaming recognizes the double-edged-sword nature of social media—that communications should be carefully framed in a manner that supports the values of the enterprise, and intermingles personal and professional elements in a way that is appropriate, personal and demonstrates thought leadership. TransGaming has social media policies that are framed by the marketing department to reinforce confidentiality in areas such as new products, trade shows, privacy and so on, and also to ensure that no off-color comments are communicated, but, beyond that, not to limit people or the channels through which they communicate.

Mobile Media

Many companies have already developed solutions for mobile devices so, rather than compete directly, TransGaming has focused on how people use mobile devices and how to incorporate these devices into customers' games-planning experience. For example, TransGaming is developing solutions that use multiple screens to allow games players to use mobile devices as controllers while watching the game on the television screen. In this way, TransGaming optimizes a game being played on the screen with personal parts of the games appearing on mobile devices which then function as a controller by making use of technologies already within them, such as gyroscopes, accelerometers and touchscreens. For example, a poker game may be split between the television screen and the mobile device so that the TV presents the poker table while each individual hand is on an individual's smartphone, from which hands can be dealt or cards played.

TRANSLINK[8]

Background

TransLink is Metro Vancouver's regional transportation authority in Vancouver, British Columbia, Canada. TransLink has developed and implemented an initiative called TravelSmart to engage with travelers in Vancouver and to help them make informed travel choices. The TravelSmart.ca website provides resources, tips and tools, and opportunities for individuals to learn travel options that are best suited to each, and to contribute and share ideas and experiences with others. Social media such as YouTube, Facebook and Twitter are also employed to engage with Vancouverites.

Demand Management

The 2010 Winter Olympics in Vancouver and the period since have presented a particular opportunity and challenge for TransLink as it has sought to manage significantly increased demand for public transit without increasing infrastructure expenditures commensurately. It is accomplishing this objective in part by optimizing system operating efficiency and in part by managing system demand. TransLink also sought to shift and spread demand away from peak periods in order to avoid the associated investments that would be required to handle peak system loading. Going beyond the TravelSmart initiative, TransLink intends to incentivize individuals through discounts and other means to shift travel from peak periods into shoulder and less well-traveled times, and even to help Vancouverites avoid traveling together on busy days and times. TransLink's new smartcard will help facilitate not only payments but also assist with demand management through tailored pricing of rates and discounts.

Behavioral Segmentation and Objectives

TransLink segments their customers demographically and behaviorally, such as according to modes of travel (public transit, private cars, bicycles, etc.). TransLink is seeking to increase the public transit share of trips from 11 percent in 2011 to 17 percent by 2020, obviously a significant increase. The organization has invested heavily for capacity to accommodate this increase but TransLink recognizes that its investments could be reduced if citizens change behaviors by, for example, riding bikes, carpooling and walking more frequently rather than taking public transit. Such behavioral change shaves system demand. TransLink's TravelSmart demand management initiative is built on best practices in other jurisdictions, as well as practices in other industry sectors that have had experience with managing system capacity such as electricity power generation and distribution—BC Hydro's Power Smart initiative, for example.

Teaching Customers New Behaviors

TransLink realizes that people don't modify their behaviors by being told to change, even when an individual's changed behaviors may benefit the society at large, such as with respect to the environment. Rather, TransLink has found that there is general support for behaviors that are environmentally sensitive, but that people need to be engaged on their own terms and benefit personally—such as by saving money or travel time—if they are to change their own behaviors. Travelers also need to know how to set about making the necessary changes in their travel plans and have peer group support to help entrench behaviors. As a result, TransLink doesn't preach "car bad, bus good," but rather recognizes and respects the transportation roles of different modes of travel while helping citizens to discover new options that fit with the lives and priorities of each person.

TravelSmart

TravelSmart's overall objective is to motivate behavioral change one resident at a time so that each individual is better off for the travel choices he or she makes. TransLink benefits from the behavioral change of travelers that reduce demand for its infrastructure and transportation services, thus putting less strain on the system and helping to avoid investments in system capacity that would otherwise be required. When citizens choose to travel by modes other than public transit, such as by foot or bicycle, they free up public transit for use by others and as a result TransLink avoids incremental expenditures.

The society also benefits from TravelSmart as the citizens of Vancouver, who already generally embrace a lifestyle of sustainability and environmental sensitivity, become even more environmentally responsible and further reduce their carbon footprints.

The initial focus of TravelSmart was to guide people to find travel options other than private vehicles. TravelSmart used its own website so travelers could register and receive information tailored to their individual requirements. After individuals register and obtain the information they want in the context of their personal requirements, TravelSmart reaches out to individuals periodically to understand how each person is behaving and whether behavioral change has occurred.

TravelSmart seeks to reinforce the public travel choices, such as by providing waiting travelers with information on the pending arrival of buses by sending real-time graphical updates to smartphones so that people will know when service is about to arrive. In addition to Google Transit, TransLink uses SMS to provide a next bus alert text message service that alerts users to the next six scheduled buses for their transit stops.

Social Media

TransLink makes significant use of social media to engage the Vancouver-area community. The organization has about 20,000 followers on Twitter and makes significant use of other social media, such as Facebook and their *The Buzzer* blog. For example, Facebook has been used to engage the local community, most recently collaborating in the naming of a new smart card to be used for travel, listening to the pet travel peeves of travelers, and setting up local meetings to celebrate transit as part of a process of helping Vancouverites begin to take ownership of the travel system. TransLink seeks to support social media in a way that customers expect, such as being able to respond to tweets quickly, which citizens would appreciate if they're waiting for a bus late at night, for example. TransLink uses a web panel of 7,000 people that is reflective of the demographics and psychographics of the region to help it examine changes, explore new opportunities and resolve existing issues, and it listens to social media commentary to track sentiment and brand impacts. TransLink supports local bloggers in order to reach out to the communities with whom the bloggers connect, providing bloggers with information they need to support their writing. TransLink encourages its employees to engage their friends and contacts in social media but naturally expects employees not to misrepresent themselves and more specifically to note that they are employees of TransLink in their social media communications.

Stakeholder Relationships and Engagement

TransLink seeks to make customer and stakeholder relationships a core competency. As part of meeting this objective, the organization has established stakeholder advisory groups to help identify and resolve issues and align the organization with its stakeholders. The advisory groups are comprised of representatives of each major constituency that has an interest in public transit in Vancouver, such as school districts, residents' associations and community associations. This form of engagement as well as more traditional forms of communication with stakeholders—such as e-mail, telephone, in-person meetings and the TransLink website—help to ensure that TransLink is well positioned to meet stakeholder expectations and potentially minimize opposition when challenges emerge. For example, recent and material fare increases have not been widely opposed, in part because stakeholders have appreciated the underlying reasons for fare increases.

Chapter 11
STRATEGY, STAKEHOLDERS AND SEMANTICS

"The privilege granted to unity, to totality, to organic ensembles, to community as a homogenized whole—this is the danger for responsibility, for decision, for ethics, for politics."[1]

Jacques Derrida (1930–2004)

This chapter considers a broad context for marketing and explores what it means to market in this socially connected era of ephemeral connections and fleeting passion for brands. This chapter first examines controllable aspects for relationship marketers to consider and then moves to arenas over which it is more difficult to assert control and where, paradoxically, control may actually be counterproductive.

Customer management implies some degree of customer control. Sales can be fostered and controlled but control of all aspects of relationships invites consideration of what it means to be in control of the mind of a customer, if this is a desirable objective and pursuit, and what the very nature of marketing ought to be with the power to know each customer better, in some respects, than customers may know themselves. If an organization seeks customer control, is it perhaps less likely that the firm actually attains this objective? Throughout this book, you will have observed that firms with considerable customer data stir controversy whenever when they find new ways to use "their" data. Conversely, it could be asked, might an organization secure more influence *with* customers, rather than *over* customers, if it limits its power and instead genuinely gives itself to customers without seeking to control any aspect of what customers think or do? Or should the organization seek balance between control and the genuine gift of customer empathy just mentioned? Apple's Steve Jobs made simultaneous control and the abandonment of control not only approachable—Zen played an important part in his life—but also evidently very profitable.[2] Serious business people ought to consider the implications of the apparent paradox between excessive customer management and control on the one hand, and the likelihood of attaining the objective on the other.

PLANNING A STRATEGIC RELATIONSHIP

This book has advocated for customer relationship planning. Chapter 2 discussed strategies for customer relationships and Chapter 3 focused on planning relationships with existing customers. Chapter 4 focused on relationships with social customers and Chapter 5 on relationships B2B. In short, you will have considered a number of issues pertinent to customers and relationships at this point and should be in a position to either develop a focused customer

Figure 31: Stakeholders and Relationship Planning

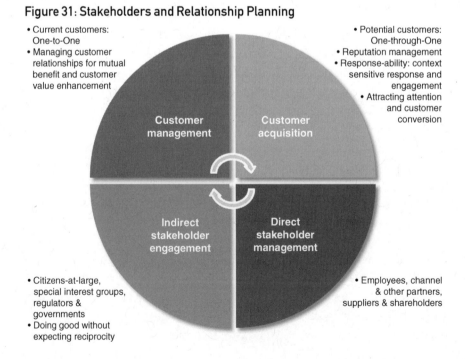

- Current customers: One-to-One
- Managing customer relationships for mutual benefit and customer value enhancement

- Potential customers: One-through-One
- Reputation management
- Response-ability: context sensitive response and engagement
- Attracting attention and customer conversion

Customer management

Customer acquisition

Indirect stakeholder engagement

Direct stakeholder management

- Citizens-at-large, special interest groups, regulators & governments
- Doing good without expecting reciprocity

- Employees, channel & other partners, suppliers & shareholders

relationship plan or enhance existing plans. Attention now shifts to integrating plan elements into a single, powerful and focused plan that brings together various stakeholder-centric elements that have been discussed in this book. Figure 31 suggests that there are four categories of planning that organizations might consider when adding relationship value to the enterprise, and each one is centered on a specific stakeholder or stakeholders. These categories are as follows:

- Customer management
- Customer acquisition
- Direct stakeholder management, and
- Indirect stakeholder engagement.

CUSTOMER MANAGEMENT

The management of current customers was discussed at length in Chapter 3 where the CREVITS model—Customer selection, Relationship objectives, Engagement, Value, Innovation, Teaching, and Sharing—was advanced as a framework for developing a plan to advance relationships with existing customers.

No plan could be complete without a feedback loop that senses customer expectations and how the organization is addressing them. Chapter 3 discussed customer sensing and issues related to this and noted that sensing is an integral element of the feedback loop that connects with, listens to, and embraces the customer for primary, remedial and secondary value creation.

A natural first question for an organization to use to gauge whether a plan is a sound one is to ask what the impact of customer relationships will be on shareholder value. A better one is to ask the reverse: if the organization focused only on transactions, what would be the results for shareholders in the near and long terms? The answer to the second question generally serves to reinforce and galvanize corporations to build customer relationships that matter and to lessen the attention the company might give to specific metrics. Few firms measure the immense cost associated with many of the things they do—like accounting, budgeting and quality control, for example. Relationship planning could be similarly engaged and this could alleviate some of the enormous pressure relationship marketers feel as they seek to deliver near-term performance improvements while simultaneously building long-term customer relationships.

It is possible that firms already feel over-planned and relationship plans could be seen as one more category of planning that shifts management time away from action and results. However, without a plan of this type, many ideas can seem good ones. Resources usually flow to those who articulate their views most persuasively or who have the ear of those in power. This leads to multiple priorities being assigned and some can have competing objectives and may not be strategically aligned without the necessary planning. A relationship plan has the potential not only to focus attention but also to free up resources from endeavors that are revealed through planning as secondary, peripheral or not strategic. It remains puzzling that organizations invest much to change things that matter very much less than relationships, arguably the most important asset of any enterprise.

In addition to the positive elements a relationship plan brings to an organization, it can also help avoid negative consequence. For example, a relationship plan has the potential to manage organizational risk should relationships not work out, a critical consideration for organizations whose business depends on a few key stakeholders. The case of a company that depended for more than 85 percent of its sales on a single, major customer serves to illustrate the point. Relatively small customer issues that could have been effectively managed became magnified when the company seemed unable to manage repetitive issues, which then escalated and caused reputational damage much like a stone tossed into a pond. The early ripples, uncontrolled, proceeded outward and more and more of them followed. Without a plan for relationship management to which both supplier and customer organizations could have subscribed, the overall relationship eventually spiraled out of control and the business relationship was terminated. This led directly and very quickly to the liquidation of the supplier, which has now gone out of business.

As important as a plan is for managing existing customers and their relationships with the organization, it is equally important for identifying and securing new customer relationships. Absent such a plan, any path will seem a good one; it will be difficult or impossible for management to effectively focus on the steps that need to be taken to arrive at a more desirable future state. Customer acquisition is discussed next.

Customer Acquisition

Chapter 4 discussed one-through-one marketing and how to engage with potential customers who are known to existing customers. This chapter noted the importance of social media planning and suggested that objectives be set in the areas of reputation management, customer management and customer acquisition. Chapter 3 and the preceding section in this chapter dealt with customer management for existing customers and their relationships with the organization.

It was suggested in Chapter 4, in a discussion centered on new customer acquisition, that organizations adopt a planning model that first reviews the current state of issues such as current customers and influencers before analyzing a desired future state for the company's relationships. It was noted that an organization might consider how each of the options it selects—such as to inform, educate, communicate, entertain, collaborate and transact—presently affect or contribute to the firm's management of its reputation, current customers and new customers. A number of thoughts were suggested regarding transitioning from the current state analysis to the future state to achieve customer acquisition and reputation management objectives. For example, suggestions were offered such as focusing on customer centers of influence, achieving message pass-through via stimulus-response approaches. Facebook's Like, Twitter's retweet, and specific tools were mentioned. Customer-specific communications objectives were also reviewed.

Customer acquisition and reputation management depend upon the strategic capability associated with an organization's ability to respond in a timely and context-sensitive manner to customer and potential customer inquiry and being able to engage effectively with the world at large. The section in this chapter entitled "Strategic Response-ability" considers this subject matter.

DIRECT AND INDIRECT STAKEHOLDERS

In addition to addressing the need to develop and sustain relationships with current and new customers, organizations also pay close attention to forming and sustaining relationships with other direct stakeholders in the enterprise. These stakeholders include employees, channel partners and suppliers such as bankers and IT firms. Indirect stakeholders include special interest groups, governments, regulators and citizens-at-large, and these stakeholders commonly receive much less relationship attention from the organization.

Indirect stakeholders are important because they have the potential to affect—both positively and negatively—the ability of organizations to succeed. Consider how class-action lawsuits faced by tobacco, mining (e.g., asbestos), oil and automobile companies have constrained growth and profits of some firms in these industries. A similar potential exists for negative attention by indirect stakeholders in industries such as chemicals, pharmaceuticals, electronics, fast-food, beverage, and banking industries, and likely a number of others. Consider, for example, constraints placed by local government in New York City on the size of sodas sold within their jurisdiction and the potential for this to be repeated in other cities with obvious consequence for the beverage industry.

No stakeholder is peripheral if that stakeholder perceives he or she has a role to play that may affect the organization, no matter how indirectly. Note that this perception is not what the organization may believe to be the case. If the stakeholder considers he, she or it is a stakeholder for whatever reasons that seem to matter to the stakeholder, then this is indeed the case. Corporate existence, growth and action require that relationships with these indirect stakeholders be considered, managed and, where appropriate, pursued. So, if the organization presently lacks a customer-specific relationship plan with indirect stakeholders, it needs one. It also needs a plan for direct stakeholders.

DIRECT STAKEHOLDER MANAGEMENT

Much of the content thus far has focused on relationships between the firm, its customers and potential customers to create, deliver and be rewarded from the value each individual wants. The unique value individual customers often want impacts not only capabilities internal to the enterprise but the contribution other stakeholders make to the end-customer relationship. This contribution comes from stakeholders committing to, and aligning with, the same relationship objectives, strategies and processes the company is trying to create and deliver to end-users. In other words, each stakeholder, whether employee, supplier, distribution channel intermediary, service company, banker or investor, has the potential to strengthen the company's relationships with its end-customers by seeing the complete picture, understanding their role and working with the company to continuously build mutual value.

If any one of the stakeholders does not advance the company's end-customer relationship, they limit or detract from the shareholder value the firm is trying to build. Worse, if the relationship between a stakeholder and the company differs in intent, intensity or nature, the outcome of the relationship between the company and its customers may be in doubt. The end-customer relationship depends on the effective alignment of the company's capabilities with the end-customer's expectations. In turn, for its capabilities, the company depends on the mutual value it creates with stakeholders other than the customer. So, if companies and customers are to continuously create and share mutual value to advance the interests of each, the company should expect and seek alignment with its stakeholders on the same basis. For example, if IT is to be a key capability in serving individual customers uniquely, the company should be aligned with IT resources that deliver the human and infrastructure capital needed to make the customer investment pay off. The firm thus depends on relationships with internal IT staff, external suppliers of computing, software and communications technologies, project managers and external consultants.

Managing the end-customer relationship may be seen as requiring management of a "chain of stakeholder relationships" that are created by the company on its own behalf and that of the customer, and are maintained and built by the company. The concept of a mutually rewarding relationship will not be hard for the company to communicate to its suppliers, most of which are likely already receptive to the concept of deepening or extending customer relationships. In fact, suppliers almost always seem more interested than their customers in developing meaningful relationships. It is the wise customer that understands that a supplier can contribute much more to the company's future than the lowest price, and that this contribution requires a relationship.

The end-customer relationship is the economic engine that provides for the company's other relationships. The deeper and more meaningful the end-customer relationship, the greater the potential economic yield will be available for sharing, leading to the potential for greater alignment with various stakeholders. Figure 32 notes the different categories of stakeholders that can influence the end-customer relationship in a "chain of direct stakeholder relationships." The diagram categorizes stakeholders into those who are directly involved with the enterprise and those with less direct or indirect involvement. It is beneficial for the enterprise to reflect, in some cases just briefly, on the current state of each category of relationship, its desired future state and how it might transition to that future state.

There are five categories of relationships with direct stakeholders that are particularly important to the enterprise, as follows:

Figure 32: A Chain of Direct Stakeholder Relationships

- Investors/owners and financial institutions
- Distribution channel intermediaries
- Employees
- Suppliers, and
- Co-venture partners.

These relationships are discussed next.

Relationships with Investors/Owners and Financial Institutions

Owners and management determine the relationship orientation of the firm. In closely held firms, owners have considerable influence and would naturally need to be committed to relationship management if such a strategy were to endure.

In widely held companies, management may play a more important role than owners in relationship management. Publicly traded U.S. companies have ownership that is characterized by numerous, relatively transient owners of stock, who manage by the value of each transaction, who each may have modest stakes, who use available public information to make rational, economic buy-sell decisions, and whose influence in the company individually and in aggregate is low. In this context, management wields considerable power. Even in companies where institutional investors have significant stakes on behalf of pension funds, and investment companies have material commitments through mutual funds they manage, it is not common for either category to be aggressively represented on boards of directors. Without the owners and managers of long-term, patient capital providing strategic rather than transactional advice, the company may lack the will to invest sufficiently in the capabilities needed for long-term customer relationships.

Firms most likely to attain meaningful, relationship-driven progress will have as many of the following conditions in place with owners and investors as possible:

- Patient, yet not undemanding, capital
- Narrowly held distribution of equity among stockholders
- Investors with similar investment profiles, with strategic investors preferred over near-term transactional ones
- A board of directors that mirrors ownership preference, and that validates relationship management in thought and deed, and
- A process of governance at the board level that values relationship management, and ensures that management is focused on this issue by having its various sub-committees, such as the personnel committee, include employee relationships in terms of reference.

Certainly, in any company where the investor community is oriented to near-term results and rapid capital appreciation, and has a board that spends more time on current financials than strategic drivers of shareholder value, management will find it difficult to advance a relationship management agenda. If the company is to achieve the promise of relationship management, it will first need a plan to develop strategic investors.

The principles illustrated in this book—especially those that focused on current customers—can be put to work with the investor community. In this context, management can assess with which investors they will be creating specific value using many of the approaches outlined in this book for customer relationships.

It is uncommon for companies to have a detailed investor relationship plan, describing, for example, the mix of investors the company seeks, the profile of investors to be targeted for retention and those to be secured as new investors, measurable objectives to assess investor relationships, the value each investor segment (and possibly, individual investor) seeks, the value the company plans to deliver, and the methods the company plans to deploy to bond with the investor community.

If the current mix of investors is not well suited to the key success factors of the industry, this plan can reshape the mix and position the firm favorably as an investment vehicle to investors with a preferred profile. In short, the investor relations function in many firms has received short shrift and represents an area of considerable opportunity for companies to build shareholder value.

Relationships with Distribution Channel Intermediaries

It is as important for companies to work together with their distribution channel intermediaries as it is to collaborate with customers to create new business value. This is so for three main reasons that some manufacturers take for granted:

1. The battle for the customer first must be won at the channel level before the end-customer can be secured
2. The intermediary adds value to products and services that the manufacturer cannot easily and/or economically do
3. The intermediary can be an enduring basis for creating new value with customers and for taking costs out of current systems

Forging meaningful relationships with distribution channel intermediaries requires that companies look for common interests and make allowances for areas of difference. For example, both companies have an interest in advancing their financial position. But the vendor often wants the intermediary to operate according to a more "strategic" set of rules, while the company in the channel, often independently owned and managed, may see financial performance as a more personal and near-term accomplishment. The challenge is to find common ground sufficient that both objectives can be attained. It is possible to find this commonality by first looking at the contribution the manufacturer makes to the business model of the intermediary.

More generally, the question arises as to how the manufacturer ought to build relationships with distribution channel intermediaries, continuously and for mutual interest. The principles for continuously developing mutual value with channel intermediaries are the same as for business customers, with a few twists. Here are the 10 main steps on which to focus:

- Step 1: Be respectful of all intermediaries
- Step 2: Establish and own a process for relationship development
- Step 3: Treat distribution channel intermediaries as though they are customers
- Step 4: Recognize distribution channel intermediaries as independent businesses where this is the case
- Step 5: Plan together with distribution channel intermediaries
- Step 6: Innovate together
- Step 7: Take out costs from the entire system rather than passing costs backward or forward in the channel
- Step 8: Align operations with an end-customer and market positioning in mind
- Step 9: Bundle services with products and recognize that the end-customer may seek a solution without paying attention to which firm provides specific components
- Step 10: Maintain consistency in treatment of intermediaries

Relationships with Employees

Employee Categorization

Relationships with customers will not typically be enduring and committed without deep relationships with employees and these, in turn, derive in part from the company recognizing that each employee is on a separate journey. Each employee ought to be treated as an individual in much the same way that the firm considers each customer. It remains curious that while many firms have embraced relationship management, few have done much more than allowing individuals to pick their own training and selected other aspects that can advance their careers, such as internal job postings. Few companies have plans that formally differentiate employees as they do customers, such as triaging employees and having development plans that reflect individual preferences and differences.

Employee-Centric Databases

There remains potential for companies to consider their people as the individuals they are. The firm might decide with which employees what type of new value will be created and how the capabilities of the company might accommodate the development of new employee value. If employees are to receive different treatment based on their individual life journeys and expectations, for example, databases and access are needed to describe, track and enable each person, and to qualify and quantify the value each creates for the company. The database ought to be at the center of an employee relationship, facilitating profiling of each person, understanding the meaning each seeks, knowing the barriers each faces, the level and nature of bonding with the enterprise, and learns more about the staff member as they make their personal journey. In many companies, this means going beyond the current state of the HRIS (Human Resource Information Systems) now used.

Employee Skills

Any company focused on relationship management has likely found that they have broadened their scope for products and services, and this has resulted in a need for also broadening their employees' knowledge. Employees now need mastery of more processes and technologies, and of how to relate to the people with whom they must interact. Companies will always require deep functional specialists but most firms need more employees who are "broad" in understanding how everything the company does comes together to create individual customer value, both for internal customers, channel intermediaries, the end-customer and other stakeholders.

Teach-nology

Organizations develop training programs and use technology support to re-skill and/or de-skill processes where employees require additional knowledge or context. For example, the bank teller who used to perform repetitive transactions for customers now receives nudges from the computer to help the customer in new ways. The teller doesn't need to remember much about each customer as the computer provides the organizational memory.

Fast-changing internal and external environments, new hires and the advance of knowledge on many fronts means that employees now, more than ever, need just-in-time training and training that occurs when it suits the employee rather than when it is best for the company.

Impact on Organizational Structures

Relationship management, by requiring more scope of knowledge from employees, may also challenge the boundaries for the business function they have historically performed. This, in turn, requires that companies take a new look at their structures to understand whether they support organizational strategies and whether the boundaries that have historically applied to specific jobs are enabling or impeding these strategies. Many firms will find that the boundaries for specific jobs are becoming more fuzzy rather than better defined, and as a result companies are becoming increasingly dependent on the goodwill of their employees to make systems work, to cater to each individual customer and adapt.

Employee Trust

Employees will need to learn new skills and be willing to accommodate the changing nature of work. For this, they need to proceed on the basis of mutual trust; the employee must be prepared to willingly, knowledgeably and happily trust his or her future to the company and the company should treat this trust as sacred because trust is a fundamental touchstone for new value creation in every company. This can be challenging for many reasons. As organizations become flatter and better informed, as knowledge proliferates, processes change, workload increases and throughput is expected to accelerate, employee oversight cannot be sustained at historical levels. Employees need new boundaries within which they are free to create value, which frames the meaning of the word "trust" in policies and procedures. Just as companies establish trust, they should have processes in place to determine when trust has been broken—but this does not mean an intolerance for mistakes. In fact, it is the very way a company handles mistakes that builds trust.

Trust can only be fostered by the trustworthy. Leaders naturally need to fall into this category in thought and deed. If leaders are to receive trust, respect and commitment, they must first give it.

Trust can be further fostered by understanding personal values and doing more than the employee expects in this regard. The development of trust starts before the employee crosses the threshold of the company. Why would people move to Redmond, Washington, for an opportunity to work at Microsoft? Microsoft looks at hundreds of thousands of resumes each year. And when it finds the best candidate among them, it goes to unusual lengths to look after individual requirements and demonstrate Microsoft's early commitment. For example, individuals concerned about the number of hours to be worked can work flexible hours, people wanting suitable accommodation are helped in this regard, and the firm even caters to unusual personal preferences, in one case locating a karate instructor for a candidate with this interest.

Unionized workforces represent a further challenge for continuous mutual value creation because value needs to be planned and created at the union level as well as at the individual one. This obviously presents a challenge because not all unionized workforces are primarily focused on the customers' interests, a situation that can be overcome using many of the same steps mentioned for building relationships with channel intermediaries, starting with mutual respect and trust-building. One company with a unionized sales force (an obviously uncommon situation) has been able to create four-way relationships—between the company, individual employees, unions and customers—by focusing on multi-stakeholder collaboration.

Relationships with Suppliers

Meaningful and continuous relationships with strategic suppliers can be fundamental to the success of a company. For example, computer companies seek to advance their relationships with chipmakers and other key components suppliers because the symbiotic nature of these relationships is so important if companies are to secure timely and cost effective access to the next generation of technology.

How, then, does a firm develop meaningful relationships with suppliers? Essential ingredients in the supplier relationship include:

1. Assessing supplier contribution to company profitability and future potential profitability, then selecting strategic suppliers from among those that add relatively less value
2. Understanding how each company is currently bonded with the other, and what objectives might be established for deepening the relationship, particularly with strategic suppliers
3. Benchmarking suppliers relative to one another, in terms important to the company
4. Assessing the company in terms of its own willingness and approach when developing relationships
5. Stating the opportunity that can be derived from increased supplier bonding, especially with the best or most strategic suppliers

6. Establishing a process to plan, implement, manage, measure and share the creation of new value

7. Establishing KPIs (Key Performance Indicators) in consultation with suppliers, tracking them and providing feedback to suppliers in a timely manner to help them affirm or rectify their performance

8. Institutionalizing a method of governance and change management for the relationship

As with all other stakeholders, relationships with suppliers require the development of mutual trust. Core values are precursors for the development of trust-based relationships. If organizations do not bond at a values level, business practices and objectives of the company and its suppliers may not align before forming a relationship, and the relationship will be more brittle than would otherwise be the case.

Once companies are bonded at the value and culture levels, then the respective leaderships should establish and publicly commit to alignment and continuous mutual value creation. Finally, the firms will be in a position to align their strategies and capabilities, to ensure that the value the company has committed to the end-customer is delivered seamlessly and rapidly. When this has happened, essentially a sort of *keiretsu* (Japanese for family-like structure of member firms) has been established.

The nature of competition is changing. In previous eras, companies naturally competed with other companies. This is no longer true for many. Now, chains of relationships often compete with other chains, sometimes in a rigid way and often more fluid in much the same way that firms get together in the aerospace industry to pursue joint projects. Sometimes the network of relationships can be reconfigured easily when one company drops out. This would be the case in the retail grocery industry, for example, where the failure of one grocery store chain would not affect a supplier such as Coca-Cola. But sometimes, as was seen when the liquidation of an auto assembler could have jeopardized many auto parts firms, networks are interdependent, and an individual component of the chain of relationships cannot be readily replaced.

With relationships in place, companies and suppliers ought to be mutually open to make both more competitive through rapid information sharing and collaboration to take time out of processes. For example, General Electric (GE) developed the Trading Process Network, which gave suppliers access to the firm's lighting unit via a secure website. As a result, GE halved procurement times, among other benefits.[3]

INDIRECT STAKEHOLDER ENGAGEMENT

Indirect stakeholders include citizens-at-large, special interest groups, regulators and local, state and federal governments. Many businesses consider stakeholders such as these to be the environment of the firm and, as such, uncontrollable. This need not be the case and could be a strategic blind spot. It may not take much for special interest groups to create flash mob protests that have the potential to create negative publicity or achieve other objectives. Citizens-at-large, special interest groups and those without particular affiliation to a cause frequently stage interventions.[4] For example, when Apple elected to comply with U.S. federal law and not sell its products to a customer who they reportedly determined had ties to Iran, a flash mob was staged. Demonstrators went into Apple's New York City Fifth Avenue store where they spoke Farsi and complained about what they considered to be profiling by Apple.[5] In another instance, Apple faced criticism over working conditions at a major Chinese supplier, Foxconn.[6] There had been negative public sentiment from advocacy groups and complaints from labor rights organizations that had been investigating working conditions, leading Apple to release lists of suppliers and engage with the Fair Labor Association (FLA) to examine working conditions at manufacturers that make Apple's iPhones and iPads, among other products. Public domain criticism such as this naturally cannot be good for brand equity. The opportunity was there for Apple to identify the importance of issues such as these earlier and to plan accordingly,[7] possibly by undertaking activities such as the following:

- Listing and categorizing the key issues likely to be engaged in the public domain over the next three to five years
- Identifying the principal actors or categories of actors that might be expected to lead or influence visibility and perception of these issues
- Framing the likely stances the principal actors would or might adopt
- Developing factual touchstones and thought pieces to engage these issues when needed
- Bridging connections to issue leaders and influencers
- Collaborating to reduce the incendiary elements or other negative context of each issue, and
- Engaging with counterweight influencers to offset negative impact, if the preceding appeared to be headed toward a fruitless endeavor.

Approaches such as those described above could also be adopted for other categories of indirect stakeholder, ranging from various levels of government to associations to the media and even to influential individuals such as bloggers. In short, indirect stakeholders can be as easily categorized and differentiated as any other, and plans can be developed to engage and advance relationships selectively and in aggregate.

Related to this consideration is a question as to whether an organization can reasonably anticipate, plan and manage every conceivable issue that might arise. Some issues might be reasonably anticipated where the issues have long lead times or where precursor triggers can be identified and monitored, such as regulatory changes. On the other hand, others can arrive in a less than fully expected way, as in the case of surprising Supreme Court rulings on the ownership, control or pricing of intellectual property, for example. Companies clearly cannot anticipate everything, try though they might. And they cannot control everything, although some may wish otherwise. This raises the issue of being able to respond strategically, quickly and effectively to issues as they emerge, as well as planning more proactively to deal with the major clouds on the horizon. Even more broadly, this raises the issue of a company's orientation toward what might be termed "infinite others," which is the concept of everything and everyone that is not the company and which is external to the organization. "Infinite others" include the many people and organizations with the potential to affect an organization's performance and future.

STRATEGIC RESPONSE-ABILITY

While plans can help organizations select from among their current customers and decide with whom and how they will develop specific kinds of relationships, it is harder for organizations to choose their *future* customers *a priori*. In previous eras, this was most certainly possible and was widely done. Companies made a target market selection decision and then tailored their marketing mix to this target market. In the age of social media and one-through-one marketing, the intent of outreach is to achieve an individual connection, a conversation, mutual understanding and value creation. That is, organizations reach out.

An ability to respond to outreach and customer-initiated connections is a strategic capability that organizations put in place to create new customer value. This capability includes sensing, understanding, interpreting and responding to individual customers. A response capability is important because customers select the enterprise and expect an appropriate response when beginning a conversation. Successful companies differentiate themselves in part by enabling an ability to respond effectively.

This ability to respond to individual customers on their terms might be termed a "strategic response-ability"[8]—an ability of the organization to respond effectively, efficiently and personally to current and potential customers. Response-ability also applies to other stakeholders, including those with a financial interest in the enterprise by virtue of being, for example, customers, suppliers, employees and investors. It may also include those who have an indirect or social interest in the enterprise such as citizens-at-large, regulators and others in the various levels of government, and special interest groups. Many organizations have an ability to engage with individuals who are customers and other direct stakeholders. Fewer are adept at engaging with individuals who are not presently customers or whose main interests in the organization are other than as customers. The ability to respond effectively and in a timely manner to all stakeholders, including indirect ones, is a requirement in the age of social media where the expectation is that the organization is transparent and fully available. Quick response can help avert reputational and other damage that is inherent in a world of viral video, micro-blogging and one-to-many communications. Remember the video about the traveler with a broken guitar on United Airlines?[9]

SOCIETY AND RESPONSE-ABILITY

There are limits to the extent to which relationships can be planned and managed. People who are not known to the enterprise at present can still affect its prospects through their communications, influence and actions. It is impossible to establish relationship objectives for those the organization does not know or comprehend. This raises the issue of maintaining reputation even among those who have had limited or no connection with the enterprise in the past. When the long-term interests of society can be affected by a corporation, and some indirect stakeholders perceive this to be the case, the business becomes responsible to society at large. For this, the organization requires a response-ability to people and organizations with which the company may not have previously had any connection, such as the following:

- Those who derive benefit directly or indirectly from the corporation's failure (examples include short sellers of shares, competitors able to grow their sales at the company's expense, and auction houses that dispose of surplus or bankrupt merchandise and other assets), and

- Those who are not part of the economic value chain of the corporation but who may nevertheless be affected positively or negatively by the corporation's decisions (examples could include people and organizations that perceive themselves to have an interest in issues that the organization might be perceived to affect, such as labor practices and wage rates, ozone-depleting chemicals, open-pit mines, defensive weapons, genetically modified agriculture, second-hand cigarette smoke and disposal of electric vehicle batteries and electronics).

Companies have generally catered to stakeholders who benefit directly from the organization's success and, to a much lesser extent, engaged those who might gain or lose from the organization's failure. For corporations to recognize and address *all* stakeholders, they would first need to reflect on two ties they presently have to existing stakeholders: ties of reciprocity and self-advantage.

Reciprocity implies that organizations are structured to derive mutual benefit in relationships with their direct stakeholders; mutual benefit and thinking about oneself to ensure benefit in one's exchanges and dealings are two key aspects inherent in a definition of relationships. A company that is more open to indirect stakeholders first needs to go beyond reciprocity and rethink what it means to benefit, as opposed to simply respond, to people and organizations with which it has had limited prior engagement. Rather than seek self-advantage from control of the marketing mix, or benefit from relationship-based reciprocity, the organization could open up and submit itself to the will of unknown others with total truthfulness, transparency and humility. It could do so respectfully and faithfully in the expectation that doing good and being seen to do good will benefit shareholders by attracting and retaining customers and employees, and creating new value with all stakeholders.

How would an organization engage with its primary stakeholders and manage this engagement for beneficial outcomes while simultaneously opening up and even supplicating itself to people and organizations the company does not now know? After all, the former requires some degree of planning and control while the latter is about having a response-ability to others and not necessarily with an expectation of a near-term return on financial or time investment. A company throwing itself fully open to almost infinite others would be open to all customers without differentiating them *a priori*—that is, before they were customers in the first place.[10] Openness, transparency and going the extra mile for stakeholders and non-stakeholders has the potential to build reputation and brand equity but management would generally perceive that opening up as completely as suggested here also has the potential to weaken near-term financial performance. According to this thinking, few organizations could afford to respond without reciprocal calculation. Shareholders require near-term performance and probably would not see openness as fully maximizing their financial results.

The challenge for most companies is not to substitute planned management of stakeholders with being infinitely open but rather to balance the two approaches so that they can co-exist, with direct stakeholders under proactive management while indirect stakeholders and unknown others become the beneficiaries of reactive and respectful engagement without the organization having an expectation of near-term benefit. In making this statement, it is recognized that genuinely embracing openness as a guiding principle runs counter to the way organizations have framed and codified relationship-based rules that guide them.

Even though there can be some difficulties in moving toward openness, especially in notoriously closed companies known for their command-and-control cultures, it is possible to move in this direction after some form of discontinuity has occurred in the firm's environment. For example, opportunities for being more open may present themselves when an organization needs to adapt to new circumstances for which it is not well prepared, such as for some unforeseen disasters, lawsuits, windfalls, one-time projects (such as new construction), or new product or market development initiatives. There can also be opportunities for more openness within the firm's existing operations by benefitting others even when it is not strictly in the firm's near-term financial interest to do so.

•   •   •

This chapter has built upon a number of concepts reviewed in earlier chapters and reflected upon what it means to be in a relationship, what an organization might give (but not necessarily get in return), and selected underlying concepts that might serve as bedrock platforms for the enterprise genuinely committed to developing and sustaining new customer relationships and sustaining its business on the basis of relating.

The discussion has been far ranging, covering issues associated with the planning of stakeholder relationships for customers now under management, acquiring new customers, and developing and sustaining relationships with direct and indirect stakeholders. This led to a discussion of management of the chain of customer relationships—all the different categories of stakeholders who together deliver value for the end-customer—and reviewed issues such as engaging with customers in social media and on their mobile devices, understanding and predicting customers' behaviors with customer analytics and teaching customers new behaviors. Much of this discussion was conducted within existing frameworks that are consistent with strategic constructs of the firm, and case studies were provided to illustrate some aspects of current practice.

This book has concluded with a chapter that considered what it means for an enterprise to be able to respond effectively to customers and potential future customers, and introduced the concept of response-ability as a strategic capability for the enterprise. This led to a review of corporate response-ability and its broader meaning for societal engagement. It was suggested that companies might consider, as a conceptual platform that precedes engagement with existing customers, reaching out to benefit the many people who currently have or might have an impact on the organization but not necessarily with expectation of benefit in return.

Attaining durable relationships with high-value customers should be the ultimate corporate objective because relationships, once forged, are hard for competitors or circumstance to disrupt and provide a pathway to the future in an uncertain world. More than products, patents or machinery, relationships with customers and other stakeholders are the most important assets of the enterprise. The value of these relationship assets ought to be the considered focus of every executive building shareholder value for the long term.

Appendix A

Selected Customer Analytics/Data Mining Software Solutions[1]

Customer analytics/data mining software[2] (and Web addresses)	Open source or commercial software	Description of selected aspects or capabilities[3]
11Ants Model Builder (11antsanalytics.com)	Commercial	Predictive analytics modeling tool to build regression, classification and propensity models.
Alyuda NeuroIntelligence (alyuda.com)	Commercial	Neural networks application for neural network, data mining, pattern recognition, and predictive modeling.
Angoss KnowledgeSEEKER (angoss.com)	Commercial	Business intelligence software product with data mining and predictive analytics capabilities including data preparation, profiling, data visualization, decision tree and strategy design functionality. Includes Salesforce.
Angoss KnowledgeSTUDIO (angoss.com)	Commercial	Modeling capabilities include linear and logistic regression, neural networks, scorecards, scoring and model code generation. Unsupervised learning techniques include cluster analysis and principal component analysis.
Angoss StrategyBUILDER (angoss.com)	Commercial	Predictive models can be integrated with the business rules that govern marketing, sales or risk business processes.
Appricon Analysis Studio (appricon.com)	Commercial	Application to improve the predictive analytical modeling process.
Bayes Server (bayesserver.com)	Commercial	Predictive analytics software to perform tasks such as classification, regression, time series prediction, segmentation/clustering, density estimation, anomaly detection, decision support, reasoning and multivariate data analysis.

Customer analytics/data mining software (and Web addresses)	Open source or commercial software	Description of selected aspects or capabilities
BLIASoft Knowledge Discovery (bliasoft.com)	Commercial	AI and fuzzy logic decision-making software to extract models from data obtained by observations or experiments.
Carrot Search Carrot^2 (carrotsearch.com)	Open source	Open source search results clustering engine.
Compumine RDS—Rule Discovery System (compumine.com)	Commercial	Data mining software for automatic discovery of prediction rules.
Data Applied (data-applied.com)	Commercial	Data mining software to visualize large data sets, build pivot charts, identify associations, detect anomalies and outliers, visualize correlations, discover similarities, categorize records and forecast time series, among other features.
Sentient DataDetective (sentient.nl)	Commercial	Data mining software functionalities include predicting, clustering, finding relationships, profiling, network analysis, fuzzy matching, creating graphs, creating maps, defining selections and creating cross tables (OLAP).
Eaagle Full Text Mapper (FTM) (wp.eaagle.com)	Commercial	Automates analysis of text information to identify patterns, opportunities and risks, among other features.
ELKI (elki.dbs.ifi.lmu.de)	Open source	Data mining software that separates algorithms and data management tasks to allow for independent evaluation. Open to arbitrary data types, distance or similarity measures, or file formats.
Gait-CAD (sourceforge.net/projects/gait-cad)	Open source	The Matlab toolbox Gait-CAD enables visualization and data mining for classification, regression, and clustering, among other features.
GATE—General Architecture for Text Engineering (gate.ac.uk)	Open source	Natural language processing including information extraction in many languages.
GenIQ (geniqmodel.com)	Commercial	Automatically data mines for new variables, performs variable selection, and specifies the model equation.
Gepsoft GeneXproTools (gepsoft.com)	Commercial	Modeling tool for function finding, logistic regression, classification, time series prediction, and logic synthesis.
Fujitsu GhostMiner (fqs.pl/business_intelligence/products/ghostminer)	Commercial	Data mining software that supports common databases and machine learning algorithms and assists with data preparation and selection, model validation and visualization, among other features.

Customer analytics/data mining software (and Web addresses)	Open source or commercial software	Description of selected aspects or capabilities
GMDH Shell—Group Method of Data Handling (gmdhshell.com)	Commercial	Predictive modeling software with features that include time series forecasting, classification, polynomial regression, curve fitting, data visualization, and automatic variables selection.
IBM InfoSphere Warehouse (www-01.ibm.com/software/ data/infosphere/warehouse)	Commercial	Data warehouse solution.
IBM SPSS Modeler (previously SPSS Clementine)— Professional and Premium (ibm.com/software/analytics/ spss)	Commercial	Data mining workbenches to build predictive models without programming, to analyze structured data to create predictive intelligence.
jHepWork (jwork.org/jhepwork)	Open source	Multiplatform data analysis and visualization framework with features that include Matlab histograms in 2D and 3D, profile histograms, parametric equations in 3D contour plots, scatter plots, neural networks, linear regression and curve fitting, clustering analysis, and fuzzy algorithm.
KEEL (Knowledge Extraction based on Evolutionary Learning) (keel.es)	Open source	Java software tool to assess evolutionary algorithms for data mining problems, including regression, classification, clustering and pattern mining.
KNIME: The Konstanz Information Miner (knime.org)	Open source	Data integration, processing, analysis and exploration platform.
KXEN Modeler (kxen.com/Products/Modeler)	Commercial	Automated data mining: classification, regression, attribute importance, segmentation/clustering, forecasting, and association rules.
MDR—Multifactor Dimensionality Reduction (multifactordimensionalityr eduction.org)	Open source	Data mining software combines attribute selection, attribute construction and classification with cross-validation to model interactions.
Microsoft SQL Server Data Mining Analysis Services (microsoft.com/ en-us/sqlserver/solutions- technologies/business- intelligence.aspx)	Commercial	Data mining using familiar tools and a comprehensive development environment for building sophisticated data mining solutions. Allows many data mining models to be tested at once, multiple, incompatible models to be built in a single structure, model analysis to be applied over filtered data and optimized near-term and stable long-term predictions to be blended.
Molegro Data Modeller (molegro.com/ mdm-product.php)	Commercial	Cross-platform application for data mining, modeling, and visualization.
Mozenda (mozenda.com/data-mining)	Commercial	Data mining tool that performs data capture, saves and organizes it to make it useful. Data extraction robots harvest information, clean and reassemble it.

Customer analytics/data mining software (and Web addresses)	Open source or commercial software	Description of selected aspects or capabilities
NovoSpark Visualizer (novospark.com)	Commercial	Visualization program that enables qualitative analysis of multidimensional data on a graphical image. Features include visually comparing individual observations and entire datasets, finding data anomalies, and identifying data clusters, among other features.
Oracle Data Mining (oracle.com/technetwork/ database/options/advanced- analytics/odm/index.html)	Commercial	Data mining functionality that enables users to discover new insights hidden in data, build and apply predictive models to target customers, develop customer profiles, and find and prevent fraud, among other features.
Orange (orange.biolab.si)	Open source	Data mining, visualization and analysis. Components for machine learning. Add-ons for bioinformatics and text mining.
Megaputer PolyAnalyst (megaputer.com/site/ polyanalyst.php)	Commercial	Algorithms for automated analysis of text and structured data that performs knowledge discovery operations such as categorization, clustering, prediction, link analysis, keyword and entity extraction, pattern discovery and anomaly detection.
R (rdatamining.com) (revolutionanalytics.com/ what-is-open-source-r)	Open source	Data mining software that performs functions such as the following: association rules and frequent itemsets, sequential patterns, classification and prediction, regression, and clustering.
RapidMiner (previously Yale) (rapid-i.com)	Open source	Data mining application with functionality that includes data integration, analytical ETL, data analysis, reporting, meta data transformation, on-the-fly error recognition and quick fixes. Multiple data loading, data transformation, data modeling, and data visualization methods.
Reactive Search LIONsolver (lionsolver.com)	Commercial	Data mining, modeling, problem solving and decision-making software to build models, visualize them, and optimize processes. "Big data" and "in the cloud" versions.
Salford Systems CART (salford-systems.com)	Commercial	Classification and regression trees, and predictive modeling.
Salford Systems MARS— Multivariate Adaptive Regression Splines	Commercial	Software that provides results in a form similar to traditional regression while capturing essential non-linearities and interactions.
Salford Systems RandomForests (salford-systems.com)	Commercial	Software for data visualization, clustering, anomaly, outlier, and error detection, classification, prediction, and generating predictive models.
Salford Systems SPM (salford-systems.com)	Commercial	A data mining platform for creating predictive, descriptive, and analytical models from databases.

Customer analytics/data mining software (and Web addresses)	Open source or commercial software	Description of selected aspects or capabilities
Salford Systems TreeNet (salford-systems.com)	Commercial	Data mining tool capable of generating accurate models, and strong performance for regression and classification.
SAP Predictive Analysis	Commercial	Data mining and predictive analysis tool with wizard-like interface to source, transform and visualize data. Algorithms for optimization. Integrates with SAP HANA and R.
SAS Enterprise Miner (sas.com/technologies/ analytics/datamining/miner/)	Commercial	Data mining application with features that include data preparation, summarization and exploration, advanced predictive and descriptive modeling, model generation, model comparisons, reporting and management.
SPAD Data Mining (usinenouvelle.com)	Commercial	Data mining and predictive analysis software with functionality that includes interactive decision trees, analysis of multiple tables and visualization capabilities.
Statsoft STATISTICA Data Miner (statsoft.com/products/ statistica-data-miner)	Commercial	Data mining solution from querying databases to generating final reports. Capabilities include clustering techniques, neural networks architectures, classification/regression trees, multivariate modeling, association and sequence analysis, simulation and optimization of models, and visual data mining.
Tiberius (tiberius.biz)	Commercial	Predictive modeling software with functionality that includes neural networks, decision tree, logistic regression, regression splines, automatic scorecard building algorithms, variable ranker, 3D data visualization, model monitoring tools, and data recoding.
Apache Software Foundation (ASF), UIMA—Unstructured Information Management Architecture (apache.org)	Open source	Component software architecture for multi-modal analytics for the analysis of unstructured information.
University of Waikato, New Zealand Weka (cs.waikato.ac.nz/ml/weka)	Open source	Data visualization tools and algorithms for analysis and predictive modeling. Capabilities include data pre-processing, clustering, classification, regression, visualization, and feature selection. Distributed under the GNU General Public License.
UMass–Boston ARMiner— Association Rules Miner (www.cs.umb.edu/~laur/ ARMiner/)	Open source	Data mining tool for finding association rules. Distributed under the GNU General Public License.

Customer analytics/data mining software (and Web addresses)	Open source or commercial software	Description of selected aspects or capabilities
UMass–Boston ARtool (www. cs.umb.edu/~laur/ ARtool/)	Open source	Algorithms and tools for mining association rules. Distributed under the GNU General Public License.
Viscovery Profiler (viscovery.net/profiler)	Commercial	Data mining solution based on self-organizing maps that provides tools for visual cluster analysis, statistical profiling and segmentation.
Viscovery Predictor (viscovery.net/predictor)	Commercial	Capabilities for linear and non-linear prediction and scoring, enabling workflow-oriented prediction, scoring, and non-linearity analysis within a project environment.
VisuMap (visumap.net)	Commercial	2D and 3D interactive data mapping, clustering and visualization of trends and patterns, among .other capabilities.
Younicycle The Online Database (younicycle.com)	Commercial	Online tools for collaboration and computation.
Zementis ADAPA (zementis.com)	Commercial	Statistical techniques and data processing application that is a service on the Amazon Cloud for predictive modeling and decision logic.

Notes

Introduction

1. The phrase "firing of customers" often evokes a visceral reaction, especially from people with long careers in sales and who know how hard it is to create a customer in the first place. But customers can and should be fired when they collectively distract the organization from achieving its vision (e.g., value-seeking customers driving the company to address their needs when the vision might be to move upmarket), when they subvert the processes of the organization for their own purposes (e.g., by taking advantage of liberal customer return policies to repeatedly return well-used items), when they are simply unprofitable and cannot be managed for greater profitability and when the people they know and to whom they might make referrals are likely to match the same profile.

Chapter 1. Managing the New Customer—and the New Customer Relationship

1. Al Ries and Jack Trout, *Positioning: The Battle for Your Mind* (Toronto: McGraw-Hill, 1980, 2000).
2. Moore's Law is named after Gordon Moore, one of the founders of computer chipmaker Intel. According to this Moore, the number of transistors that can be placed on an integrated circuit doubles every 18 to 24 months. This accurate observation has led to significant improvements in the price/performance ratios of the processors that underpin

computing devices and, accordingly, not only the functionality of those devices but also entirely new generations and types of products, and increased use of computing in appliances, vehicles and in other products where microprocessors were not previously employed. See Gordon Moore, "Cramming More Components into Integrated Circuits," *Electronics* (April 19, 1965).

3. While the Marketing Concept focuses on the philosophy of identifying and satisfying customers' needs and wants, the Customer Concept pays attention to the individual customer and the philosophy of putting each chosen customer first to engage him or her on his or her own terms in a virtuous cycle of connection, bidirectional communications and interplay, value creation, collaboration and value sharing.

Chapter 2. Strategies for Better Customer Relationships

1. For example, see Don Peppers, Martha Rogers and Bob Dorf, "Is Your Company Ready for One-To-One Marketing?," *Harvard Business Review* (January–February 1999).

2. The Balanced Scorecard is an approach to performance management that uses metrics in areas such as financial, customer, internal business processes, and learning and growth to provide a rounded perspective on organizational performance. See Robert S. Kaplan and David P. Norton, "Using the Balanced Scorecard as a Strategic Management System," *Harvard Business Review* (January–February 1996). Net Promoter Scores are discussed in Chapter 8.

3. For example, using the Relationship Ladder approach to setting and measuring behavioral objectives as described in Chapter 3.

4. ERP stands for Enterprise Resource Planning but is now generally taken to mean the software the company uses to run its business. SAP is one of the larger ERP vendors.

5. Company filing with the Securities and Exchange Commission (SEC), Form S1, June 10, 2011.

6. Facebook's President, Mark Zuckerberg, implied a variant of this view that focused on usage and cumulative data provision and processing (naturally expecting this to benefit Facebook), as follows: "I would expect that next year, people will share twice as much information as they share this year, and next year, they will be sharing twice as much as they did the year

before. That means that people are using Facebook, and the applications and the ecosystem, more and more." See Saul Hansell, "Zuckerberg's Law of Information Sharing," *The New York Times* (November 6, 2008).

7. Likely a paraphrase from Lewis Carroll's *Alice in Wonderland*.

Chapter 3. Planning Relationships with Existing Customers

1. One of the most common models used for planning relationship management is the IDIC model, which is an acronym for Identify, Differentiate, Interact and Customize, as described in Don Peppers and Martha Rogers, *Managing Customer Relationships* (Hoboken, NJ: John Wiley & Sons, 2004, 2011), first and second editions. This chapter provides the CREVITS model as an alternative to the IDIC model to make specific aspects of relationship management explicit for relationship planning purposes.

2. Sociographics seeks to understand society according to a taxonomy and consideration of societal and group structure, affiliation and connection in much the same way as demographics focuses on people according to who they are and other personal characteristics and aspects, such as what they have done. Applied to an individual, sociographics seeks to understand each person in a societal, community and group context.

3. See company website for detail: www.klout.com.

4. Parts revenues are calculated on revenues for the car company, i.e., the dealer's costs. Service revenues accrue to the dealer.

5. Justin Bieber has 18 million followers on Twitter and received 30 messages per second on his 18th birthday. See Seth Stevenson, "Popularity Counts," *Wired Magazine* (May 2012).

6. Lady Gaga's and President Obama's Klout Scores were both reportedly 91. See Lan Nguyen, "Forbes' Most Powerful Women with Klout," The Official Klout Blog, October 21, 2011, http://corp.klout.com/blog/2011/10/forbes-most-powerful-women-with-klout and Note 5.

7. President Obama has a Klout score of 99 and Justin Bieber, 92. See Sarah Mitroff, "Now Barack Obama Can Brag About His Klout Score With a (Slightly) Straighter Face," *Wired Magazine* (August 14, 2012), http://www.wired.com/business/2012/08/klout-updates.

8. Robert C. Blattberg and John Deighton, "Manage Marketing by the Customer Equity Test," *Harvard Business Review* (July 1996).

9. Ibid.

10. "Supersize loss could bother some," *Chicago Tribune* (March 07, 2004), http://articles.chicagotribune.com/2004-03-07/business/0403070497_1_mcdonald-s-corp-harris-nesbitt-gerard-oak-brook-based.

11. Customer Retention Model as described in F.F. Reichheld and W.E. Sasser, Jr., "Zero defections: quality comes to services," *Harvard Business Review* (September–October 1990).

12. Subsequent to the initial transaction

13. "Organizational listening" and related terms, such as "customer feedback," are sometimes referred to as "voice of the customer" or "VoC." VoC may also be used to include customer experience, customer loyalty and customer satisfaction.

14. Although this is a good illustration of customer-specific innovation, after less than a decade in business, Streamline sold out to competitor Peapod, apparently the victim of losses and insufficient financing. This example therefore illustrates some of the challenges associated with being the first. It also shows that relationships must be mutual—benefiting neither the customer nor the enterprise exclusively. More specifically, not only must any innovation create customer value, it had better create shareholder value too.

15. See Lear's website, http://www.lear.com.

16. An acronym for "Identify customers, Differentiate customers according to their needs and value, Interact with customers uniquely and Customize goods or services for each." See Don Peppers and Martha Rogers, *Managing Customer Relationships: A Strategic Framework* (Hoboken, NJ: John Wiley & Sons, 2011), second edition.

Chapter 4. One-Through-One: Engaging Social Customers

1. Barton George, "Dell opens its Social Media Command Center," Inside Enterprise IT (December 16, 2010), http://en.community.dell.com/dell-blogs/enterprise/b/inside-enterprise-it/archive/2010/12/16/dell-opens-its-social-media-command-center.aspx.

2. Erica Swallow, "Dell To Launch Social Media Listening Command Center [EXCLUSIVE]," Mashable, December 8, 2010, http://mashable.com/2010/12/08/dell-social-listening-center.

3. Adam Ostrow, "Inside Gatorade's Social Media Command Center," Mashable, June 15, 2010, http://mashable.com/2010/06/15/gatorade-social-media-mission-control.

4. For additional reading in this regard, the reader is referred to Bernard J. Jansen, Zhe Liu, Courtney Weaver, Gerry Campbell and Gregg Gerry, "Real time search on the web: Queries, topics and economic value," *Information Processing and Management* (2011).

5. For additional information on competitive intelligence and strategy, the reader is referred to two of the author's other books: *Beat the Competition* and *Competitor Targeting*. For details, see Convergence Management Consultants, http://www.converge.ca.

6. One of the better known categorizations of conversation enablers is from author Brian Solis, The Conversation Prism, http://www.theconversationprism.com.

7. MMORPG: Massively Multiplayer Online Role-Playing Game

8. United Airlines has apparently learned from the experience, as have many other companies that benefitted from this early lesson in the importance of social media. See "Broken guitar song gets airline's attention," CBC News July 8, 2009, http://www.cbc.ca/news/arts/music/story/2009/07/08/united-breaks-guitars.html.

9. Erica Swallow, "Dell To Launch."

10. As of December 2011, according to Facebook's IPO, S1 registration.

11. Facebook and Twitter were apparently banned in China in 2009 but a recent increase in users suggests the ban may have been relaxed to some extent.

12. Syncapse is one such capability. See http://syncapse.com.

13. Facebook's major markets, according to Socialbakers.

14. The other owner of Ketel One Worldwide is The Nolet Group, the Dutch founding family's eponymous company.

15. *Matchstick Inc. Word-of-Mouth Marketing (A) and (B)*, Richard Ivey School of Business, The University of Western Ontario, 2010, and Matthew Stradiotto, Matchstick Inc., http://www.matchstick.ca.

16. Facebook CEO Mark Zuckerberg said that more than 1 billion stories are being shared from Open Graph apps per day. See "Facebook introduces new structured status updates to help users share what they're feeling, watching, eating and more," Inside Facebook, July 26, 2012, http://www.insidefacebook.com/category/open-graph.

17. "Social Plugins," Facebook Developers, https://developers.facebook
    .com/docs/plugins.
18. Ted Greenwald, "Facebook's Timeline," *MIT Technology Review* (May–
    June 2012).
19. See "Plugins Overview," LinkedIn Developers, https://developer.linkedin
    .com/plugins.
20. For additional suggestions, see sites such as those mentioned earlier in
    this chapter, including Alexa.
21. Chris Lee, cofounder of Meeteor, as quoted in David Zax, "Fast Talk:
    With Meeteor, Facebook-Stalk For The Job You Want," *Fast Company*
    (February 14, 2012), http://www.fastcompany.com/1815993/fast-talk-
    meeteor-facebook-stalk-job-you-want. See also Meeteor, http://www
    .meeteor.com.
22. Based on information presented in Robert B. Cialdini, "The Science of
    Persuasion," *Scientific American Mind* (2007).
23. Tim Simonite, "What Facebook Knows," *MIT Technology Review*
    (July–August 2012).
24. Ibid.
25. Customer-supported is not the same as customer-controlled. A number
    of firms have learned that they need to monitor customer communica-
    tions to ensure it is not abusive or profane and does not defame, among
    other considerations. They have also learned that customer complaints
    and reasonable criticism ought to be tolerated and addressed.
26. Drew Neisser, "Twelpforce: Marketing that Isn't Marketing," *Fast
    Company* (May 17, 2010), http://www.fastcompany.com/1648739/
    twelpforce-marketing-isn%E2%80%99t-marketing.

Chapter 5. B2B Relationships

1. Examples of content many companies don't wish to share with customers
   include a rating of relationships that executives have with their counter-
   parts in a customer account, but even content like this would ideally be
   shared with customers to help ensure full and open information exchange
   and alignment.
2. Casey Hibbard, "How Social Media Helped Cisco Shave $100,000+ Off a
   Product Launch," Social Media Examiner (August 30, 2010), http://www
   .socialmediaexaminer.com/cisco-social-media-product-launch.

3. Although now in fairly wide circulation, the origin of the term "gamification"—meaning the application of games and gaming principles to other than games—has been attributed to Nick Pelling in 2002.

4. At the time of writing, their "Future of Shopping" YouTube video had been seen nearly 7 million times.

5. Widgets: pre-packaged code to enable ready sharing.

6. Hibbard, "How Social Media."

7. Jacqueline Renfrow, "Small Business Owners Get Intimate with Visa's New Network," *Response* (December 1, 2008).

8. Information about the Visa Business Network is available at http://www.visa businessnetwork.com.

9. Trackur's company website: http://www.trackur.com/why-trackur.

10. Infomediaries: information and content intermediaries

11. Indeed, even in the development of this list, I found companies had ceased operations between the time the lists were first written and when the manuscript was finalized. It is quite likely therefore that this list will also be obsolete by the time of publication, which serves to highlight the challenge of discussing specific technology solutions in a book such as this.

12. Sources for comments made here are primarily or exclusively the company's own websites. This list is not intended to affirm the performance or appropriateness of specific solutions, nor is it intended to be a complete list as this would naturally not be possible for a book such as this.

Chapter 6. Relationships with Mobile Customers

1. PDA: Personal Digital Assistants, such as Apple's iPod Touch.

2. Tablets typically employ solid-state memory and other capabilities such as touch-sensitive glass screens to serve as both a means of data input and presentation, quite different from other forms of mobile computers that have separate keyboards. An example is Apple's iPad.

3. According to "World POPClock Projection," United States Census Bureau, http://www.census.gov/population/popclockworld.html.

4. According to ITU (International Telecommunication Union), a United Nations agency that focuses on information and communication technologies. See "The World in 2011," ICT Facts and Figures, http://www.itu.int/ITU-D/ict/facts/2011/material/ICTFactsFigures2011.pdf.

5. Google Inc. Securities and Exchange Commission (SEC) 10K filing, December 2011.

6. Google Inc. SEC 10K filing, and *Global Mobile Statistics 2012*, mobiThinking, February 2012, http://mobithinking.com/mobile-marketing-tools/latest-mobile-stats.

7. E-learning can be provided in a manner that is synchronous or asynchronous, meaning that teaching and learning occur either simultaneously with the educator engaged while the learner is online (synchronous) or in a forum-like situation where the learner responds to questions and submits documents for handling by the instructor when the instructor chooses to respond.

8. Although a number of specific applications are mentioned, the fast-changing nature of technology, applications and firms suggests that these should be viewed as illustrative rather than all-inclusive for the categories that are reviewed.

9. See Note 4.

10. 3G access: 3G is generally considered necessary for broadband mobile Internet usage.

11. See Note 4.

12. 8.49% of website hits come from mobile devices, excluding tablets according to "Mobile Internet usage is doubling year on year," StatCounter, January 2012, http://gs.statcounter.com/press/mobile-internet-usage-is-doubling-year-on-year.

13. Ibid.

14. On Device Research, December 2010, http://ondeviceresearch.com/ondeviceresearch/blogPost/9 and "Global mobile statistics 2012", mobiThinking http://mobithinking.com/mobile-marketing-tools/latest-mobile-stats#mobileweb.

15. This compares with 6.9 trillion SMS messages in 2010. SMS had a 63.5% share of mobile messages in 2011. See "Mobile Messaging Futures 2012-2016," Portio Research, 2011. http://www.portioresearch.com/en/reports/current-portfolio/mobile-messaging-futures-2012-2016.aspx.

16. Mobile Instant Messaging.

17. SMS hubbing intermediates SMS communications between operators, making it possible and easier for consumers to connect with one another wherever they are.

18. *Mobile Messaging Futures*, Portio Research 2012, sixth edition.

19. Ibid.
20. "Gartner Says Worldwide Mobile Advertising Revenue Forecast to Reach $3.3 Billion in 2011," Gartner Group, June 16, 2011, http://www.gartner.com/it/page.jsp?id=1726614.
21. Zynga's SEC 10K filing for the fiscal year ended December 31, 2011.
22. Ibid.
23. "The New Dot-Com Boom," *Canadian Business* (February 14, 2011).
24. EA has revenues of about $4 billion. Its titles include FIFA, Madden, NHL, Battlefield: Bad Company, and The Sims.
25. Free pricing makes apps and usage available without cost, while the company benefits from alternative revenue streams, such as in-game sales and advertising. Freemium pricing occurs when software is given away free in basic versions but upgrades are available at an additional cost to the consumer.
26. Projection for 2014: $12.7 billion. See "Press Release: Mobile Location-Based Services Market to exceed $12bn by 2014 driven by Increased Apps Store Usage, Smartphone Adoption and New Hybrid Positioning Technologies, According to Juniper Research," Juniper Research, http://juniperresearch.com/viewpressrelease.php?pr=180.
27. Among other benefits, Google Latitude plots users' locations onto Google Maps using GPS data. Consumers can decide how much or how little of their location information to reveal to other users.
28. Near field communications facilitates the connection of smartphones to one another and other enabled devices, like readers, that are nearby.
29. *Mobile Betting: Game On!*, Juniper Research, May 2012.
30. Ibid.
31. Jeffery M. Jones, "Gambling a Common Activity for Americans," *Gallup News Service*, March 24, 2004, http://www.gallup.com/poll/11098/gambling-common-activity-americans.aspx.
32. 81.8%, based on the average of provincial gambling surveys as reported in the *Canadian Gambling Digest 2007–08*, Canadian Partnership for Responsible Gambling, 2008, p. 17, http://www.cprg.ca/articles/Canadian_Gambling_Digest_2007_2008.pdf.
33. *British Gambling Prevalence Survey 2010*, The UK Gambling Commission, The National Center for Social Research, 2011, http://www.gamblingcommission.gov.uk/pdf/british%20gambling%20prevalence%20survey%202010.pdf.

34. *Gambling,* Productivity Commission Inquiry Report, 2010, http://www
    .pc.gov.au/_data/assets/pdf_file/0010/95680/gambling-report-volume1.pdf.
35. MIT Center for Mobile Learning: http://mitmobilelearning.org.

Chapter 7. Mass Customization

1. Called Andersen's "Window of Knowledge," the kiosks enabled customers
   to design their own windows, a major breakthrough when the initiative
   was introduced in 1994.
2. Andersen's 400 Series Casement Windows: http://www.andersenwindows
   .com.

Chapter 8. Customer Analytics

1. For example, the app for the Obama 2012 campaign. David Talbot,
   "Facebook: The Real Presidential Swing State," *MIT Technology Review*
   (September–October 2012).
2. This discussion has been informed in part from Tim Simonite, "What
   Facebook Knows," *MIT Technology Review* (July–August 2012).
3. The author was the subject matter expert of a team that studied Harrah's
   in the mid-1990s as part of a best-practice review. For more information
   about Harrah's use of decision analytics (and unrelated to the author's
   experience), the reader is referred to Lauren Keller Johnson, "Defying
   the Odds: Using Decision Analytics to Win Big in the Gaming Business,"
   Balanced Scorecard Report (January–February 2007).
4. Shyam V. Nath, *Customer Churn Analysis in the Wireless Industry: A Data
   Mining Approach,* 2003, http://download.oracle.com/owsf_2003/40332.
   pdf.
5. CRISP-DM: Cross Industry Standard Process for Data Mining.
6. Brian Christian, "The A/B Test," *Wired Magazine* (May 2012).
7. Ibid.
8. For more information, the reader may want to read Tudor Bodea and Mark
   Ferguson, *Pricing Segmentation and Analytics* (New York, NY: Business
   Expert Press, 2011).
9. 4Q Survey website: http://www.4qsurvey.com/about-us.
10. For example, you may wish to review the list provided by David
    Berkowitz, vice president of Emerging Media at digital agency 360i: "100

Ways to Measure Social Media," Marketers Studio, November 17, 2009, http://www.marketersstudio.com/2009/11/100-ways-to-measure-social-media-.html.

11. Jim Sterne, *Social Media Metrics* (Hoboken, NJ: John Wiley & Sons, 2010).

12. Ibid.

13. 47% of data miners use R according to *2011 Data Miner Survey*, Rexer Analytics, 2011, http://www.rexeranalytics.com/Data-Miner-Survey-Results-2011.html.

14. The Data Mine website: http://www.the-data-mine.com/Software/DataMiningSoftware.

15. Kashmir Hill, "How Target Figured Out A Teen Girl Was Pregnant Before Her Father Did," *Forbes* (February 16, 2012).

16. One such example is IBM's SmartCloud services.

17. Frederick F. Reichheld, "The One Number You Need to Grow," *Harvard Business Review* (December 2003).

18. Frederick F. Reichheld, *The Ultimate Question: Driving Good Profits and True Growth* (Boston, MA: Harvard Business School Press, 2006).

Chapter 9. Teaching Customers New Behaviors

1. Portions of the following discussion and selected other content in this chapter are drawn in part from Ian Gordon, "The Marketer's Challenge: How to Teach Customers New Behaviors," *Ivey Business Journal* (September–October 2008).

2. Edward C. Baig, "Digital pen lets fly with high-tech cool," *USA Today*, Personal Tech, November 30, 2005, http://www.usatoday.com/tech/columnist/edwardbaig/2005-11-30-fly-pentop_x.htm#.

3. G.R. Morrison, S.M. Ross and J.E. Kemp, *Designing Effective Instruction*, (Toronto: John Wiley & Sons Canada, 2004).

4. Benjamin S. Bloom, *Taxonomy of Educational Objectives* (Boston: Allyn and Bacon, 1984).

5. M. Evans, A. Jamal and G. Foxall, *Consumer Behaviour* (Toronto: John Wiley & Sons Canada, 2006).

6. Social pedagogy as noted here includes elements of constructivism, the theory by which learning occurs when information is filtered and becomes personal before being converted by the recipient into individual-specific knowledge.

7. As an example of the Myers-Briggs Type Indicator, INTJ is an acronym that stands for Introversion, Intuition, Thinking, Judgment. People with this personality seem self-assured and almost arrogant. Their assurance helps make them opinion leaders to their peers but their knowledge can be narrow and situation specific, and their perfectionism off-putting.

8. "I am like a teacher who enjoys hearing your ideas, who enjoys telling you his own, but has no plan to make you think as he does.... That is just the difference between education and indoctrination." Alan Paton, *The Land and People of South Africa* (Philadelphia, PA: J.B. Lippincott, 1955).

9. *Oxford American Dictionary and Thesaurus* (New York, NY: Oxford University Press, 2003).

10. Kunur Patel, "All the World's a Game, and Brands Want to Play Along," *AdAge Digital*, May 31, 2010, http://adage.com/article/digital/world-s-a-game-brands-play/144154.

11. Ibid.

12. Gabe Zichermann and Joselin Linder, *Game-Based Marketing* (Hoboken, NJ: John Wiley & Sons, 2010).

13. Gabe Zichermann, "Cash is for SAPS," Gamification Corp, October 18, 2010, http://gamification.co/2010/10/18/cash-is-for-saps.

14. Chris Anderson, *Free: How Today's Smartest Businesses Profit by Getting Something for Nothing* (New York, NY: Hyperion, 2010).

15. Author is the source for the iso-profit curves and chart as presented. Copyright © Convergence Management Consultants Ltd, http://www.converge.ca.

16. For example, providing consumers with rewards that enhance consumers' perceptions of the volume and nature of status, access, power and stuff (SAPS). See: Gabe Zichermann Gamification Corp., http://gamification.co.

Chapter 10. Case Studies: Making it Happen

1. The case is based on an interview with Dan Trott, Business Development Executive, Unified Clinical Archive, Dell, October 5, 2011.

2. PACS, or Picture Archiving and Communication System, facilitates storage, retrieval and access of medical images. Once large medical images are compressed and encoded with patient information, images are stored using PACS imaging software, which enables clinical department-specific access to digital images when healthcare professionals need them.

3. DICOM software (Digital Imaging and Communications in Medicine) is used for PACS image storage and transfer.
4. The case discussion is based on information provided by NHS Leicester City and an interview with Tim Rideout on December 16, 2011. At the time of the initiative discussed here, Mr. Rideout was Chief Executive, NHS Leicester City. He is now on assignment with the UK's Department of Health.
5. The case is based on an interview with Isidore Sobkowski, CIO, Health and Human Services, New York City, and Executive Director, HHS Connect, December 21, 2011.
6. GIS: Geographical Information Systems—essentially apps with location information.
7. The case is based on an interview conducted with Vikas Gupta, President and CEO, TransGaming, on December 6, 2011.
8. The case is based on information provided by, and an interview with Robert Paddon, Executive Vice President, Customer & Public Engagement, TransLink, on December 28, 2011.

Chapter 11. Strategy, Stakeholders and Semantics

1. Jacques Derrida interview as reported in *Deconstruction in a Nutshell*, John D. Caputo, ed. (New York: Fordham University Press, 1997).
2. The opposite of control is an interesting issue to contemplate. Is it faith that an absence of control will not prove deleterious? Could the opposite of control be respect for others, in the belief that control has as an implicit assumption that others need to be controlled for outcomes to be beneficial? Might control's opposite be its abandonment or simple acquiescence to forces uncontrolled?
3. "Big, boring, booming: Business-to-business e-commerce is a revolution in a ball valve," *The Economist*, May 8, 1997, http://www.economist.com/node/596342.
4. Information sharing and interventions may be enabled by websites such as flashmob.com, for example.
5. See video uploaded by mmshtube (user), "Iranians Flash Mob Against APPLE's Discriminatory - Havaar," YouTube, June 21, 2012, http://www.youtube.com/watch?v=tdG4K5nrz4k.
6. Foxconn makes over 40% of the world's electronics products—including for such brands as Amazon, Dell and Hewlett-Packard—and is China's

largest and most prominent private employer, with 1.2 million workers. See Charles Duhigg and Steven Greenhouse, "Electronic Giant Vowing Reforms in China Plants," *The New York Times*, March 29, 2012.

7. Ibid. The were early signs that this was a material issue, going back to at least 2006 when Apple discussed labor compliance with its Code of Conduct.

8. Usage of the term "strategic response-ability" is intended to be associated with the concept from post-modernist philosopher Jacques Derrida, who discussed "infinite response-ability" as being able to respond to the requirements of infinite Others, both stakeholders and everyone else.

9. Discussed in Chapter 4.

10. After people become customers, the theory in this book suggests that an organization would differentiate customers according to their value, needs and influence. Here the reader is invited to consider how the notion of differentiating customers could be in opposition to being fully open, supplicating the company respectfully to all—stakeholders and non-stakeholders alike. The question then arises: which approach should assume primacy?

Appendix A

1. This list is necessarily incomplete as companies and their products come and go. Like other lists in this book, this table is obviously not intended to recommend any specific solution or affirm performance or appropriateness in any context.

2. All companies, trademarks and brands referenced here are considered registered to their respective owners.

3. Sources for comments made here are primarily or exclusively the companies' own websites. Selected extracts are presented or synthesized in this table. The reader is invited to visit the websites listed for current and more complete descriptions than can be provided here.

About the Author

Ian Gordon is a management consultant with over 25 years of marketing and strategy consulting experience. He is president of Convergence Management Consultants Ltd., a Toronto-based customer relationship and revenue acceleration consulting firm (www.converge.ca). Prior to founding Convergence in 1996, Ian worked for 14 years with Ernst & Young's Toronto office, where he was senior partner responsible for the marketing, research and strategy consulting practice and the firm's focus on technology and manufacturing companies. Ian has been employed in executive management positions by multinational companies in the consumer products and software sectors.

Ian pioneered and formalized strategic relationship marketing principles and documented his perspectives and experience in his book entitled *Relationship Marketing: New Strategies, Techniques and Technologies to Win the Customers You Want and Keep Them Forever,* published by John Wiley & Sons Canada in 1998. Ian conducts strategic relationship management consulting assignments to help companies reimagine, reframe and pursue customer and stakeholder relationships. He has worked with global, intermediate-sized and emerging clients around the world, including four of the ten largest firms in the United States and many companies in diverse industries in the United States, Canada, Europe, Japan, Asia, South America and Africa. His experience includes working with organizations in industries such as chemicals, consumer services, electrical utilities, financial services, governments, manufacturers, not-for-profits, office products, primary metals, printing and publishing, retailing, technology (hardware and software), telecommunications, and transportation and distribution.

Ian has chaired and addressed numerous conferences on the subject of relationship management. He presents to open market forums and to senior management groups in in-house sessions.

In addition to *Relationship Marketing*, Ian has authored books on competition and competitively superior customer relationships. His first book considered principles for waging and winning a business war using competitive intelligence to help chart the way. It dealt with the challenge of retaining and gaining market share in a competitively intense marketplace. Entitled *Beat the Competition: How to Use Competitive Intelligence to Develop Winning Business Strategies*, it was published in 1989 by Basil Blackwell, Oxford, UK, a John Wiley & Sons company. It is in Spanish translation.

Ian also authored *Competitor Targeting: Winning the Battle for Market and Customer Share*, published in 2002 by John Wiley & Sons Canada. This book considered the competitive context and strategies for developing customer relationships. The book is in multiple translation.

Ian has documented his views in over one hundred articles that have appeared in leading U.S., Canadian and Asian publications, including 12 articles for the *Ivey Business Journal* and *Business Quarterly* (as it was previously known). He is an electrical engineer, MBA, past president of the Industrial Marketing and Research Association of Canada, and a founder and first president of the Association for the Advancement of Relationship Marketing. He has lectured in relationship marketing and customer relationship management as well as other marketing subjects to undergraduate and MBA students at three universities in Toronto, Canada.

Ian welcomes an ongoing dialog with the reader. If you have any thoughts or ideas about the content in this book, Ian would be very excited to hear from you. He can be reached at the following e-mail address: igordon@converge.ca.

Index